Psychoanalysis and Religion

GREGORY ZILBOORG

1890 - 1959

Psychoanalysis and Religion

*Edited with an Introduction
by Margaret Stone Zilboorg*

London
GEORGE ALLEN AND UNWIN LTD

FIRST PUBLISHED IN GREAT BRITAIN IN 1967

This book is copyright under the Berne Convention. Apart from any fair dealing for the purposes of private study, research, criticism or review, as permitted under the Copyright Act, 1956, no portion may be reproduced by any process without written permission. Enquiries should be addressed to the Publishers.

© *Margaret Stone Zilboorg 1962*

PRINTED IN GREAT BRITAIN
BY JOHN DICKENS AND CO LTD NORTHAMPTON

Contents

Introduction, vii

The Fundamental Conflict with Psychoanalysis, 3

Psyche, Soul, and Religion, 19

Psychoanalysis and Religion, 54

A Psychiatric Consideration of the Ascetic Ideal, 63

Sigmund Freud, 80

Scientific Psychopathology and Religious Issues, 104

Love in Freudian Psychoanalysis, 117

Some Denials and Assertions of Religious Faith, 140

The Sense of Guilt, 169

Psychiatry's Moral Sphere, 189

Freud and Religion, 195

Introduction

GREGORY ZILBOORG was born in Russia of Orthodox Jewish parents on Christmas Day of 1890. He studied medicine and psychiatry, took part in the first (Social Democratic Party) Revolution, fled Russia shortly after the Bolsheviks took control. He came to this country at the age of twenty-nine, studied medicine and psychiatry again, and finally psychoanalysis. He was engaged in private practice in New York City, and in writing and teaching, until his death in September of 1959.

Gregory abandoned the faith in which he was born soon after he reached maturity. When he came to the United States, he set himself the task of learning English in three months (he knew only "Yes," "No," and "Bolshevik" on his arrival in 1919). At the end of the third month he gave his first lecture, in English, and in his audience was Jesse Holmes, Professor of Philosophy at Swarthmore, a devout member of the Society of Friends. The young lecturer was approached by Holmes at the end of the evening and asked if he would be free to join the Chattauqua Circuit, which Gregory did. He admired and respected, and soon grew to love, Jesse Holmes. Before long, Gregory himself had become a member of the Society of Friends.

I first met Gregory in the Spring of 1940, when he needed a new research assistant. The bare details of my qualifications and experience were very shortly disposed of; they appeared to both of us to be satisfactory. The more important imponderables of my suitability and possible aptitude for the work to be done remained; Gregory asked me how I liked the book he had earlier noticed me reading, Henry Link's *Return to Religion*. We were off.

He wanted to find out as much as he could about the religion I was "returning" to, and his approach was that of the devil's advocate; I found myself first mildly defending beliefs I had only just begun seriously to think about, then somewhat sharply attacking the views that this interesting and interested Quaker was expressing of my own Episcopal faith.

The "interview" ended on a slightly discordant note. Later I wondered whatever had possessed me to *argue* with a man from whom I wanted a good job; but his interest in whatever I had to say had been profound. I did get the job.

A year before, Gregory had first touched briefly on the subject of psychoanalysis and religion, in a critique of Mortimer Adler's *What Man Has Made of Man*. He discussed the relationship between the philosophy of St. Thomas and the principles and practice of psychoanalysis—and took issue with Adler's variety of neo-Thomism which led him to dismiss most of the findings of Freud.

In the same year, 1939, Gregory's article, "The Fundamental Conflict with Psychoanalysis" (the first in this book), appeared in the English *International Journal of Psychoanalysis*. It was the opening salvo in a battle which he fought with constantly increasing interest and effectiveness for the next twenty years, until his death.

"Psyche, Soul, and Religion," the concluding chapter of Gregory's *Mind, Medicine and Man* (1943), was an inspired and clear presentation of his thoughts on the subject up to that time. In answer to a published criticism of this chapter (and of his criticism of Mortimer Adler), Gregory was to write: "I did not deny Freud the right to assume the attitude toward

Introduction

religion which he did. I merely pointed out that in analyzing the psychological dynamics of religion Freud, by way of . . . erroneous, individual-social parallelism, drifted into measuring and evaluating religious belief by scientific methods of reasoning; that is to say, he overlooked the fact that religion and even ethical values are not measurable by scientifically weighing their phychological components. Were we to do so consistently, then such things as saluting the flag, standing up when we sing or hear sung the national anthem, kissing when we love, and taking off our hat out of respect to a person or a gathering, should be condemned as irrational, infantile, passive homosexual, and oral neurotic bits of behavior—for no one would deny that these conventions and activities are made up of the above-mentioned infantile components, which have become ritualized. . . . Instead of opposing religion, instead of rejecting it as unscientific or as a cultural neurosis (the use of the latter term is hardly more than a polite pseudoscientific name-calling), I believe we shall understand it better and view it probably with greater sympathy, if we concentrate our attention on the study of its psychocultural function as one of man's fundamental ways of living and of meeting life."[1]

"Psyche, Soul, and Religion" attracted the attention of many theologians, among them the Dominican Father Noël Mailloux, himself a psychologist. Soon the two men met; it was Gregory's first intellectual encounter with a Roman Catholic priest.

The intellect of Father Mailloux, and of most of the other priests—primarily monks—whom he began to encounter, delighted and excited Gregory's own intellect. Their humanism, their devotion to man as an individual, were vibrant echoes of his own attitude.

For many years Gregory's interest in the Church remained

[1] *The Psychoanalytic Quarterly*, Vol. XIII, 1944, pp. 96, 97, 99, 100.

primarily an intellectual one. He tried hard to become interested in my faith, and enjoyed talking with Episcopal priests, but his intellect was never seriously involved. He had ceased to attend Meetings of the Society of Friends shortly after World War II began; now the Episcopal faith too was found lacking for him. Though he continued occasionally to go to church with me after our marriage, in 1946, he was never truly touched: "It's the scholarship that's lacking; they just don't have the scholarship."

He was not entirely correct, but then it would have been difficult indeed for anyone to find the "scholarship" which he encountered constantly in the monks who came to him to discuss this business of religion and psychoanalysis.

Late in 1953 Gregory became convinced that he wanted and needed to join the Roman Catholic Church; a year later, he did.

It was a matter he preferred not to discuss with even his closest friends; he thought his faith a purely personal matter. Moreover, he was concerned lest his future writings on the indeed possible rapprochement between religion and psychoanalysis would be deemed merely the prejudiced thinking of a convert to the Church, despite the fact that he had been thinking and writing about the subject for more than fifteen years.

Gregory died a good psychoanalyst and a good Catholic. A few days before his death, when he was already in the hospital, he was deeply moved by the present of a small and beautiful crucifix which a former patient, herself Jewish, had sent to him; it was the only thing he kept on his bedside table— besides his glasses and pen, for he hoped until the very end that he would be able to continue to write.

The afternoon before he died, he asked me to bring to the hospital a lamp he had ordered from Denmark, which had made its trip from Europe without a plug at the end of the

Introduction

wiring. I brought the lamp that evening, with a plug, pliers and a screwdriver. The last words, it turned out, he was able to say to me, with an exhausted smile, were: "Good, good. You know, dear—*arbeiten und lieben*." It was Freud's answer to what he considered the ideally normal person, a person whose life consisted of "work and love."

MARGARET STONE ZILBOORG

New York City
October 21, 1961

Psychoanalysis and Religion

The Fundamental Conflict
with Psychoanalysis

PSYCHOANALYSIS has had its fiftieth birthday. Half a century is but a brief moment in the history of a scientific discipline. It is long enough, however, in this age of ultra-rapid developments to perceive the major trends of a new science which indicate, perhaps, its historical destiny. Other therapeutic endeavors saw light in the course of the same period. A number of procedures, more "sound" than psychoanalysis, came and went with the utmost dispatch. Pyretic therapy, for instance, malarial inoculations by the followers of Wagner-Jauregg, insulin and metrazol, the dental and abdominal surgery of Cotton, the neurosurgery of Walter Freeman, all were used for the cure of psychoses and neuroses and all have been discarded or are about to be abandoned as soon as the brief and naïvely spectacular claims prove false at the first contacts with the grim realities of clinical psychopathology. The precipitate birth, ephemeral life and sudden death of these procedures are primarily due to the fact that they came into existence not as the results of empirical observations based on analytical scientific thinking, but instead were derived from the perennial obsessional belief that "there must be something anatomical and physiological at the root of

First published in *The International Journal of Psychoanalysis*, 1939.

this or that." This "there must be," persisting in medicine from the days of Hippocrates until now, is the only constant feature of the *ad hoc* method in medical psychology. Its external manifestations vary with the traditions of the ages. Hippocratic psychiatry inaugurated or authorized the tradition of "touristic" and pharmacological psychotherapy: long voyages and hellebore, a potent laxative, and hypnotics. Medieval psychiatry followed this tradition and elaborated upon it through the development of dietetics and the *Dreckapotheke*. The age of physics brought the gadget into psychotherapy, the twirling chair (*Drehstuhl,* producing vertigo and unconsciousness), the psychiatic "noyade" (half or almost complete drowning), and finally blood letting. From the beginning of the nineteenth century on, through the great strides made by chemistry, we have returned imperceptibly to the pharmacological ages of yore (metrazol), to the *Dreckapotheke* and Hippocratic humoralism, as represented by that overworked and never working mono- and polyglandular therapy. Except for a few cases, these therapies with their induced convulsions, fever, states of unconsciousness, with their lobectomies, sigmoidectomies and direct castrations of men and sterilizations of women, represent the expression of an ancient trend of conscious and mostly unconscious hostility against the mentally ill. This hatred is sufficiently repressed to assume a variety of guises but always it betrays signs of the return of the repressed either in the form of a death threat against the patient (drowning, cutting, inducing convulsions, artificially prolonged sleep) or in the form of the obsessional conviction that "there must be something organic, something constitutional," the sick individual must be a contemptible cripple of some sort. The sincerity of these therapeutic convictions cannot be questioned, nor should the industry and the inventiveness of the traditional therapy of mental diseases be disparaged. Yet it is easy to observe that the history of this psychiatry

The Fundamental Conflict with Psychoanalysis

is not that of a scientific discipline, but rather a manifestation of a secular repetition compulsion which always rises despite its ever conspicuous proclivity to fall and which inevitably falls despite its inherent tendency to rise. The history of a truly scientific system is not characterized by such compulsive repetitiveness. It has its own historical rhythm, to be sure, but it does not appear to be a victim of such rapid ups and downs.

Every scientific system begins as a revolutionary idea. Opposed at first, it gradually crystallizes into a set of accepted dogmatic principles; an orthodoxy is then established which creates a rapidly growing harvest of heterodoxies. These heterodoxies, for the most part eclectic compromises, give violent battle to the prevailing system of thought. On the other hand, the established dogma defends itself with considerable vehemence but ultimately degenerates into a set of authoritarian, lifeless postulates which prove very brittle in the hands of an objective investigator. In the wake of this *débris,* there is left as a permanent heritage of knowledge the few data which are truths and therefore are able to withstand the storm of events. Hippocratic medicine and its offspring, the Galenic system, went through this series of developmental stages until they finally yielded, not without bloodshed and passionate stultification, to modern scientific principles.

Psychoanalysis, like any other scientific system, also started as a revolutionary idea but, unlike any other medical system of thought, it struck at the very heart of the age-long pharmacosurgical obsession. It presented at once such a radical departure from the compulsive neurotic thinking about the cure of the mentally ill that there is reason to doubt if it will ever completely overcome universal resistance as, for instance, the heliocentric theory finally surmounted the geocentric prejudice. The very nature of the opposition psychoanalysis had to meet forced it into a revolutionary attitude toward the prevailing systems of thought. This fact accounts for a great deal of the atmosphere of conflict with which it is surrounded in relation to medicine, sociology, theology and psychopathology, but it is highly doubtful whether this factor alone could be held responsible for the sustained opposition.

Psychoanalysis appears already to have lost its sparkle of newness. Even the name has become sufficiently familiar to all civilized tongues for the term to be applied with an ever increasing lack of discrimination to a variety of procedures which deserve more precise and more pungent denominations. There are purple and red neon signs glowing in some streets of Hollywood which proclaim the virtues of psychoanalysis along with those of hair tonics and sure-fire laxatives. Such conspicuous and cheap popularity is usually a sign of decay. It signifies that a system of thought or a world view has already settled into sanctimonious dogmatism and, as a result, a loud eclectic wave begins to hit the rock of dogma. One may, therefore, legitimately ask whether psychoanalysis, despite its revolutionary observations and formulations, has already fallen or is showing signs of reaching those developmental stages of disintegration which forewarn of rigid doctrinairism. If this were true, it would explain not only the appearance of aggressive heterodoxies and boastful eclecticism, but also the general opposition which frequently hides itself behind such rationalizations as: "How can we accept or agree with psychoanalysis when the psychoanalysts don't agree among themselves?" After all, the sustained revolutionary attitude of psychoanalysis may be no more than a façade for aggressive dogma. A careful and objective scrutiny of the history of psychoanalysis will easily disabuse us of this suspicion, for the characteristic peculiarity of the founder of psychoanalysis and his worthiest pupils, like Ferenczi, Abraham and Ernest Jones, is their unwillingness to consider their formulations final. For almost fifty years Freud refused to overvalue his own statements and, from his earliest observations on neuro-psychoses

The Fundamental Conflict with Psychoanalysis

to *Inhibitions, Symptoms and Anxiety* and his most recent *Moses and Monotheism*, he has continued to study and revise his own opinions in the light of newer observations and discoveries. There has been and still is no sign that psychoanalysis is being jellied into a set of immobile laws. This being the case, it is more probable that the dissension within and the opposition from without psychoanalysis are rather indications of vitality, of the fact that psychoanalysis is still in the phase of scientific revolution.

We have thus arrived at a state of unmistakable confusion: psychoanalysis is a vigorous system of thought; it is very popular, at times too popular; it has become widely accepted by many scientists, practicing physicians and even some political philosophers; yet it is combated by an ever increasing mass of people and affects. It is disputed not because it is a new thing and not because it is getting old and dogmatic, not because it has abandoned its therapeutic intent and not because it is unmindful of human ills. What is it then that seems to promote the war against psychoanalysis? As psychoanalysts, we may well ask ourselves: What are the chief instinctual sources of the conflict with psychoanalysis?

There was a time when the question was disposed of by the simple answer: sex. The individual and society as a whole are unwilling to face their own sexual drives. If this were the final answer, the opposition to psychoanalysis should now be definitely on the wane. Even the *New York Times* now allows the word "homosexual" in its columns; it calls syphilis by name instead of gyrating with vague euphemisms. Some news agencies, in a report of a Polish-German incident, used the word "castrated" when describing an alleged mutilation of a soldier. An authoritative Catholic guide for Catholic doctors[1] admits that certain neuroses have something to do with the

[1] A. Bonnar, *The Catholic Doctor*, New York, 1938.

sexual difficulties of certain individuals. The phrase "psychosexual maladjustment" is common usage in scientific and quasi-scientific circles; such terms as "father attachment," "mother attachment," "auto-erotism," are heard almost as commonly among the enlightened and not so enlightened laity. Problems of male and female homosexuality are discussed with increasing frequency and frankness in literature and the theatre. People are not so frightened of direct and some indirect manifestations of sex as they used to be. The answer "sex" appears at least to have become inadequate.

Perhaps the discovery of the unconscious should be looked upon as an important source of antagonism. Striking as it does at the heart of man's narcissism, it may be responsible for the chronic resistance which surges up when one is invited to consider psychoanalysis objectively. We do not like to admit that we do things unknowingly. This is another way of saying that we persistently assert our omniscience and the sadistic omnipotence of our thoughts; what we do not think, what we are not conscious of, does not exist; it is dead—as we unconsciously wish it to be, of course. It is true that a great deal of opposition to psychoanalysis was and still is due to our unwillingness to recognize the role of the unconscious, yet today it is more or less universally acknowledged that it is not merely an abstract and benevolent concept of the doings of the Author of All Evil.

Moreover, despite the obvious unwillingness to honor the unconscious as an integral part of ourselves, the concept is not entirely unfamiliar to the mind of the common man and to the history of biology, medicine and psychology. "I said it without thinking," "it slipped off my tongue before I could think," "before I even thought, I could hear myself say ...," "I said it automatically"—all these are everyday expressions.

Theories of sex and the unconscious have been touched upon, played with and guessed at from the days of the ancients.

The Fundamental Conflict with Psychoanalysis

Aristotle was apparently at least partially aware of the problem when he related a certain story in his *De Anima:* a young colt, while grazing in the field, covered a mare but later, on recognizing that the mare was his mother, he jumped off a rock and killed himself. The connection between hysteria and the invisibly and imperceptibly wandering uterus was asserted for over two thousand years. All the literature on the examination and persecution of witches overtly recognizes the sexual substratum of the neuroses of the day.[2] Paracelus was more specific when he stated that St. Vitus's dance should be renamed *Chorea Lasciva,* the cause of which he ascribed to unconscious factors *(ein angenommen imaginatz)*. This *imaginatum,* says Paracelsus, is the cause of the disease not only in adults but also in children, for they too have this kind of imagination which comes not from understanding. "The child's sight and hearing are so keen that it fantasies unconsciously *(es fantasiert unwüssende).*"[3] Such unconscious fantasying produces symptoms. In the middle of the eighteenth century, Jean Astruc asserted that men and not women alone suffer from hysteria, and his statement met with the same haughty skepticism that confronted Freud when he presented similar findings before the Vienna Neurological Society toward the end of the nineteenth century.

The observations of Heinroth, the references of Janet to the unconscious and the main theses of Bergson's early works are manifestations of the same order, of almost conscious familiarity with the unconscious. The subsequent discovery of the unconscious and even the oedipus complex[4] could thus be

[2] Ernest Jones, *On the Nightmare,* 1931; Zilboorg, *The Medical Man and the Witch during the Renaissance* (The Hideyo Noguchi Lectures), 1935.
[3] Aureoli Theophrasti Paracelsi Schreyben von den Kranckheyten, 1567, Book I, Chap. 3.
[4] Zilboorg. "The Discovery of the Œdipus Complex: Episodes from Marcel Proust," *Psychoanalytic Quarterly,* Vol. VIII, 1939.

viewed as the ultimate and dramatic culmination of a series of imperceptible, culturally subliminal steps toward a deeper understanding of mental phenomena. Similar observations can be made of many discoveries in other sciences. Newton's discovery becomes less of a revelation and more of a summation when it is considered as the outcome of suggestions and assertions made by students from Archimedes to Galileo and the immediate predecessors and colleagues of Newton in the Royal Society. These facts do not, of course, detract from the genius of Newton or Freud, but their historical sequence does help to place psychoanalysis in its appropriate historical setting and to explain to a degree why, despite severe resistance, it has succeeded in penetrating so many strongholds of thought and so many fields of scientific endeavor.

Considering the historical factors and the cultural transformations of the past quarter of a century, one might expect greater responsiveness to psychoanalysis rather than increased antagonism. Yet actualities confute this expectation notwithstanding the apparent popularity of Freud's teaching.

Groping for an answer to this puzzle, one's mind turns to the well-known phenomenon of dissensions and deflections which prevails among certain students of psychoanalysis in and outside the psychoanalytic movement. At the outset these students accepted psychoanalysis as Freud formulated it. They did not for the most part reject Freud's views on sexuality and none refused to recognize the unconscious. For many years they studied psychoanalysis sympathetically, and they certainly could not escape the sense of enlightenment which the knowledge of new facts always brings to man. Yet, sooner or later, a number of these sympathetic students turned away from the empirical and theoretical foundations of psychoanalysis, some overtly, others covertly, some by means of condemnations, others with more or less oblique praise. Two

The Fundamental Conflict with Psychoanalysis

earnest thinkers, Roland Dalbiez and Mortimer Adler, have recently added to the representative array of deflections and dissenting criticism.[5] The thought suggests itself: If some of those who are thoroughly familiar with the theory and the practice, the subject matter and the method of psychoanalysis, ultimately rise in protest against it, the cause or causes that make for the deflection must bear an especial kinship to the fundamental source of the general opposition. If we disregard the various, purely individual determinants of particular dissenters and if we find that all or most of these dissenting opinions show an essential uniformity, a psychological unity in their opposition, then it is not impossible that in their attitude a clue will be found to the solution of the vexing problem.

The psychoanalyst is well aware that external variations in attitudes do not exclude the possibilities of internal unity or uniformity. External manifestations may be multifarious while the determining instinctual source of conflict may well prove to be one and the same throughout. Despite the variety of styles of expression and modes of thinking, the bewilderment over mental diseases which prevailed from the days of Pythagoras, through Hippocrates and Galen to St. Augustine, St. Thomas, Vesalius, Harvey and Descartes and throughout the nineteenth century right up to the time of Freud, presents one cardinal characteristic trend: Man has a soul. At times it appeared that this soul and the intelligence and will, which are its major vehicles, were ill. Yet the indisposition of the soul was truly unthinkable and, therefore, impossible. This general attitude was best expressed by the later medieval scholars, and it found its conscious, scientific adherents among the best psychiatric students of the nineteenth century—Heinroth, Reil, Griesinger. It ran as follows: The soul is perfect and immortal; illness is an imperfection; the soul cannot

[5] Dalbiez, *La méthode psychanalytique et la doctrine freudienne*, 1936; and Adler, Mortimer J., *What Man Has Made of Man*, 1937.

be ill because what is perfect by definition can never become imperfect by accident. The body, marvellous though it may be as an organic phenomenon, is not perfect and therefore it is susceptible to all sorts of imperfections. There is no such thing as mental illness; all allegedly mental diseases are nothing other than physical diseases, particularly brain diseases.[6] Reduced to its simplest terms this contention, a purely emotional conviction, may be said to represent the only convincing denial of death man has ever invented. It has determined the major direction of psychological science from time immemorial and perhaps for centuries to come. Man has made of immortality a psychologically incontrovertible fact.[7] Yet while he carries on the business of living, of catering to his mortal body, the postulate of immortality gives insufficient comfort to his mostly unconscious anxiety, his sense of helplessness. He must find a way to rid himself, to a degree at least, of his anxiety, otherwise he feels like a child, biologically and sociologically frustrated. A child cannot but observe that his elders do whatever they please, that their will is law. The passive submission to this law imperceptibly generates the need for passivity but also the counterpart, an escape into the fantasy that when the child grows up he will be as free as all grown ups. His will shall then be free, for a man's will is always free. Without this conviction, man would find it difficult, if not impossible, to maintain intact the companion conviction of immortality.

The instinctual narcissistic inevitability of these two con-

[6] A detailed review of the psychology of this attitude will be found in three articles by the writer: "Overestimation of Psychopathology," *American Journal of Orthopsychiatry*, Vol. IX, 1939; "The Border Lines of Knowledge in Present-day Psychiatry," *New England Journal of Medicine*, Vol. 261, 1937; "What Man Has Made of Man," *Psychoanalytic Quarterly*, Vol. VII, 1938.

[7] Cf. the writer's "The Sense of Immortality," *Psychoanalytic Quarterly*, Vol. VII, 1938.

victions is obvious to any student of psychoanalysis, but this inevitability no less obviously becomes a potent force which leads the rebellious opposition against psychoanalysis. Psychoanalysis, with its "inventions" of the psychic apparatus, does injury to this inevitability and undermines the security of a free will and an immortal existence. It arouses enormous masses of anxiety, re-awakens the sense of helplessness, and leaves no alternative but to fall back into a stage of infantile passive submission to that which is law and to rise in protest and accuse psychoanalysis of being immoral, of removing the only basis for ethics and of disturbing law and order. It is this vicious circle of anxiety which leads the thinker back to the Thomistic philosophical dogma demonstrated by Dalbiez and, more explicitly, by Mortimer Adler, who adopts the slogan, "Back to St. Thomas."

If one sees this reaction in the light of these inner psychological motivations, it becomes clear that one need not be an official adherent of orthodox Christian apologetics to feel the pull in the direction of free will and immortality, for they are the inevitable expressions of the eternal conflict of man, and they are the age-long components of all apologetics, both ecclesiastical and secular. They spring not from reason or even revelation, but from postulative dogma, from a *conditio sine qua non* which produces some semblance of inner security. That is perhaps the reason why such students as Karen Horney, rediscovering the total denial of Freud's theory of the instincts as the basis for the understanding of the psychic apparatus, find it possible to claim that this denial restores the human personality, morality and religion "to their original dignity." That Freud never dealt with the soul seems to be overlooked; general confusion arises because these opinions disregard the fact that Freud introduced the concept of the psyche as a biopsychological unit and, far from being a denial of the "organic," as a part of the total organism in its minutest functions. Even those keen thinkers who try to arouse an inspired and conscious nostalgia for the return to Thomas Aquinas disregard this fact; they fail to observe the major principle of St. Thomas which saved Aristotle from being reforgotten after he had been rediscovered. This principle presents perhaps the greatest contribution of St. Thomas. He adapted Aristotle to the prevailing apologetics by means of a new postulate: That which is true in philosophy may not be true in theology, and *vice versa*. By confusing soul with psyche or psychic apparatus, a distortion of thought resulting from profound anxiety, the opponents of psychoanalysis found themselves unable to apply the Thomistic principles to the Freudian studies and unable to comprehend that what is true in psychology may not be true in traditional apologetics, Catholic, Protestant or secular, and *vice versa*—that the psychic apparatus is not the soul and the soul is not the psyche.

Descartes came very close to freeing himself from this confusion but, sensing the dangers of his century, he fell back upon the tradition of generations and set himself the task of finding a seat for the soul. His was the smallest seat that had been named up to that time, the pineal gland; but nevertheless it was a very definite seat. As long as the soul has a seat, it is set apart, it remains an independent unit free of blemishes. Since it cannot be ill, it is the body's business to keep the seat of the soul as nearly well as possible. It is the body, the anatomy, the physiology that must be watched, cared for, cured. We are thus led back into a world without psychology, a world which made Möbius proclaim with false pride and a pontifical bow to the microscope "the hopelessness of all psychology."

Adler and Jung, the two earliest objectors to Freud, present the typical deviations from psychoanalysis which are implied in this outline. Adler's system starts with the organic, which is conceived rather naïvely as superficial anatomy ("organic in-

The Fundamental Conflict with Psychoanalysis 15

feriority"), and presents the accentuation of the trend of free will. Social organization is the most important factor; it is one directly visible structure of our culture. In other words, Adler has a good deal to say about the environment in the most diffuse yet simplest sense. We ought to be masters of this environment; we are in fact the determiners and, if only we think well, we find that we know how to assert ourselves, how to fashion and dominate the world we live in, and how to exert perfect control over ourselves. This voluntaristic, sociological philosophy is but a modern edition of the old defense against that anxiety from which we attempt to save ourselves by the proclamation of free will. Social organization and current economic and political conflicts take the place of the traditional anatomico-physiological discussions of the past; they are the screen for the relentless craving to maintain the identity of the soul and to find an appropriate seat for it. From the psychological point of view, it makes little difference, of course, whether this seat is the pineal gland, a trade union, or a parliament. Once the seat has been located, all the problems involving the function of the psychic apparatus recede into the background. When and as the instinctual life of man becomes a serious hindrance to the serenity of his conclusions, the soul becomes dislodged and the current superficial conflicts, if duly stressed, enable him to hold himself at the greatest possible distance, and thus he avoids the discomforts involved in "looking at himself." In many respects, this is exactly the position occupied by Alfred Adler, and it is particularly and more explicitly characteristic of the views recently evolved by Karen Horney.

On the other hand, should the point of effective emphasis fall upon the essence of the soul rather than upon free will, the "seat" is displaced from the purely sociological elements to the tradition of metaphysical heritage. The universal, the eternal, the endless continuity of the spiritual past with the spiritual future, the identity of these two in their pantheistic wholeness, come to the fore. In essence, the present is but an insignificant link in this continuity. The conflicts between the microcosm and the macrocosm, between the small ego and the universal, the discordant personal and the cosmic Nirvana, become the source of all ills. The concept of culture becomes transformed: whereas purely sociological psychopathology stresses man and his will and conceives of culture as something freely malleable that may be cut, measured, fitted and rearranged, the pantheistic psychopathology conceives of culture as a universal and indivisible external soul that is fundamentally independent of man, though it may occasionally seek him out and manipulate him for self-expression. This second road away from anxiety will already have been recognized as that indicated by Jung.

All the other major and minor deflections from psychoanalysis reveal themselves as based on the same fundamental conflict, and they present only variations on the adaptations which Adler and Jung first expressed. Rank, for instance, stresses the separation from the universal, the pantheistic—organic birth; man must avoid the anxiety he would feel should he discover himself a separate unit, weak and mortal. The most recent views of Rado, underlining the *scientific,* seem to reflect the ancient need to find firm support in the physiological, the biological, in other words the thing that, theoretically at least, is subject to manipulation. The so-called pure scientist seeks to find comfort in the exercise of his power over the physiologically palpable and visibly measurable. To him science is the manifestation of control, of free will, and it also serves him by providing proper quarters for the soul—the physiological system. Under the guise of overt materialism, the ardent pure scientist in psychology is actually completely independent of matter. True, it is always the biological, anatomical and physiological units that preoccupy him. The psychic apparatus, when consciously conceived as soul, is discarded, repressed, and, when unconsciously conceived as soul, is concealed under the screen of skepticism. When in doubt, he says that we know only the biological, the reflexological, the scientific; what the rest is, we do not know. Paradoxical attitudes are very familiar to the psychoanalytic clinician, and it will surprise no one if we conclude that the most materialistic physiological views in psychology, like those of Pavlov for instance, are actually based on the scientist's inability to overcome the fear that the acceptance of the concept of a psychic apparatus, as evolved by Freud, might persuade him to give up his conscious or unconscious religious faith in the independence and immortality of the soul and in free will. It is not the validity of the physiologist's findings that are questionable; these may be perfectly correct. It is the exclusivism of the so-called pure scientific psychologist that does injury to scientific fact, for it makes him blind to a number of essential findings that have been discovered by psychoanalysis. It is not a passive blindness, a mere inability to see. It is rather an amblyopia constantly fed by anxiety and therefore a combative distortion which always insists on its exclusive right to remain scotomized in a self-made halo of scientific clairvoyance.

Unless this underlying anxiety is sufficiently dissipated and a truly scientific differentiation between psyche and soul is made, a proper understanding and acceptance of psychoanalysis is practically impossible. I am afraid that the followers of Freud who consciously or intuitively fulfilled this prerequisite overlooked the full significance of man's most profound narcissistic tradition to make a megalomanic introjection of the father (free will) and a similarly megalomanic projection of his unwillingness to die (immortality, soul). The relationship of the general resistance against psychoanalysis to the mechanisms of introjection and projection is very instructive. The sociological objector to psychoanalysis utilizes primarily the mechanism of introjection and is, therefore, biased in favor of the motor expression of life, social changes and social controls. To him, behavior is mostly motor activity. He is the adept of the syntonic current action (Adler, Horney, to some extent Wilhelm Reich). On the other hand, projection leads to cosmic contemplation, to a kind of quietism and speculative constructions which acquire the value of realities. It produces an autistic orientation (Jung and, in part, Rank). The physiologico-reflexological point of view appears to utilize both mechanisms alternately and with equal cathexes. The value of realities of human motor behavior are displaced on to the physiological equivalents of psychological activity and by means of deduction rather than induction a hypothetical individual is created (Rado).

The groundwork on which the structure of true psychoanalysis should be built may well be fashioned in the pattern of St. Thomas. The manifestations of our struggle against the anxiety aroused by our investigation of the psychic apparatus should not impinge upon the philosophy (validity) of our psychological science, no matter what truths they might represent in theology or its unconscious equivalent. A confusion of the psyche as a scientific concept and the soul as a theological one mobilizes in us a complex mass of narcissistic cathexes which constitutes the fundamental source of the well-nigh invincible opposition to psychoanalysis.

Psyche, Soul, and Religion

AMONG the numerous controversies which were aroused by psychoanalysis, the question of Freud's negative attitude toward religion played no minor role. There are few aspects of cultural expression about which Freud was bitter, but he was bitter about religion. From the very outset the Church, Catholic or Protestant, was hardly less condemnatory of Freud. There were some among the Protestant clergy—notably the Swiss minister Oskar Pfister—who contributed much to psychoanalysis and its literature, although they disagreed with Freud's views on religion. However, all religious denominations were and for the most part still are opposed to Freud and to psychoanalysis. Their opposition dates far back, to the time when Freud formulated his theory of sex and first expressed rather tentatively the opinion that an obsessional neurosis could be considered a "private religion," and religion, a universal obsessional neurosis.

Freud's religious opponents found it easy to draw the rather superficial conclusion that psychoanalysis is basically irreligious and that psychoanalysts are all atheists. Freud's overt

First published in 1943. Reprinted from *Mind, Medicine and Man* by permission of the publishers, copyright © 1943 by Harcourt, Brace and World, Inc.

rejection of religion after almost twenty years of psychoanalytic research was taken generally as the natural outcome of his erroneous observations and as the inevitable, logical conclusion of his false psychological premises. It was as if the Church had said: "We never accepted Freud's psychology, because we always knew that it led to atheism; now, when Freud has pronounced himself unequivocally an atheist, it is even more clear to us that we were right all the time; Freud has proved our point beyond any further doubt." That Freud's views on religion might possibly have been only an expression of his personal attitude was apparently not considered. That unconditional opposition to religion, or any opposition to religious belief, was not inherent in the Freudian system of psychology seemed unthinkable. That Freud contradicted himself even when he took a stand against religion remained unnoticed. That his contradictions on the subject of religion were both logical and psychological has not been properly pointed out by either his opponents or his followers.

It is not difficult to detect an element of welcome in the general attitude toward Freud's antireligious platform, as if this stand added obvious and irrefutable substance to the violent criticism of psychoanalysis, which was general, sustained, and almost unshakable. Freud's views on religion were accepted or rejected too uncritically and too readily. Injury is always done to truth, and violence to justice, when in the midst of a serious controversy we welcome a logical misstep of an opponent merely to ease our conscience, which would otherwise reproach us for lack of curiosity and failure to understand what our opponent has to say.

Let us recall and fix in our minds that Freud was a rather unskilled philosopher and that he was not a social scientist. He was a doctor and a psychologist and a great artist, a master of the written word and a lucid, incisive, although at times a

Psyche, Soul, and Religion

little morose, intellect. He was a great humanist, but his was also a strict mind. Superficiality disturbed him. The question of how man lives within himself and with others fascinated him. He was absorbed in his own work and deeply preoccupied with the vastness of his field and the ramifications of psychoanalysis in all branches of life as well as in scientific and speculative thought. It is extremely curious that Freud, who delved so deeply into the human mind and whose method of study of the individual was so strictly historical, never seems to have been interested in the origin and history of his own ideas on the unconscious, repression, and the instinctual drives. The historical psychophilosophical continuity of his thought seems to have been of no concern to him. He never made a study of Herbart, Schopenhauer, or Nietzsche, who in many respects anticipated certain of the concepts which he created and developed in the course of his work. Freud was an empiricist and a medical psychologist. Even in his nonmedical writings—such as his brief study of Leonardo da Vinci, his article on Jensen's novel *Gradiva*, his anthropological study *Totem and Taboo*, his sociological work *Civilization and Its Discontents*, or his purely speculative writings such as *The Unconscious* and *Two Principles of Psychic Functioning*—Freud had but one problem in mind: How does the psychic apparatus work, and under which conditions does the psychic economy get out of balance and produce neurotic disturbances or psychotic disintegration?

A profound humanist and libertarian, Freud looked on the world only from the point of view of the individual. He saw true values only in the individual's creative forces and in his normal existence, in his aspirations for a better life. He found that two leviathans stood in the path of the individual: nature, which had to be conquered, and civilization, which was always a source of discomfort. Like a true Christian, Freud loved and pitied man. But also like a true Jew, he was always proud of man in a melancholy way and rather serenely anxious when he contemplated the biological strivings and limitations of man and his inordinate aggression. The central point of Freud's fascination was man's great capacity for love, and with considerable pessimism he wondered about man's inordinate capacity to hate, to kill, and to seek death. He was stirred by the vistas which revealed themselves before him when he studied the transformation of man's self-love and hedonism into love for others and altruism. In this preoccupation Freud was the true descendant of Aristotle and St. Thomas Aquinas. He lent more than casual support to these two men by the mass of empirical data which was unknown to Aristotle or St. Thomas and which he accumulated during six decades of assiduous and productive work. Yet Freud would have been the last man in the world to admit the affinity of his findings and ideas with the thought of Aristotle and St. Thomas. He would have been the first to say that it was Plato from whom he derived greater inspiration, that he was neither Christian nor monk, and that he felt foreign to St. Thomas, even if he had ever cast a casual and uninterested glance at the cover page of the *Summa Theologica*.

Broad philosophical systems and the inner empire of religion were of little value to Freud, because in them the individual seemed to him lost. Anything that threatened the autonomy of the individual he treated with skepticism, suspicion, and even contempt. It is not difficult to see where Freud made his mistake when he was confronted with the major phenomena of human living—civilization and religion. Freud was always so careful not to judge man that he left the question of values to be answered by the healthy individual himself; consequently, he betrayed a methodological weakness in his estimation of the values of civilization and religion in their proper perspective. One almost senses in Freud reverberations of the eighteenth century. The French political philosophy of *Le Contrat Social* demanded the utmost freedom for man within the broad limitations imposed upon him by the voluntary contract which he was supposed to have concluded with his fellow men. Civilization insofar as it restricts and hampers man appeared to Freud a violation of this contract. Religion as one of the most restrictive forces in our civilization was, therefore, injurious both in form and in content.

Freud, who never failed to stress the polarity of human nature, the tendency to be passive and submissive as well as active and domineering, overlooked the immense role of religion in relation to man's passivity. Perhaps it is this error that also made him overlook, or pass over in silence, the relationship between the intensification of manifest homosexual drives whenever religion shows signs of losing its hold on a given civilization. This phenomenon has become particularly obvious since the last war, especially in Germany under Hitler. Freud was more interested in the psychological parallelism between the individual and certain aspects of civilization; therefore he centered his attention primarily on the psychological mechanisms of culture and religion insofar as those mechanisms could also be found operative in the individual as an autonomous unit. Whenever he saw in civilization a psychological constellation which was similar to that of an individual neurosis, then it was a neurosis of civilization. A neurosis in an individual must be cured—a neurosis in society must be rejected. It is to be noted that it was not cure that Freud advised, but rejection on the basis of purely intellectual analysis of the psychological components of the alleged social neurosis. In relation to civilization, he appears not as the therapist but as the bearer of severe protests. Freud was the greatest representative of the Renaissance which humanity was fortunate enough to have in the otherwise gruesome and bloody half-century of our age. Like Erasmus, he was keen and challenging and libertarian and critical. But unlike Erasmus and many other great and pious humanists, Freud was closer to the classicist and the rationalist; he opposed religion because he honestly believed that "religion decries the value of life." It may be repeated that it is on the problem of values that Freud's methodology was stranded or even shattered.

In order to understand the true relationship of psychoanalysis to religion, we must keep definitely in mind what it is we discuss when we use the term "psychoanalysis." Is it psychoanalysis as a therapeutic technique? A technique of treatment of a disease, a rational, empirical, and scientific technique based on causal principles, cannot be of any worth in evaluating anything but the efficacy of its curative power. It is obvious that the technique of psychoanalytic treatment has nothing to contribute to problems of estimating social and religious values.

Is it psychoanalysis as a philosophy? This we cannot consider, for the simple reason that there is no such philosophy. There are many people, among them this writer, who derive certain social, religious, and philosophical considerations out of the body of facts accumulated by psychoanalytic research, but this does not make psychoanalysis a philosophy. Botany and zoology present an enormous mass of factual material; philosophers might make use of these facts, but this use would not elevate botany and zoology to the status of philosophies.

Is it then the body of empirical facts and the accompanying working hypotheses that we have in mind when we use the word "psychoanalysis"? This should be the case. It is quite obvious that we ought to limit ourselves to the consideration of the facts which psychoanalysis has to submit; we ought to postpone consideration of the question of philosophical or religious values until we are in full possession of that which has been observed and described. This is the prerequisite of any learning; we should comply with it and avoid that carping state of mind which rejects in advance any or all of the facts of

Psyche, Soul, and Religion

psychoanalysis only because Freud himself happened to have his own way of estimating certain rules of life.

Moreover, facts, like faith, cannot be rejected. Facts stand, no matter how much one may insist that they do not exist; and faith stands in the mind of man, no matter how sharply many people may choose to reject it.

Freud's attitude toward religious values is a highly interesting psychological phenomenon. He treated religion now as if it were an expression of the nature of man which he did not particularly like, and then as something superimposed on our culture and as something highly undesirable because it is infantile, neurotic—an illusion. He gave no evidence of being interested in the actual function of religion in the frame of our cultural growth. He did not go beyond pointing out that the psychological mechanisms of religious expression were those of a neurosis, and on the basis of these mechanisms he rejected religion. Yet Freud described in similar terms the psychological mechanisms involved in the creation and application of art and assumed a totally different attitude. "The substitutive gratifications [of unconscious, forbidden, and infantile drives], such as art offers, are illusions in contrast to reality, but none the less satisfying to the mind on that account, thanks to the place which fantasy has reserved for herself in mental life." Freud did not decry the psychological infantilism of art, nor did he call art a cultural neurosis, nor did he reject it on the ground of its being an illusion.

Even in his consideration of religion, Freud contradicted himself. He stated in his *Civilization and Its Discontents:* "Nor may we allow ourselves to be misled by our own judgments concerning the value of any of these religious or philosophic systems or of these ideals; whether we look upon them as the highest achievement of the human mind, or whether we deplore them as fallacies, one must acknowledge that where they exist, and especially where they are in the ascendant, they testify to a high level of civilization." Unfortunately Freud, who almost admitted in this passage that his own judgment concerning the value of religion might be a purely personal bias, never pursued the matter any further. It would seem that having dealt all his life with problems of psychopathology and having continuously occupied himself with the effort to disperse the nonrealistic fantasies and illusions of neurotic and psychotic patients, Freud confused neurotic, false belief with faith, particularly religious faith. In addition, he seems to have accepted his personal opposition to religion as one based on his scientific psychology. Scientific knowledge is essentially different from religious knowledge, and it is impossible to measure one by the other; they have no common methodological denominator.

It is totally outside the scope of our discussion to try to analyze the psychological and philosophical relationships between science and religion. Such an analysis would inevitably lead us into a discussion of theology, and the writer is not a theologian. His contribution to such a discussion would only enhance the confusion of the issues involved. Moreover, whenever science has worked to put theology on a scientific basis, and whenever theology has attempted to put science on a theological basis, so much strife has been generated that the dignity of both has been considerably tarnished and humanity has suffered, not only intellectually, but spiritually and physically as well.

There is a great deal of feeling in religious faith. The psychologist of the future will probably acquire both the courage and the insight necessary to enlighten us on the deeper psychological forces and mechanisms underlying religious faith. All faiths, except perhaps the Mohammedan to some extent, are pervaded with such a spirit of humility and of service to God and man that one is fascinated and yet frightened to see

Psyche, Soul, and Religion

how much aggression and intolerance are aroused as soon as a religious controversy is kindled. Religion does appear to be a repository of great masses of aggression and therefore, from the point of view of its psychological function, religion does seem to be the force which harnesses a greater amount of aggression than any other spiritual agency. This aggression comes out of its repression with the utmost intensity as soon as some unknown element is touched to disturb or to question a given religious faith. The cynic might merely point to the floods of blood and waves of hatred accompanying religious strife as signs of the very incongruity of religion, of its basic instability; he therefore might reject it as irrational and useless and even injurious. The less cynical and more contemplative might wonder whether some forty centuries of monotheism is really a sufficiently long time for the human race to learn to be faithful to religious belief, and whether the religious crises were not a direct result of our general cultural, economic crises. Human history bears ample proof that it was not religion that produced these crises but a number of potent factors which merely engulfed the religious life of the race in their stormy waves. This was the history of the Kingdom of Israel and of the Roman Empire. Not Luther, not even Savonarola, certainly not Henry VIII, represented purely religious issues, although their struggles, which grew out of the very essence of the march of civilization, produced great religious controversies, schisms, hostility, calumny, combat, bigotry, and perversity. We must again defer our hopes to the future psychologist who may be able to decipher this tragic puzzle. Clear it is for the moment that when religious individuals or groups act in such a manner as to give full vent to all the human weaknesses, it is not their religion but their human deficiency that makes them victims to the disrupting trends of life.

It is of little scientific or philosophical value to point to what many scientists, including Freud, have called the "fallacies of religion." One cannot consider the postulates of religion scientific fallacies and feel that some point is proved, for religion was never based on scientific proof.

There is more than a lurking suspicion in one's mind that the fundamental anxiety of man, his deep-seated insecurity, plays its rather cynical, Mephistophelean role in both scientific and religious questions. The scientist in all his sagacity sooner or later reaches a blind alley wherein he is lost in the mist of the unknown and perhaps unknowable; he then defends himself against the trembling voices of anxiety by demanding that religion either give him scientific proof of its validity or desist from beckoning his troubled mind. The religious man who, in all his faith and devotion, stumbles upon the fullness of his anxiety demands that science either accept his religion and then give him succor, or desist from trying to seduce him with the obviousness and tangibility of all that is measurable and gives one such an illusion of power and mastery over the universe. One wonders whether some ingenious critic of empirical and experimental science might not turn the tables and say, not entirely without right and plausibility, that science ought to be rejected because it is an outlet for man's inordinate infantile, peeping, sexual curiosity, because it is merely a formalized expression of his faith in himself and in his ultimate mastery over nature and man. Such a critic might even assert that science is an infantile, neurotic adaptation which leads us to destroy life while claiming that we aspire to achieve the opposite.

Very few in our age of mass production of Flying Fortresses would countenance such an argument about science, for we are too thrilled with self-adulation over our mass production, and we overlook the bomber-and-tank aspects of it. We *must* overlook the destructive forces of our scientific civilization, because we cherish our delusions of scientific goodwill, of light in the midst of darkness. It is hardly necessary to remark

Psyche, Soul, and Religion

that this imaginary argument about science is as tenuous as Freud's about religion. Freud's argument, we must repeat, involves a consideration of values to which science has no answer and never will have. The problem of values belongs to that inner and anxious longing for the re-establishment of that true brotherhood of men on earth which may have existed for a fleeting moment in the remote past and then disintegrated as a result of the reciprocal aggression and common sense of guilt which came from the primal murder of the father.

Both religion and psychoanalysis—the former by way of inspiration and revelation, the latter by way of psychological investigation—seek to solve the difficult problems which impose themselves upon man in his constant state of anxiety and sense of guilt. Both seek the path that would lead to serenity and attenuation of the sense of guilt. Each uses a terminology of its own, but both seem to have solved the problem on the basis of the same principle. Both give the principle the same name—love. One sees in love the means for ultimate salvation, the other, the means for ultimate health. This, it would seem, is a point of contact between religion and scientific psychology which no other science has ever had. Yet religion and psychoanalysis have kept apart throughout the history of psychoanalysis, largely on what seems to have been the initiative of Freud himself, but not without the most active co-operation on the part of religion. This antagonism, particularly in the light of what they have in common, is at first not easily explained. What Freud's psychological and methodological error might have been has already been suggested. Moreover, in discussing religion, particularly when he said that it decries the value of life, Freud was too general and, entirely in contradistinction to his usual succinct way of looking at things, rather diffuse and dogmatic. He confused the ideational content of religion with its ritualistic expression, its psychological elements with its institutional aspects.

While Freud was not entirely explicit on the subject, he seems to have had foremost in mind the Catholic Church; he lived most of his long life in Vienna and in the atmosphere of ancient Catholic tradition. Of liberal Catholicism he was apparently not aware. His judgment of Protestantism he never stated, but it is doubtful whether he felt more kindly toward it. Because of his individualism, Freud chose religion as the symbol of the anti-individualistic forces of our culture. That is perhaps why he concentrated his criticism on religion and overlooked many much more potent cultural forces which neglect, reject, and injure the wholeness of man as an individual. He overlooked, for instance, the maelstrom of modern capitalistic industrialism and its pressure on the individual. Modern industrialism—whether in Catholic or Protestant countries—sacrifices the individual with increasing frequency and ever growing efficiency in favor of the whole. It does so without any formal guiding ethical authority but through the sheer pressure of the material power of man over man. It is highly doubtful whether the nonindividualistic theology of Catholicism has actually impeded the growth of man. While capitalistic industrialism does standardize man almost as much as automobiles, it is essentially irreligious in its striving for possessions and power; while it does not officially decry the value of life, it circumscribes it sufficiently to hamper man's inner creative freedom.

Freud, the profound individualist, did not express himself so violently, or at all, against this economic aspect of our civilization. What seems to have aroused his bitterness against religion is apparently something more than and different from his individualism, which he used only as a point of departure for his antireligious considerations. One wonders whether Freud, had he lived longer and preserved his analytical powers, or had he come to the examination of religion sooner, would not have revised his views on religion, or at least have corrected them to the extent of apperceiving in the religious "escape from realities of life" not a neurotic illusion but one of man's most natural functional adjustments to many of the inner realities with which he is always confronted.

Freud resented the restrictions which religious tradition imposes upon our biological urges, particularly the erotic ones, yet he could have considered the fact in a somewhat different light if it had occurred to him that these restrictions and taboos are older than our historical civilization, older than our monotheistic religions. As he himself said, they arose from a number of primitive needs which are controlled with the same difficulty as any other basic need of man. Freud looked upon religion as the proponent of asceticism; yet if one considers the theoretical but logical possibilities of turning one's love outward to the utmost, a situation might obtain which Freud himself described so very well when he spoke of "that way of life which makes love the center of all things and anticipates all happiness from loving and being loved." If and when this way of life is ever reached by man, he naturally feels humble and serene, and he expresses the totality of his relationship to life in terms of loving God and everything living, and of being loved or striving toward being loved by God.

Freud had St. Francis in mind when he spoke of the way of life which makes love the center of all things, and it is the mystical quality of the imagery which accompanies this way of life, the mysterious, magic concomitants of ceremony and prayer, that Freud felt necessary to reject because he felt all this was none the less infantile and illusory. In this Freud was in error, and religion in reply committed its error in relation to Freud. Stated briefly, this reciprocal mistake could be outlined as follows.

I walk to church. In order to reach church I use my legs. I bring into play those nerves and muscles which supervise and are involved in locomotion. I walk across the street to shoot a man. I use the same set of nerves and muscles and the same brain nuclei for this purpose. I enter church, still using the same part of my neuromuscular apparatus, and I light a candle; in order to light the candle, I use my right hand, especially my thumb and forefinger, and that part of my neuromuscular system which moves my forearm, arm, and hand. I enter the office of the man I am to kill and shoot him. To shoot, I use my right hand, especially the thumb and forefinger, and the same set of neuromuscular units.

He will be insensate who will conclude on this basis that going to church and lighting a candle are equivalent and perhaps equal to entering a man's office and shooting him, because the anatomic and physiological units used to carry out these two most divergent acts are identical. Let us assume now, no matter how preposterous the invitation may seem, that Freud and the Church both agree on one point—that the anatomical and physiological instruments of walking to church and lighting a candle and walking into a man's office and shooting him are identical. Each would draw his own inimical conclusion. On the basis of the above-established identity, Freud would say: "I reject religion and all it stands for because it is anatomicophysiologically criminal and murderous." The Church on the same basis would say: "I reject Freud because he describes the anatomicophysiological apparatus which we use to walk to church in the same terms as the neuromuscular apparatus which we use to commit murder. I further reject Freud because his anatomy is wrong, his physiology is wrong, his theology is wrong, and consequently his whole system is erroneous and sacrilegious."

Preposterous and incongruous as such imaginary reasoning might appear, Freud and the representatives of religion have repeatedly approximated this error in relation to one another. This impasse of mutual misunderstanding is so definite and final that one would have real cause to despair of ever bringing any warmth of reconciliation into this cold atmosphere of settled divergence were it not for a number of similar problems in the past which offer considerable hope in the manner of their solution. When the great minds of Islam, Averrhoes and Avicenna, introduced Aristotle, the established Church rejected the great founder of the Lyceum. Averrhoes and Avicenna were followers of a great enemy of Christianity, and Aristotle was a pagan; consequently, Aristotle's physics was condemned in 1209, and his *Metaphysics* in 1215. At that time no one could have suspected that thirty-five years later Aristotle would be taught in the University of Paris with the full approval of the Church, and that less than fifty years later the philosophy of Aristotle would become the very foundation of the immortal system of St. Thomas Aquinas and of Christian theology itself.

The biological and psychological instruments at man's disposal are limited. On the borderline between that which he can learn to know and the unknowable, man appears to try to surpass himself, and his aspirations seem to make him trace for himself a path far beyond the limits of his ability. He is limited in his ways and means of comprehension and, particularly, of expressing himself. The ways and means at his disposal are always the same, and he can use them for physical and intellectual, good and bad purposes. Freud formulated his concept of the psychic apparatus as the reservoir of man's psychobiological ways and means. He inferentially mistook the psychic apparatus for what is called the "soul." Religion glanced at Freud's formulation and demurred, for it was not the soul as religion understood it. It was then easy for religion to affirm that there was no such thing as the psychic apparatus. That Freud on certain indeterminate occasions inferentially equated psyche and soul was one of the methodological mistakes which he seems to have been unable to escape, even as a majority of people mistakenly assume that psychology has something to do with the soul.

As has already been mentioned, this same methodological mistake was for some reason duplicated by the religious opponents of psychoanalysis. We must divest ourselves of the consequences of this mistake, and we shall succeed in doing so if we recall certain events in the history of thought. For many centuries the Church relied on the principles of Thomistic philosophy, which recognizes two sources of knowledge: reason and revelation (science and theology). St. Thomas, following the principle, had no difficulty in incorporating the knowledge which the pagan peripatetic philosopher had outlined over three hundred years before the birth of Christ and more than fifteen hundred years before St. Thomas wrote his *Summa Theologica*. Nor did St. Thomas have any difficulty in accepting the scientific findings of the Mohammedan Arabian scholars. The paganism of Aristotle and the heresy of Mohammed were matters for purely theological consideration. One could reject the religious, or if you wish the irreligious, beliefs of Aristotle and the Mohammedan Avicenna and still consider their scientific conclusions acceptable, without impairing the integrity and the consistency of the Catholic dogma.

In the same manner, the scientific and sociological views of some popes could not be considered as a part of the theology which they represented as heads of the Church. Boniface VIII opposed the study of anatomy, but this was in an age when many in less lofty places and more scientifically minded assumed the same attitude; one cannot on this basis say that the Church as a religious faith opposed the study of anatomy. The Church as an institution could not but reflect the scientific and cultural struggle of each given epoch. Today no Catholic would even imagine that it is imperative to oppose the study of anatomy in medical schools. The meteorological views of

Psyche, Soul, and Religion

Innocent VIII, who ascribed storms and droughts to the machinations of witches, were as much an expression of the culture of his day as was the superstitious attitude toward witches on the part of some of the greatest medical scholars of the fifteenth and sixteenth centuries. Today Catholicism would not say that modern meteorological science encroaches upon the theological foundation of the Church. The anti-Jewish laws of Marcellus II, which in many respects parallel the Hitlerian Nuremberg Laws, were characteristic both of the man and of the times. They are sufficiently outweighed by the serene simplicity of Pius XI, who denounced anti-Semitism without mincing words and stated that the tradition of the Catholic Church is Semitic and that she considers Abraham her patriarch. One wonders why, by the same token, some judicious and contemplative and scientific Catholic mind, whose Catholicism would be as profound and unshakable as that of St. Thomas and whose breadth of vision and scientific taste would be as universal and catholic, could not undertake a careful restudy of Freud and his followers and see for himself wherein the scientific findings of these unbelievers are truly scientific and therefore, like any true science, do not, as they cannot, encroach on the theology of the Church.

Let us take as a simple example St. Thomas's assertion that sensuality is the source of evil and misuse of reason. The scientific findings of Freud demonstrated that hedonism, infantile sexuality, if persisting beyond a certain period of life leads to mental illness and other forms of maladjustment. Here we have the scientific corroboration of the claims made by both Aristotle and St. Thomas. That St. Thomas on the basis of his attitude toward sensuality chose to take orders against his father's will and lead a saintly, monastic life, and that another person on the same basis would today choose the secular life of a family man, in no way contradicts the psycho-philosophical conclusions of St. Thomas or the biopsychological findings of Freud.

The concept of sensuality which was in the mind of St. Thomas might well have been the concept of sexual indulgence in the narrow sense of the word, although his age intuitively sensed that other, seemingly nonsexual forms of sensuality, such as gluttony, are of the same sensual order. In the light of scientific, psychological investigations, Freud found it possible to establish the common nature of all sensual drives, which he called "sexual," "erotic"; the term cannot be considered alone and by itself and be forcibly re-established in its narrow sense of pertaining to the sexual organs. Any drive which provides pleasure and which is used or utilized primarily for the pleasure it provides is termed "erotic"; aggression, when it becomes coupled with pleasurable apperceptions, conscious or unconscious, is considered erotized even if it does not take the form of a sadistic perversion. The fact that for many centuries the word "erotic" made men think only of something related to the reproductive organs is undeniable and understandable, but perhaps no less regrettable. Plato's conception of Eros was certainly more broad and profound. It is a matter of taste, not truth, whether we accept the Freudian term "sexual" or the Thomistic "sensual." Freud was no more pansexual in his attitude toward and hopes for man than St. Thomas was pansensual. By the same token it matters just as little whether we use the Aristotelian term "self-love" or the Freudian term "narcissism," provided we understand the psychological structure and the dynamics of narcissism as they are understood by modern psychological science. They encroach upon the dogma and the basic theological principles of the Church no more than the discovery of the benzene ring by the chemist or of the electric charges in the stormy clouds of the firmament by the physicist.

We may now go beyond the mere consideration of terms

and take a close look at the libido theory, or the "theory of sex," as it is sometimes called. The conclusion which imposed itself on Freud was that man cannot be considered grown-up or normal unless all the component infantile drives become fused into one genital constellation. Only then does the libido acquire the capacity and quality of turning toward the outside world, toward people and things. Only then, in other words, does man become capable of true love. The term "love" from now on loses its narrow, selfish, sensual meaning; even the purely erotic aspect of this love, in the narrow sense of the word, is no longer dominated exclusively by the sensual elements of which it is composed. The child, if we look upon him from the point of view of our adult standards, is not capable of this adult love; in all his innocence, he is what Freud called "polymorphously perverse." The grown-up is alive with his filial, brotherly feelings for others, and his love flows outward; the psychological maturity of the individual leads to mature psychological fatherhood and motherhood. This change must occur even before physiological maturity sets in. Love becomes the mainspring of our psychological energy and the cornerstone of that edifice which represents our social, esthetic, and spiritual life. Love becomes the master drive which keeps permanent vigil, holding back and trying to neutralize the aggressive, antisocial drives coming from within as well as the aggressive impulses aroused by the impacts of reality coming from without. Love is the source and substance of our conscience. The anxiety with which our sense of guilt is pervaded and the severity of our conscience may appear to us to be made up only of fear and aggression, but if it were not for our unquenchable need to love and be loved there would be no conscience; there would remain only animal fear and animal aggression.

It matters little which terminology Freud used. It matters little whether or not Freud, in describing the biopsychological evolution of the individual from the cradle to puberty and maturity, stopped to consider the mysterious transformation of that which we perceive and feel into cognition—consciousness. It also matters very little whether or not Freud took into consideration the religious aspects of the growth of man. From the point of view of our argument, it is perhaps an advantage that Freud failed to consider all these questions, for his conclusions could then be viewed as even more objective. In his study of the individual's development from the narcissistic, polymorphous perverse stage to the level of mature love, Freud took into consideration the mystery of human life as little as the anatomist, who dissects the various organs of the body, concerns himself with the mystery of death. What does matter is that Freud, unconcerned with ethics or religion, arrived at the conclusion that the life of man is based on creative love, on constant domestication of his aggression, on constant harmonization of the animal within him with his humanness, on the constant living of his life on the basis of love and reason instead of hate and impulse. These conclusions imposed themselves upon Freud by the very evidential force of the psychological phenomena which he observed clinically. It is not necessary to call upon complex philosophical speculations or to exercise much logical strain to see that Freud, unbeknown to himself, thus established an empirical basis of life which is in total conformity with the Christian ideal.

It is baffling, and often confusing and even embarrassing, to note that our Christian thought has failed to accept and wishes to reject a scientific finding and conclusion which not only lends support to the fundamental precepts of its own ethicoreligious teaching but also brings a biological, observational, scientific proof of the revelatory intuition which has inspired religious teachers since the time of St. Augustine.

It is not accidental that the objective, biological terminology of psychoanalysis designates being in love as "being fixated on the love object." It describes the sense of oneness of adult love as different from the infantile or neurotic state of being *fixed* on the infantile object or source of pleasure, different from the disrupting, essentially non-loving, purely biological, purely animal egotism. Nor is it accidental that psychoanalysis describes the love for others than the adult sexual partner as *desexualized* and the love for the adult sexual partner as imbued and motivated by the need and wish for children, for adult parenthood. These nonaccidental designations demonstrate how our disorganized and selfish and anarchic drives arrange themselves in a harmony in accordance with an inner law, which religion has expressed in terms of morality, the sanctity of monogamy and ethics, and unity with the will of God. That psychoanalysis nowhere seems to occupy itself with problems of morality and ethics is, of course, true. But it is also true that the physiologist is concerned little if at all with the ethical and religious implications of his experimental findings. Nor does the logician consider the ethical and religious implications of his system; he studies the forms of reasoning and leaves the problem of their ethical or unethical directions to the religious preceptor.

Science has always concerned itself very little with questions of religion and morality. The scientist as a person may or may not be a good man; he may or may not be religious; he may or may not offer his own ideas on the relationship between his scientific observations and his religious feelings; he may be indifferent to the problem; he may even be antagonistic to religion. Whatever he feels in this respect he will feel not as a scientist but as a person, pious or unbelieving, who even at the height of his scientific greatness remains a mere human being. The greatest scientist may be and usually is a very poor theologian and if an unbeliever, a rather naïve one. One of the most flagrant mistakes religious thinkers make is to assume inferentially and implicitly that a good scientist, to be scientifically right, must be either a good theologian or at least an adherent of the theological tenets of an established religious institution. That this is unnecessary and that the opposite, far from injuring religion, may become one of its chief sources of factual support, has been proved time and again by the history of medicine, physics, and chemistry, which have never yet succeeded in refuting and still less in undermining the dogma of the Church.

Freud might well be placed in the same relation to Christian dogma as St. Augustine stood in relation to Plato, and Thomistic religious philosophy in relation to Averrhoes and Aristotle. Even from the strictest philosophical point of view, Freud as a scientist does not contradict the fundamental principles of the descriptive, philosophical psychology of St. Thomas. Freud observed and described what he observed. At no time did he touch upon the question of how our animal drives and our sensory reactions become transformed into thought and comprehension. He was not concerned with, nor did he advance any facts or any arguments against, that principle which St. Thomas called the "acting intellect" (*intellectus agens*), which produces reasoning by way of forming abstractions (*per modum abstractionis*). Where St. Thomas speaks of "phantasmas" Freud speaks of "representations"—that is, the inner images we make for ourselves of the objects of the outside world.

It would not add to the clarity of our discussion if we engaged in a detailed consideration of Thomistic psychology and compared it with the Freudian. To retranslate St. Thomas's scholastic terminology into purely modern language and then to recast Freud's own terminology into its more tangible equivalents is no easy task, yet in the opinion of the writer it is feasible, scientifically justifiable, and philosophically tenable. Suffice it to say here that Aristotle and St. Thomas were and numerous generations of philosophers since have been preoccupied with the problem of how our perceptions become transformed into thought and action. Purely materialistic explanations failed to provide a satisfactory answer, and the sharp dichotomy of body and mind succeeded as little. The search for a center in which all sensations meet (*sensorium commune*) and become integrated has always been a matter of concerted preoccupation and has never yielded really satisfactory results. Whether we place this *sensorium commune* in the heart or in the brain matters little; the riddle remains unsolved.

It is Freud's momentous contribution to the solution of this riddle that seems to be overlooked. Science probably never will be able to provide the final answer, but Freud's conception of the psychic apparatus made it easier for us to understand the dynamic process of the transition from the purely physiological to the purely mental. The psychic apparatus is apparently the actual *sensorium commune*, the central, intermediate, obscure and yet so dynamic zone of functioning by virtue of which man is able to make the transition from automatic animal to human behavior. It is perfectly logical to look upon the psychic apparatus, particularly the area between the id and the superego, as the functional biological stratum in which man is no more a mere animal and not yet fully a human being. The psychic apparatus is just what it etymologically means: It is the apparatus, biological in nature, through which filter the conative and cognitive elements of the human personality. One cannot repeat too many times that psychoanalysis knows and claims to know as little about the soul as the religious opponent knows about the psychic apparatus. These two entities cannot be united and confused with or substituted for one another. Any attempt at such a unity or substitution is an attempt to construct a contentious artificiality, something like a scientific theology or a theological science—which is a contradiction in terms, in concepts, and in basic subject matter.

The emotional fog of mutual suspicion and open hostility which surrounds psychoanalysis has produced unserviceable controversies and some singular paradoxes. Religious dogma looks upon psychoanalysis as the essence of incorrigible materialism denying the existence of the soul; the modern dogma of Marxism accuses psychoanalysis of being too idealistic for acceptance by a historical materialist. Religion assumes that Freud is too mechanistic; Marxism, that he is too metaphysical. Both accusations are obviously unjustified; both are based on the misunderstanding of the basic scientific premises of psychoanalysis. One can answer the accusation raised by religion merely by saying that the phenomena of life and living, being what they are, manifest themselves to us in a certain way; Freud described these phenomena not only as they appear to the outside observer but also as they subjectively appear to those observed. One can answer the economic determinist by saying exactly the same thing with the added observation that the psychology of man is not only a cultural but also a biological phenomenon, and biology is something more than mechanical physicochemical physiology. Psychoanalysis as a body of facts and working hypotheses neither explicitly nor implicitly denies economics or religion; psychoanalysis cannot deny them, because it cannot deny anything that represents human living. Both economic materialism and religion deny psychoanalysis not because they know that it is wrong but because they do not yet understand it.

A point has been reached in this discussion at which one is tempted to proceed along the lines of philosophy, particularly that part of philosophy which is preoccupied with religious problems. If one were to give in to this temptation, one would run the double risk of abandoning the field of observation for that of speculation and of intruding into a domain in which, to say the least, a scientific observer is apt to find himself highly inexperienced. The writer has endeavored to the best of his ability to make clear how little psychoanalysis as an observational discipline really does encroach upon religious philosophy, and how it even lends empirical support to some of this philosophy's precepts as he understands them. He has neither the right nor the equipment to venture beyond the limits thus far reached.

It must be borne in mind that no attempt has been made here to seek a psychoanalytic solution of theological problems, or a theological solution of psychoanalytic problems. The only thing that appears really important in this discussion is to establish clearly that the psychic apparatus, or the psyche, is not the soul, that it is the instrument of the soul as much as our neuromuscular system is the instrument of our sensorymotor system. It is not a separate, anatomical entity; it is a functional instrument, charged with energy, and it works, reacts, and behaves in response to stimuli. These stimuli come from without (from the outside world) and from within (from our instinctual drives). The instinctual drives come from special organs and from the organism as a whole. These drives may be speculatively identified with the "life force," or the *élan vital*, or whatever it is that makes a living thing a living thing, whether it is an ant, a lion, a snake, or a man.

The instrument which we call the "psychic apparatus" is limited in its manner of expressing its reactions in the same way as any other instrument in our body is limited. The lungs cannot jerk as the muscles do, and the heart cannot secrete bile as the liver does. The psychic apparatus expresses its biopsychological responses by means of unconscious imagery and representations; that is its own language as much as the language of the muscles is motion and the language of the stomach lining is fermentation and the breaking-down of food.

What we find in the psychological content of the psychic apparatus is a struggle of images, self-contradictory fancies, the battle of drives plastically and dynamically represented. That the psychic apparatus is not reason, not intellect, not "mind" in the usual sense of the word, is clear. When the psychic apparatus expresses itself on any matter, it expresses itself in the intimate paralogical, irrational manner of primitive representations and imagery, which are nonrealistic. Thus, realistically we know that we are voting for one candidate for the Presidency and against another. We also know realistically our reasons, particularly if we happen to be nonneurotic. But our psychic apparatus, the unconscious core of it, knows nothing about Presidents and democracies and it reacts and feels; *it does not think*. It plays and struggles with the image of patricide. This is irrational, nonrealistic; this is the paralogical nature of our unconscious. In this case the greatest psychological achievement for us, ideally of course, is to become able to differentiate automatically between the irrational, fantastic, and unconsciously fantasied patricide and the casting of our vote for President. But even at the height of this achievement, the unconscious still speaks its own primitive language of patricide, incest, and its concomitant anxieties.

No wonder, then, that Freud found the unconscious, irrational language in which man couches his religious faith and the performance of his religious service to be the language of primitive, irrational, infantile imagery. He could not have found anything else, for the psychic apparatus cannot express itself in any other way. But one cannot deny the civic value of democratic elections, the social and moral value of honoring a leader at a banquet, or the pervading value of religion, merely because our psychic apparatus is unable to designate them successively in any other way than a patricide, a primitive feast of oral passivity to the leader, or a passive infantile, self-castrative dissolution before the father.

Psyche, Soul, and Religion

The idiom of the unconscious in no way affects the substance of civilization, any more than the idiom of the Chinese language affects, changes, or nullifies the meaning of the history of the American Revolution when it is told in Chinese. What goes on in the unconscious, the unconscious tells in its own manner. Gustav Mahler once said, in rejecting programmatic commentaries on music: "If it could all be told in words, one would not have to say it with music." If one could say it all in the words of our conscious, there would be no unconscious. It is not on the literal meaning of the unconscious language that we must base our rational evaluation of life, but on the direction which our drives take in the process of our development.

One should not overlook the fact that even the concept of original sin or of the original fall of man finds its empirical counterpart in the findings of psychoanalysis. We may recall a French abbot of the middle of the twelfth century, the Abbot of Stella, who in order to discuss some psychological problems with one of his pious and inquiring friends, and in order to avoid any pitfalls of possible sacrilege, decided to consider the soul without touching upon the question of "what it was before sin, or is in the state of sin, or will be after sin." He thus excluded theology in order to be empirical and pragmatic. This is what Freud tried to do, although he was not entirely successful. Without knowing it in advance, Freud soon discovered that he was studying the psychological reactions of man *in the state of sin;* he was at once confronted with the anxiety, the sense of guilt, and the sexual conflicts which burdened his mental patients. He discovered that there is no man living who is not burdened with what he called "the precipitate of the oedipus complex"—man's perennial, unconscious sense of guilt. Again, it would appear that if we remove the purely terminological objections which religion raises against

Freud, its dogma would find itself supported rather than denied by Freud's factual psychological findings.

This point is stressed here so repeatedly not because the fundamental precepts of religion need scientific support. As has been said, religious beliefs need no scientific proof, nor are they made less valid by scientific refutations. Science can refute superstition, but not religious faith. It is true, of course, that at various stages of our civilization superstition was so intimately interwoven with established religion that the undiscerning mistook one for the other. But it is also true that the Church itself discarded numerous superstitions which were dispelled with the advance of science, while the fundamental principles of faith naturally remained. There was a time when the mentally ill whose psychotic delusions and trends were related to religious imagery were considered as especially blessed; today we know quite well that religious ecstatic trends in a schizophrenic represent merely the utilization of religious pseudorevelatory fantasies in the service of the psychopathological process. A schizophrenic may weave into the system of his paranoid delusions any psychological material—sexual, social, philosophical, or religious.

To remove the paranoid trends which are couched in religious terms does not mean to touch the fundamental principles of religion. This leads us directly to one of the most pronounced causes for the opposition of religion to psychoanalysis. It is claimed that psychoanalysis is based on a philosophy which when accepted invariably destroys religious faith. One could deny this assertion flatly and with a clear conscience, but it is worth while to point out here that this misconception is based on an anxious misunderstanding which motivates even the irreligious layman and not only the sincere believer. This misunderstanding could be expressed approximately as follows:

"You as a psychoanalyst claim that I am suffering from a

Psyche, Soul, and Religion

sense of guilt because of my sexual conflicts. You will treat me and you will presumably relieve me of this sense of guilt. I have heard and myself believe that psychoanalysis is like a confession. I shall confess to you everything. And then what? Am I not in danger of being cured of my sense of guilt and then leading a life which I consider bad and incompatible with my conscience? Does it mean that I shall be relieved of my conscience and that this relief is the goal of psychoanalysis? Isn't this a very high price to pay for feeling well? And isn't it much more decent and moral to continue to suffer rather than to become a lascivious person whom society would condemn?"

The answer to this seemingly legitimate query is that the query is not rational and that the goal of psychoanalysis implied is not its goal at all, and cannot be.

Psychoanalysis is not confession, nor is it like confession. Confession is a conscious act of repentance, and a ritual. Man can confess only that which he consciously knows, that which makes him consciously guilty; as a result of confession and the officially given absolution man feels relieved, and he is admonished and inspired not to sin any more. In psychoanalysis the patient cannot confess in the usual sense of the word. The patient gradually reveals the unconscious sense of guilt of which he has been unaware; he is not given absolution, nor does the psychoanalyst have any means at his disposal to relieve the patient of this guilt. What the psychoanalyst does do is listen and watch how the patient learns, gradually and almost imperceptibly, to differentiate fantasy from reality, infantile from adult impulses. The patient then obtains relief from feeling guilty about things of which he is not guilty at all, and he continues to feel guilty about those things of which one usually does and should feel guilty. If the patient has criminal or suicidal trends, he learns to know that his fantasied aggression against his father or mother is a leftover of his infantile past; he learns to know that the poor old grocery clerk or his foreman is not his father, and that he wishes him no evil; consequently, he no longer has the unaccountable impulse to kill him, nor does he wish to execute himself by way of suicide.

Man cannot be cured of those ethicomoral and religious demands of his personality which live in him and make him what he is. Only the morbid, the useless, the unrealistic can be analyzed; only the unconscious conflict between the infantile and the adult—which is useless and injurious, which cripples man's psychological, integrated functioning—can be analyzed. The deepest psychoanalysis is unable to reach and analyze those personality traits and fundamental human adjustments which serve the socioethical purposes of true adulthood in the psychological and social sense. Nor can religious belief, unless it is but a mark for a neurosis and therefore not truly religious faith, be touched by psychoanalysis.

It is knowledge of what is real in this world and what is endowed with a fantasied reality that one seeks to discover and can acquire by psychoanalysis. The power to discern when reason is clouded and guided by those unconscious drives which vitiate our understanding of reality is real power indeed, but it is weakened by neuroses and almost emaciated by psychoses. We thus can see that reason, instead of being excluded from the sphere of therapeutic effort, is put at the very center of the procedure. Reason cannot function properly when one has a severe physical illness. It is impaired in certain cases of brain tumors or other cerebrospinal diseases. But in no illness is it so impaired as when the psychic apparatus is disturbed in the quantitative relationship of its parts, for the psychic apparatus is evidently a much more important organ of the human *personality* than the heart, the stomach, or the brain.

The discoveries of psychoanalysis make it possible to in-

Psyche, Soul, and Religion

troduce a clarifying correction in the old schematization of how our personality functions. The scholastic philosophers and those who followed them in the wake of Descartes and Leibnitz looked for the seat of the soul somewhere in the body. An intermediate area between the body and the soul and yet within the perishable frame of man seemed to them unthinkable. They not only divided man sharply into a body and a soul, but they sharply divided their own thoughts; they were purely materialistic when they looked at the body, and as purely idealistic when they contemplated the soul. Their minds searched for a connecting link, but they did not know their own minds. The discoveries of psychoanalysis seem to have done away with this conceptual discontinuity. Life is a continuous phenomenon, and it cannot be fragmented. The visualization of the psychic apparatus, which uses all the organs and yet favors no one special organ, re-established from the biological and, if you wish, philosophical point of view the very continuity of all the so-called parts of man. It re-established the wholeness of man which thinkers and religious philosophers of all ages always sensed but never truly comprehended. The old, simple, untenable formula, body and soul, can now be modified to read body—psychic apparatus—soul. This schematic presentation seems most natural, and it would also seem in no way to impair even the strictest Thomistic tradition. But no matter how fitting it does appear, such an outline may nevertheless prove totally unacceptable to religion unless the major objection to psychoanalysis, an objection heretofore not mentioned, is met.

Psychoanalysis advanced the theory of psychological determinism. This theory appears to clash most sharply with the dogma of free will. That this is a true and undeniable clash is accepted by all concerned. The psychoanalyst who rejects religion points to psychological determinism and the alleged Darwinism of psychoanalysis in support of his rejection. The

Catholic stands on his firm ground and points to psychological determinism as a denial of his most fundamental postulate. This is a sharper parting of the ways than any other aspect of psychoanalysis can produce.

One need not indulge in sophisticated constructions of logical and metaphysical formulae to reconcile these two apparently irreconcilable positions. The writer is a poor philosopher and a poorer theologian. He does not know the subtleties of scholasticism, nor the heavy armors of scientific materialism. He has only a speaking acquaintance with them, and he cannot boast of being able to use them as tools of argument with any degree of ease. This is a theoretical disadvantage which he is happy to acknowledge and accept, but he finds himself unable to accept the apparently general agreement on the part of psychoanalysis and religion to disagree and to disregard one another with mutual suspicion and reciprocal contempt. Science cannot be contemptuous of life or of any part of it, and religion, even the most irreligious would admit, is an integral part of life. To treat it as a superstition or a disease means no more than to cloak ourselves with scientific respectability for purposes of denying that which we do not understand. On the other hand, to snatch at the term "psychological determinism" as the last word, as the slogan of a scientific attitude, and then reject the science as a whole is not in harmony with the seeking of truth. History knows many examples of bloody strife because science in the exuberance of its power and perspicacity seemed to challenge the postulates of man's faith. It must be said in full fairness that the bloodshed and the strife never were initiated by science; science always turned the other cheek until truth ultimately prevailed. Like Savonarola, only less impetuously and less flamboyantly but not less tragically, the fate of science elevated it repeatedly from apostasy to sainthood; seldom if ever did it move in the reverse direction.

The Freudian system is too young to be able to establish itself on a solid philosophical footing, but even now it can be said with certainty that insofar as it can be considered related to any biophilosophical trends it is closer to Lamarck than to Darwin, to vitalism than to mechanistic structuralism, to idealism than to materialism. The Freudian system is, moreover, not a system of thought but a partially systematized set of observations of facts not yet sufficiently correlated with any uniform theory. It is a real misfortune that the uncertainties and anxieties which have always surrounded man's attitude toward psychological problems have kept psychoanalysis in a state of isolation. Traditional science—so inept in matters psychological and so anxious to protect its dignity within the realm of that which is only directly visible and immediately tangible—has contributed perhaps more than religion to this isolation. It was left for psychoanalysis to stand alone and by the sheer power of obstinate, scientific integrity to maintain itself and display before the thinking world the rich mass of fact which it accumulated. In this struggle for scientific existence psychoanalysis itself was forced into an attitude of defense and was compelled to use its very isolation for purposes of maintaining its self-reliance. The result, as inevitable as it was deplorable, was a form of exclusivism and pride in being rejected.

Theoretically, these circumstances should have delayed the proper scientific evolution of psychoanalysis. They probably did, and yet psychoanalysis has made enormous strides in the short span of some fifty years. These years were not peaceful years. They were darkened by two profound crises that shook the very foundation of our culture; one of them is now at its height, and the end is not yet in sight. Yet psychoanalysis has made enormous strides despite all the ill winds and well-nigh insurmountable obstacles. This process is a testimony to its vitality, to its true appeal to reason despite all the confusing misconceptions with which its opponents and ill-advised friends have surrounded it.

To dismiss psychoanalysis despite the fact that so many of the objections to it which have been raised can be met with comparative ease, to dismiss it without further examination because it seems to be in conflict with the postulate of free will, means to disregard the fact that psychoanalysis is not a philosophy, nor has it ever discussed seriously the question of free will. Psychological determinism can be as acceptable as physicochemical determinism if we do not forget that the adjective "psychological" is used in the sense of the functioning of the psychic apparatus and not in the sense of "spiritual," of pertaining to the soul. If one looks upon the psychic apparatus as an organ and not as a psychoanalytic substitute for the soul, the misconceived controversy about psychoanalysis and free will will easily recede. Man's free will cannot come to expression without free reason; reason cannot be free unless the organic or biological system within which the human personality is destined to function does function without the impediments which we, for want of any other term, call neurosis, or illness. Freud's psychological determinism never went and never could go beyond the limited frame, the *closed system,* of the psychic apparatus. The deficiencies or malfunctions of the latter vitiate the free exercise of the will as much as do deficiencies and pathological changes of the brain.

There is a characteristic story about Freud. He was asked once whether a man could be held responsible for his dreams, and he answered: "Whom else would you hold responsible?" There is also Freud's profound sense of respect for reason, which he sought all his life to liberate from the fetters of the infantile, nonrealistic fog of a malfunctioning psychic apparatus. He wished to secure for man the true ability of free choice, which he thought impossible when the psychic apparatus is not fully integrated and harmonized, even as it is impossible to make the free choice to take part in a race if one is legless or paralyzed or ataxic. This striving for the opportunity of free choice is inherent in psychoanalysis. If psychoanalysis does not explicitly accept the postulate of free will, it does not deny it; if anything, it supports it by its striving to liberate man's reason and will from the frailties which his biological, and therefore psychological, imperfections impose on him in his daily life.

Freud's system of facts as differentiated from his fleeting excursions into fields which were foreign to him, the manner in which he struggled to disentangle these facts from the unknown, the curative faith which prompted him, the persistence with which he sought to make man inwardly free from the impediments of delusions and the disharmony of misconceiving life, his steadfast claim that adulthood, love, and a free reason are a unit and the hope and the goal of life—all these bear testimony to an unshakable faith in man's will and in his ability to make his choice freely when unfettered by disease.

Psychoanalysis and Religion

SOME fifty years ago, when Freud's views on human psychology were first made known, they were given a rather hostile and contemptuous welcome by all professions, sacred and profane. Fifty years of psychoanalytic research seem to have conquered a number of the earlier prejudices, but the atmosphere of contentiousness still surrounds psychoanalysis—despite the fact that psychoanalysis has been gaining ever increasing professional and academic recognition. The spirit of contentiousness with which the uninitiated continue to approach psychoanalysis concerns the major issues of morality and religious faith.

When Freud finally (in 1927) issued his *Future of an Illusion*—in which he termed religious faith an illusion, its practices a form of compulsion neurotic ceremonial, and religion as a whole a manifestation of a neurosis—the suspicious attitude of the moralist became a conviction, for from then on he could quote Freud himself to prove that psychoanalysis is antagonistic to religion and to the morality which religion preaches and demands.

The line of battle was drawn almost spontaneously. On one

First published in *The Atlantic Monthly*, 1949.

Psychoanalysis and Religion

side were the psychoanalysts who felt that the acceptance of Freud's clinical findings and his method of treating neuroses imposed upon them the need to accept his philosophical excursions as well. On the other side there were those who felt that since they found it necessary to reject Freud's psycho-philosophical excursions into the field of religion, they also had to reject everything that Freud had ever discovered about the human mind: the dynamic power of the unconscious, the psychoanalytic method of treating neuroses, any "Freudian" clinical finding or procedure.

This conflict has not been resolved with the years. If anything it has become more intense and—as is always the case with any conflict in which reason and emotion, experiment and faith, are confused and intermingled—a great deal of passion and misunderstanding has been generated, so that problems have accumulated upon problems, but solutions (lasting solutions at any rate) have not been forthcoming.

Before World War II the problem of psychoanalysis versus religion seemed to be—to put it in psychoanalytic terminology—repressed or partially repressed. There appeared to be peace—but it was an armed one, with all participants alerted. The psychoanalysts went on with their tasks in a spirit of official unconcern but occasional rationalist antagonism against religion; and the religious teacher, the minister of the Gospel, and the priest adopted similar attitudes toward psychoanalysis. It must be said that neither the indifference nor the antagonisms seem to have been based on any clearly defined principles. Evidently there was some emotional undertone that united the objectors, but once they embarked upon their respective tasks, each chose his own customary and preferred set of objections.

However, there were some among the clergy, mostly Protestant, who found themselves in little conflict with Freud's basic findings. Among the Catholic clergy or laymen there were fewer adherents of psychoanalysis, for the tradition of Catholic scholarship has always been that of patient and at times almost exasperatingly slow examination, contemplation, re-examination, and testing. The revolutionary views of Freud required careful evaluation; the new facts about the human mind were so extraordinary and even shocking that they could not be easily tested, and Catholic thought seemed at best to be patient, at worst indifferent in a challenging way. The current reverberations of the conflict between Christianity and psychoanalysis have come mostly from Catholic sources, and the most recent publicity on the subject from certain pulpits and microphones might give the impression that Catholicism is irrevocably opposed to Freudian psychoanalysis, that it stands ready to combat it with all the spiritual might and moral authority at its disposal.

This general impression is erroneous. First of all, the rather violent intolerance regarding psychoanalysis, the various and loud incriminations which are heard from certain quarters, seem to be limited to a small group. As recently as last May, the American Psychiatric Association devoted a part of its annual meeting in Washington, D. C., to the problem of Psychopathology and Faith. One full afternoon and one full evening were given to free, dispassionate, interested, and interesting discussion of the problem. Two rabbis, a Dominican priest, and an Anglican priest of the Oratory of the Good Shepherd led the discussion. The Roman Catholic representative was far from antagonistic or combative, and he viewed the basic issues raised by psychoanalysis with sympathy and discernment.

The two rabbis expressed no quarrel with psychoanalysis; on the other hand, their support of psychoanalysis seemed to be based on purely utilitarian, philanthropic grounds. They supported psychoanalysis for the good it can do to help religion to produce the peace of mind which every one of us is supposed to be seeking. The problem of religion versus psychoanalysis cannot be solved by way of this pragmatic approach, and, as was suggested in the course of the Washington discussion, the ideal of peace of mind seems to be a reverberation of the ancient Oriental tradition. The Western religious tradition is more concerned with the relationship of man to his fellow man, to his God, and to himself—a complex set of problems to which Western Christianity has devoted all its energy from the very birth of the Church.

It is natural perhaps to find that the Mosaic tradition should prove less sensitive to the innovations made by psychoanalysis. Both the Anglican and the Catholic priests, who as far as positive dogma is concerned have no quarrel, found it therefore necessary to face squarely the principal issue: Is the body of psychoanalytic knowledge fundamentally antireligious, and is the Christian doctrine fundamentally at absolute variance with any of the findings and tenets of psychoanalysis? It may come as a surprise to many to learn that at the Washington meeting neither the Anglican nor the Catholic priest was opposed to psychoanalysis, nor does either consider psychoanalysis a threat to his faith or pastoral vocation.

The psychoanalyst has learned a great deal about the development and the workings of the human mind; he has learned a great deal about the psychological mechanics of thinking and feeling, and of worshiping God and of religious ecstasy. This knowledge does not of course provide him with any new rational, experimental, scientific tool to disprove the existence of God. He cannot disprove the existence of God scientifically, any more than the physicist can. Good astronomer that he was, Laplace stated with an overtone of rationalist superiority that God is a hypothesis which cannot be proved. But Robert Boyle was as good a scientist as Laplace, and he was unable to observe a single natural phenomenon, to discover a single chemical or physical law, without seeing in every one of them the work of God. Boyle's theology is as lofty and passionate as his science is cool and objective. And there is no reason to believe that psychoanalysis, with or without Freud, has discovered a single new fact or any new method which would enable it to refute, verify, corroborate, or otherwise assess the existence or the nonexistence of God by purely psychoanalytic means.

Yet many psychoanalysts, like the majority of serious scientists, are subject to a fundamental error: They really believe that greater intellectual understanding of life and living will make people *better*. They would exclude moral values and similar considerations from the field of their interest because they believe inherently that to understand means to be good. They do not state their belief in such a blunt and almost naïve way, but they do express the belief just the same.

To know a great deal, and to be non-neurotic, does *not* mean that one is possessed of or endowed with moral values by virtue of this knowledge and lack of neurosis. It is not Einstein's mathematical genius that makes him such a noble person and devout representative of modern humanism. It was not Freud's great intellectual sagacity and scientific boldness that made him an almost heroic figure of tolerance, his detractors to the contrary notwithstanding. Neither Göring nor Goebbels lacked great intellectual powers, but these powers did not make them good.

That science and moral values do not always coincide, that most frequently they are far from one another and are phenomena of different orders, can be easily seen in the problems faced by so many nuclear physicists who, when they became atomic bomb scientists, were horrified by the use to which their new scientific discoveries could be put.

Psychoanalysis, a new and young and revolutionary science, found itself able to go along officially without moral values not because it rejected these values but because it carried them implicitly and inherently as everything human carries them. But psychoanalysis prefers to insist that the good and the just for which it strives are but rational goals rationalistically arrived at. It is a chronic, enviable, and very noble blindness, this belief that our striving for the general good and our altruism and self-sacrificing struggle for the betterment of man and mankind are a purely dispassionate rational thing, merely because we *know* the psychological, erotic roots of love of one's neighbor, and the masochistic roots of our readiness to die for a cause or for our country.

It is this blindness become a little aggressive that contributed a great deal to the conflict of psychoanalysis with religion. Yet it should not be forgotten that among the members of the American Psychoanalytic Association there are God-fearing Protestants and devout Catholics, who are also Freudian psychoanalysts. These psychoanalysts have not found it necessary to follow Freud in his amateur theology, or to follow the bigot in his amateur psychology.

Self-righteousness, even the self-righteousness of a scientist, breeds ignorance. The ignorance of what traditional religious doctrine represents did not help the psychoanalyst to create a rapprochement between the newest psychology and religion; for, despite his seemingly cool, objective, rational and rationalistic divorcement from religion, the psychoanalyst stood with passionate inspiration ready to defend his own new knowledge at whatever cost.

Passion, even noble passion, provokes one at times to great extremes. It was such a passion that led William Lloyd Garrison to proclaim the Constitution of the United States "a covenant with death and an agreement with hell" and to burn it in public. When the passion of a libertarian is aroused, he will fight even liberty in the name of liberation; a Fisher Ames will exclaim that "our country is too big for Union, too sordid for patriotism and too democratic for liberty." What some psychoanalysts have said about religion as a human function and what certain religious leaders have said about psychoanalysis would make as much sense as these passionate exclamations of Ames and Garrison, if they were taken literally.

The zealous religious opponent of psychoanalysis may insist that psychoanalysts are too loose in their moral views, and that many of them are bad. The fact that there are bad and unconscionable lawyers and doctors and priests certainly does not make jurisprudence, medicine, and religion bad and unacceptable to a morally sensitive person.

In anti-analytical passion a great many silly things have been said by a great many intelligent people, and one of those things, often repeated from platform and from pulpit, is that psychoanalysis wants to do away with confession and make itself a substitute for the Sacrament of Penance. In my practice and professional contacts as a psychoanalyst, I have heard of only one occasion when a psychoanalyst believed (and I must submit quite erroneously) that confession would interfere with the prospective patient's psychoanalysis. The patient refused even to start with the prospective analyst, and he went to another with no harm to psychoanalysis or to his faith. Neither officially nor unofficially does psychoanalysis interfere with confession.

The fear existing in some religious circles that the very fact of being psychoanalyzed and therefore "telling all" prevents the faithful from going to confession is not founded on any reality. There can be no more authoritative pronouncement on the subject than that of Jacques Maritain, who is among the leaders in Catholic philosophy and who is an opponent of many a psychoanalytic principle. In his *Quatre Essais sur l'Esprit Humain dans Sa Condition Charnelle,* there is an essay on Freud and psychoanalysis. In this essay Maritain says:

Psychoanalysis and Religion

One hears occasionally that psychoanalysis supplants or is an ersatz of confession. This seems quite incorrect. On the one hand it would be an illusion to believe that confession has the power of curing neuroses and psychoses. The object of confession and its ultimate goal are in no way psychotherapeutic. Furthermore, the memories presented at confession are conscious, or preconscious, and they are brought out by voluntary effort. If the penitent at confession tends to push his will further into the sphere of the unconscious, he runs the risk of suffering from pathological scruples. . . . When a neurotic or a more severely mentally sick person comes to confession, he does not uncover the roots of his neurosis or his delusions. Instead, he burdens his confessor with the (abnormal) constructions created by his neurosis or his delusions.

On the other hand, confession is in itself an act of our rational life, an act of reason and will. . . . The penitent surrenders the secret of his heart to the confessor as to an agent of God, and the confessor withdraws his individual personality to stand before the penitent only as a minister-judge.

This statement of Jacques Maritain, in addition to being authoritative and exact, should put an end to irresponsible and unfounded confusion about the psychoanalyst's wishing to steal into the Sacrament of Penance, in the manner of a conventional Satan in modern dress.

Modern Catholic thought has been showing of late both a great interest in and a great understanding of psychoanalysis and its positive relation to religion. This new trend has not yet become properly noticeable in America, but in Europe, particularly among the French-speaking people, it has become rather pronounced both in psychoanalytic and Catholic circles.

We find more and more attempts made to consider psychoanalysis as a source of information and better understanding of man's functioning in this our world. Thus Etienne de Greef, in Louvain, has little if any quarrel with Freud's views on human instincts. Also in *La Vie Spirituelle,* Vol. 75 (1946), there is a thoughtful appraisal of Freud's views by Dr. Nodet, in the article "Psychisme et Spiritualité." And in *Mélange Théologiques* (1946) Yves de Montcheuil writes on "Freudisme et Psychanalyse devant la Morale Chrétienne," in which among other valuable things we find an excellent explanation of why confession and psychoanalysis are and remain different, and why they do not interfere with one another.

It is regrettable that the promising trend toward co-operation between Catholic theologians and psychiatrists has not yet established itself in this country, where mutual intolerance between psychoanalysis and the Catholic Church is pretty much the rule. When a few years ago a well-known psychoanalyst was asked to give a series of lectures on psychoanalysis in a Catholic university, a rabble-rousing publication accused the analyst of "turning over" psychoanalysis to the Catholic Church to be devoured. On the other hand, some free-lance and professional proselytes are sufficiently misguided to turn away from many real sources of evil in this world and denounce psychoanalysis as one of the major enemies of mankind.

As a healing art, psychoanalysis is by its very nature the opposite of the enemy of mankind. As a mass of factual data about human beings and their behavior, it can serve both God and man, for facts do no harm unless they are perverted by prejudice—and then they are no longer facts. As a philosophy, psychoanalysis does not exist. It is a systematized, scientific, working hypothesis about human behavior, and as such it has stood the test of half a century. It threatens religion no more than the heliocentric theory or Newtonian physics threatened religion. Man's faith and man's need for moral values are not overthrown by scientific discoveries, although they may be destroyed by wars and concentration camps.

A Psychiatric Consideration
of the Ascetic Ideal

WHY should psychopathology impose itself, even intrude itself, into the field of purely religious experiences? And what can it teach the religious believer about faith and self-denial which the believer does not learn through direct religious experience? These are not idle or purely formal questions; they are questions which must be answered not only for the sake of the believer but for the sake of the scientific psychopathologist as well.

The first answer that suggests itself is both obvious and practical. It is important to be able to differentiate abnormal from normal mental states. It is important, therefore, for the believer as well as for the psychiatrist, to differentiate between the refusal to accept food on the part of a pathologically depressed individual and the fasting done as penance. It is important to note the differences between the reflections of the faithful layman or priest about his unworthiness while he carefully examines and re-examines his relation to God, and that state of ruminative, obsessive, self-tormenting doubt which is known at times as scrupulosity and which is a manifestation of a depressive, obsessional state. Such differential

Written in 1950 for delivery before a conference of representatives of French monastic orders. *L'Ascèse chrétienne et l'homme contemporain,* Paris, Les Editions du Cerf, 1951.

diagnosis is important, of course; psychiatry here has a utilitarian pragmatic value, as much as medicine would have in differentiating hypertension and a state of being ashamed although both make a man's face red.

However, the purely utilitarian value of psychopathology is not the only one that could interest those dealing with religious problems; it is not even the most important one. The issues are much more complex and more profound, and both psychopathology and religion have common concerns. These concerns are not easy to enumerate but they are numerous and important. In a general way one may state that that which goes on in the human mind, both from the point of view of content as well as form, has been learned empirically mostly through psychopathology. What appears normal is not usually seen by the psychopathologist or by anyone else, for that matter; it is through the deviations from the normal functions that medicine (and this does include medical psychology, of course) learns a great deal. It can then reconstruct the concepts of the normal which it is never able to observe directly, but by which it is always guided in the evaluation of human functions.

Psychopathology has enriched immensely our knowledge of the human mind, particularly since the discoveries of the dynamics of the psychic apparatus, which is mostly unconscious. But unfortunately psychopathology, and especially psychoanalytic psychopathology, developed an undue partiality for the abnormal and became inclined to consider as neurotic—pathological—every mental phenomenon which seemed to utilize the same psychological mechanisms as the neuroses. But it is not true, for instance, that everything that follows the laws of chemistry as we observe them in organic disease is pathological. The laws of chemistry are the same in organic disease as in health, and health and disease do not differ from one another in this respect. The difference be-

A Psychiatric Consideration of the Ascetic Ideal

tween health and disease lies in the arrangement and constellations of the by-products and their combinations, which the human individual is at times unable to tolerate biologically and which at times threaten his life. The fact then that the same laws of physics, chemistry and psychology are found in disease, physical and psychological, does not make health and religion a disease when we discover in their human manifestations and unconscious dynamics the same laws of physics, chemistry and psychology. The fact that many if not all human instincts play an active role in our religious experience does not make religion an instinct. "It is wrong to speak of an instinct of religion or an instinct of worship. Religious behavior has an instinctive basis but is not itself a primary instinct. Were it so, we should be able to trace its counterpart in the lower forms of animal life, where it would be even more clearly defined than in man."[1]

Since we have mentioned instincts we might state now that a great many of our instinctual wishes, i.e., either the instinctual tensions themselves or the goals to which they aspire, are frequently repressed; they remain outside the field of consciousness, in a primitive state of primitive impulses and primitive goals. They would do neither harm nor good and would be of no interest (scientific or spiritual) to anyone were it not for the fact that in their repressed state they retain all the psychological energy which they possessed originally; under certain circumstances, these psychological energies attach themselves to some of the higher and therefore less disturbing functions of our lives and thus "break through" to expression. In other words, these repressed impulses remain constantly dynamic; when they seem most static, they are actually in search of an outlet; they are always, therefore, either "almost" kynetic or fully kynetic, and are actually never

[1] R. S. Lee: *Freud and Christianity*, London, 1948, p. 44.

static. It is this that must be considered as Freud's greatest discovery.

In view of the above it will be clear if we join with a writer who said: "Symbols capture repressed tendencies because the unconscious seizes upon the symbols to get displaced outlet for repression. Religion thus draws the forbidden impulses to strengthen belief or action which consciously was intended to have a different character."[2] This would lead one to agree with another statement by the same writer: "A life of self-sacrifice, for example, may be the expression of a free and highly developed personality; on the other hand, it may be the outcome of a strongly repressed masochism—a tendency or impulse to seek suffering because of the unconscious pleasure which is derived from it, and which is neurotic. . . ."[3]

Perhaps because of the admixture of neurotic trends in the religious practices of many people, perhaps also because deeply religious states frequently seem to fail to bring happiness to man, so many among the psychoanalytic psychologists began to consider religion itself a neurosis, or a pathological illusion. Perhaps, therefore, I may be permitted to quote once more from R. S. Lee, who said: "We should not look for life to be made easy for us. Some people are disheartened when in genuine sincerity they have made some active profession of faith, been converted or confirmed, and find that they still have to struggle against temptations to do evil. Such people have a mistaken idea of what true Christianity offers. It offers the grace and power that comes from communion with God to reach heights of living, of self-realization, and so of happiness, that are impossible without them. But the heights cannot be reached without struggle. To suppose that conversion will make us good in the sense that we shall not have to struggle against sin any more is to indulge in

[2] *Ibid:* p. 91.
[3] *Ibid:* p. 55.

a form of the womb[4] fantasy, for it looks for a spiritual life of security and bliss that comes without our putting forth effort. The Christian cannot hope to find life easier than Christ found it, and the Gospels bear witness to the fact that all that He did cost Him great effort."[5]

To religious people the above is, of course, self-evident. It bears repetition, however, insofar as there is danger because of this very self-evidence of a tendency both on the part of the psychopathologist and the religious to misunderstand one another rather completely. Present-day psychology, the one enlightened by the findings of psychoanalysis, not infrequently mistakes religion for a restrictive moral discipline which stands up in arms to combat man's instinctual life. Since psychoanalysis recognized the cardinal importance of sexuality in human psychology and behavior, any serious attempt systematically to restrict the expression of the basic human instincts is considered wrong and even pathogenic, and therefore, overtly or covertly, psychoanalysis seems to have found itself opposed to religion. On the other hand, psychoanalysis appeared to the uninitiated to be based almost solely on principles of hedonism and, it would follow, of unrestricted sexuality; religion, therefore, found it necessary to turn away from psychoanalysis, because in the eyes of religion it was a newer agency of unbridled hedonism which could not be accepted as a guiding principle of life.

Anyone who takes pains to try to solve this conflict, which seems at times hopelessly unsolvable, is at once struck by the fact that the problem is really not so difficult as it appears, that the misunderstanding is not justified by the empirical, clinical findings of psychoanalysis, nor is it justified by the demand which a true and healthy religious attitude makes on a person.

It is true that psychoanalysis, like any medicobiological

[4] intra-uterine.
[5] Lee, *op. cit.*, p. 105.

discipline, is based on the mechanistic principle of a utilitarian or, if you wish, hedonistic teleology and determinism. This is as it really should be, because a science always works within a closed system, and this restriction represents both the advantages as well as the limitations of any science. But despite these limitations psychoanalysis has made a great contribution to the labors of those who are in search of a true philosophy of life. Psychoanalysis itself, like physics or mathematics, permits of a number of generalizations and syntheses; but not a single one of these scientific disciplines, nor all these disciplines taken together, can be made into a philosophy of life. It is the mass of empirical data which these disciplines offer to philosophy and religion which represents their true contribution to philosophy and religion. In this respect, despite its desultory excursions into materialistic philosophy and even antireligious intellectualism, psychoanalysis has made a major contribution to the greater understanding of religious life. This again is as it should be, because no true empirical findings of facts in human nature can contradict the fundamental religious truths; what is more, the more correct and the more fundamental these facts are the more they are bound to support rather than to contradict the religious truths dealing with the destiny of man. The confusion and mutual suspicion and distrust that surround the relationship of psychoanalysis and religion are due to many causes; without considering any of these causes in particular, we may say that they would all fall under the heading of reciprocal ignorance resulting in most cases in an active opposition to learning something about one another.

Freud did not exclude unhappiness, suffering, from health. A man may be psychologically healthy and yet have to struggle with many forces within and outside himself, and suffer the pain of the struggle, and *live* the suffering as an integral part of his life. It is not true, therefore, that every suffering within

A Psychiatric Consideration of the Ascetic Ideal

the supposedly normal person is a neurotic symptom. It is still less true that every suffering when it is constant and perhaps a direct result of the given activity chosen is masochism—as so many would mistakenly insist. Suffering is masochism only when it is a perversion, when it leads directly to sexual gratification or when it is a singular substitute for it. This type of suffering is deeply neurotic from the point of view of psychoanalysis, and this type of suffering was specifically recognized by the Church as not leading to sainthood and as being unworthy.

Freud's conception of a normal person was (briefly) the person who in his growth and development from childhood reaches *genital* adulthood. By "genital" Freud meant not the physiological-sexual maturity which is commonly known as genital, but that state of psychological development in which the various infantile, partial, hedonistic ("sexual" in the Freudian sense) impulses become synthesized in such a way that the sensual-egocentric (infantile-sexual) drives become adult-altruistic and the infantile, exclusive love for the object outside oneself (father and/or mother, and/or sister or brother) becomes adult love for other people. The earlier infantile impulses are all characterized not only by an egocentric, narcissistic sensuality, but by a sort of utilitarian, mercenary love bestowed on others only if and when one gets something for it. This utilitarian love is also an unsteady love, which becomes hate rather easily at the first experience of frustration; it is a mixed, ambivalent love in which anxiety and anger, aggressiveness, fear and cowering passivity are all combined in unequal proportions and in a state of considerable lability.

All these states and processes are unconscious, of course, and their psychological representations are unconscious. The behavior of the individual is subject to direct observation, but the unconscious can be uncovered only by special psychoanalytic techniques. The adult, object-libidinous state is also unconscious. And, of course, it never reaches its absolute completion; the weight of the infantile drives and of the various stages of adolescence, with all their unconscious constellations and charges and countercharges of psychological energies, is carried over in varying degrees into the adult, object-libidinous stage. If too many of these early burdens are carried over, either the object-libidinous stage is never reached or its proper function is interfered with, and then we deal with neuroses of varying severities. But if the primacy of the object-libidinous state is established, the adult lives a normal life, and within the frame of this normal life the adult has to struggle to live with or overcome some of the left-overs of socially modified infantile drives. This struggle is apparently what Freud had in mind when he spoke of "the unhappiness common to mankind."

In other words, "normality" or "adulthood" is not a state which can be attained once and for all, and once attained basked in without any difficulties or concerns. At its very best it is something which must be maintained, sustained, held on to, to avoid regressions to earlier levels, to avoid too much anxiety, to avoid being thrown into too much psychological passivity which thwarts initiative and original thought and independent activity, to avoid the mobilization of too much unconscious hostility which robs one of the object-libidinous, altruistic, paternal and fraternal attitude toward one's equals. Such unconscious hostility makes a man live on the forces which give him a sense of power over others. This sense of power may be expressed in many ways: for instance, through the acquisition of unnecessary wealth, or through a sense of megalomania which thwarts a man's rational choice to exercise his will in the direction of object-libidinous interest and instead evokes in him the captious, impulsive, yet persevering,

A Psychiatric Consideration of the Ascetic Ideal

all powerful egocentricity which gives the illusion of great will power.

This is as far as Freud went in his psychological findings with regard to man's place in the world and in the society in which he lives. Freud's Eros is an Eros which painfully grows from the state of purely biological urges and whims of the infant to the altruistic, creative synthesis of adulthood. Neither Freud nor the Freudian analysts went any further, not because they did not consider it important, nor because they considered it difficult (although some of them did), but because this is the natural limit of psychoanalysis. Its sphere is man's relationship to Eros from the crib to complex social life, and the vicissitudes of Eros from the relative simplicity of childhood to the synthesized complexity of adulthood. Caritas and Agape have remained outside the field of psychological analysis; it is to be hoped that Caritas and Agape, their psychological dynamics and place in the life of man, will be the subject of study of future psychoanalysts. Certain it is that in order to study Caritas and Agape one will have to learn to observe them and then study their phenomenology as well as their dynamics. Heretofore, the Freudian adult Logos and adult Eros seemed to be the limits of psychoanalytic studies, and Caritas and Agape were left to the religious as purely unscientific. This attitude, while it estranged analysis from religion and from true religious psychology, was nevertheless a good thing, because Caritas and Agape are intimately interwoven with the problem of values, and a science which preoccupies itself with highly evaluative problems, particularly such a young science as psychoanalytic psychology, is apt to get lost in confusion between the psychological phenomena as they are and the moral values they either represent or flout.

That is why the deeper religious problems have hardly ever been touched by psychoanalysis. In its whole literature we find, for instance, only one article on asceticism, which was published a quarter of a century ago. As could be expected, the author did not understand the problem very well; to him asceticism meant primarily self-denial of sexual pleasure, and he saw in it a particular form of search for power, overlooking the fact that the ascetic in his self-denial of genital-eroticism also denies himself the will to be rich as well as the will to have power.

However, the cardinal psychological problem with which one is confronted in the consideration of the ascetic ideal and the striving to fulfill it is not so much which psychological mechanisms are involved in the formation of this ideal and which in its exercise. As has been said, mechanisms *per se* do not yield much information as to true psychological characteristics; it is the total constellation of man's primary instincts which matters. It is obvious that I do not feel qualified to subject asceticism to a proper psychoanalytic examination. Neither my personal experience nor the neurotic experiences of those religious persons who have come to me for medicopsychological help suffice. They do not suffice for the formation of a definitive formulation, but they do permit me to attempt to formulate a few preliminary conclusions, some tentative thoughts on the subject.

A few years ago, while studying the psychological dynamics of current social prejudice, I made a list of things the prejudiced say about those who are the subject of their prejudice. This list proved surprising and, for a moment, both disconcerting and revealing. I was interested in what the anti-Catholic has to say about the Church and its priests, what the anti-Semite says about the Jews, the Southerner in the United States about the Negro, the capitalist about the workingman, and the workingman about the capitalist, the Communist about the capitalistic bourgeois, and the capitalistic bourgeois about the Communist.

Whatever is said, it all could be summarized as follows:

A Psychiatric Consideration of the Ascetic Ideal

The prejudiced usually acuses the group against whom he is prejudiced of being rather keen intellectually, but ill-willed, perverse, well-organized, power-seeking. He accuses it of being a closed group whose members stand together to acquire all riches and power at the expense of others and to keep them for themselves in order to enjoy life "fully," that is, to enjoy the full sensual gamut of one's instinctual urges. The members of the group are accused in short of sexual incontinence and promiscuity, of accumulating worldly riches, and of seeking to establish and keep their power over others. What struck me in all this is the essential psychological uniformity with which blind prejudice would accuse a monastic order and the Communist regime of exactly the same things—a drive for sexuality, riches and power.

But what impressed me even more was the unique characteristics of monastic vows, which demand chastity instead of unrestricted sexuality, poverty instead of riches, and obedience instead of power. As one thinks of it all, one is impressed with the depth of intuition which the Christian ascetic ideal displays (I am speaking here, of course, only in psychological terms). I was led to the conclusion that prejudiced people always project into others those things which they themselves are unconsciously tempted to have and to be and to which they do not dare to confess within themselves. I was led to the further conclusion that the ascetic ideal is inwardly cognizant of this fact, and that it demands conscious and deliberate renunciation of those drives which various non-ascetic individuals and groups factually accept but ultimately project into others who are the victims of their prejudices.

I was led to one further conclusion which I did not state at the time I published my paper on "The Psychopathology of Social Prejudice," namely: Only the struggle of various partial sexualities for expression, only the incomplete synthesis of Eros in the adult, makes prejudice (hate) possible and makes possible the contingent projections of the pseudo-socialized, pseudo-sublimated erotic drives, such as drives for power (in its form of extreme sadism), drives for worldly possessions (in its form of extreme lecherous avarice) and orgiastic restlessness which becomes sensual depravity. All three of these drives or groups of drives came to their tragic and catastrophic expression in the Nazi philosophy and practice, which was acquisitive, sadistic and sensual to the point of reducing male and female humans to machines for the mass production of future German guardians of Nazi-exclusivism.

That the crassest drives of man are usually projected into others by the aberrations of prejudice is more or less a normal phenomenon. Therefore, as long as we stop and do not go beyond the limits of formal normalcy established by psychoanalysis, it is really impossible to visualize a greater and deeper ideal. It is impossible not because psychoanalysis does not recognize one, but because the business of psychoanalysis is to investigate the human psychic apparatus and to establish the psychobiological level which it must reach to be healthy—and that is all. However, psychoanalysis does demonstrate that there is no health without the transformation of our sexual instincts into the constellation of an altruistic ego; therefore, in the final analysis, psychoanalysis points not only to that which is healthy but to that which is good.

The whole concept of Eros in Freud is Platonic in origin, and it is nothing against Freud if we find that his Hellenic Eros coincides with the psychobiological unit that is man but does not cover the formation of those masses of trends which we might call ego ideals and which, while rooted in Eros, do in our utopias and religions transgress beyond the confines set by Eros. Father M. C. d'Arcy, S.J., quoting Simmel says: "The Hellenic Eros is a will-to-have, even when it is used in the nobler sense of the desire to have the loved person as an object for ideal instruction, ethical training and education in culture.

It is for this reason that love for the Greeks is a middle-state between having and not having, and consequently must die when its aim is attained."[6]

We cannot go here into the details of differentiation between Eros and Caritas and Agape, and we shall have to limit ourselves to the more or less dogmatic statement that Caritas and Agape are not states that can be fully reached without one's having reached a sufficiently high level of psychobiological erotic organization. If we were to limit ourselves to the purely phenomenological and formal aspects of human behavior, we might fall into a pit of truly miserable errors. For instance, a very anxious, neurotically frightened person who unconsciously runs away from genitality might become impotent. Pragmatically, his lack of exercise of his genital functions may be looked upon as being the same as that of the one who is abstinent on moral, religious grounds, but I need not point out how vast a difference there is in psychological content and dynamics between abstinence and impotence. The neurotically impotent is a passive individual unable to love, unable to achieve erotic adulthood; the abstinent individual must first achieve erotic adulthood to be able to abstain from the exercise of its demands. The healthy sexuality which psychoanalysis has in mind is not the sexuality which must constantly express itself, but the one which is capable of expressing itself fully if one permits it to do so. There is no question of conscious will in a case of impotence. The same and similar differences can be found between shy, neurotic passivity and inability to be independent, and that powerful self-control which enters into the practice of conscious obedience. The same and similar differences can be found in the aspirations to be rich and in the self-conscious acceptance of the ideal of poverty.

Man does not necessarily become happy, free from suffering,

[6] M. C. d'Arcy, *The Mind and Heart of Love.* New York, 1947, p. 61.

through the mere acceptance of the ascetic ideal of chastity, poverty, and obedience. Acceptance of the ideal carries with it the need for a constant struggle with those genital and pregenital forces into which our personality breaks up, or to which our personality is drawn, or which come up within us as unwelcome irritants as soon as we voluntarily and deliberately suppress one of our major instinctual drives. There is always, therefore, a certain amount of suffering present, as Regamey pointed out when he said: "The absence of suffering in the practice of the vow of poverty shows that the degree of detachment has not gone far enough." (Mgr. Ancel.)[7] There is not only suffering but discomfort, that state of a sense of privation which Freud found to be present in our daily civilized life. "In the idea of religious poverty there will be, for some, the appearance of excessive unreasonableness. There is no real religious poverty without difficulty and inconvenience; let us say even, with Father Chevrier, without 'suffering,' without a certain 'uncomfortableness.' "[8] The fundamental struggle between what man is psychobiologically and psychosocially, and what man aspires to be by accepting Agape as an ego ideal, is very simply and very beautifully stated by Regamey when he quotes Fr. Chevrier and says: "He who has the true spirit of poverty has always too much. He tends always to retrench. He who has the spirit of the world never has enough, is never satisfied. He must always have something more."

In this simple description, more than merely one of the principles of the ascetic ideal is stated; the root of the psychological problem is exposed to our view most poignantly. One cannot repeat too often that the ascetic ideal of poverty does not represent the absence of the acquisitive instinct, nor its

[7] P. R. Regamey, "La pauvreté religieuse," *La Vie Spirituelle,* Paris, 1948, p. 380.
[8] *Ibid.,* p. 379.

A Psychiatric Consideration of the Ascetic Ideal

atrophy, nor a neurotic overcompensation covering its hypertrophy; it represents rather a conscious rejection of a "healthy" acquisitive instinct and a refusal to obey its demands.

Father Yves de Montcheuil has said about the ascetic ideal: "It is not a question of making oneself in one's own image, of making oneself a wise man or a saint, but of freeing all one's powers for Caritas."[9] In other words, the ascetic ideal is not a narcissistic, egocentric ideal, not a form of neurosis which springs from one's anxious inability to accept life. Rather, it is an object-libidinous ideal coming from other sources which have not yet been sufficiently studied. And the neurotic denial of life has nothing to do with it. Father Montcheuil has stated this with unique psychological acumen when he said, as if foreseeing the objections of some psychologists: "Christian asceticism is not born of the conviction that the world is evil. It is not inspired by contempt for life and for joy. We must deliberately reject this sad, morose, defiant, suspicious asceticism, which is nothing but a caricature of true Christian asceticism."[10]

This growing up to life and acceptance of the ascetic ideal is a complicated process, because "the idea of asceticism carries with it the idea of a painful, difficult exercise, an exercise that has something of the obstinate and methodical in it."[11] This testimony of someone who himself espoused the ascetic ideal with profound devotion and success is serious and ample testimony of great psychological value. For the problem with which scientific psychoanalytic psychology is confronted here is quite complex and perhaps even baffling.

But let us look again at Fr. Montcheuil before we attempt a tentative final formulation. We know what it is to be in the throes of human actualities despite one's complete abandon

---
[9] Yves de Montcheuil, *La Vie Spirituelle*, Paris, 2nd ed., p. 142.
[10] *Ibid.*, p. 142.
[11] *Ibid.*, p. 136.

to Caritas, for he tells us: "Caritas encounters obstacles to its expression in our lives. There is in us a spontaneous love of evil, and consequently an antipathy for good, which does not simply evaporate as a result of our receiving grace. There are in us those lower appetites which search for their satisfaction at the expense of our higher ones. There are egotistic tendencies which force us to serve ourselves at the expense of our neighbor, make us pass him by or subject him to our own ends. There is a tendency to distraction which prevents the peaceful contemplation necessary for prayer. There are the stresses which transport us, or the indolence which immobilizes us . . . One could continue the enumeration indefinitely."[12] It would be difficult, if not impossible, to summarize the whole mass of instinctual struggles which Fr. Montcheuil so compactly enumerated. He uses evaluative terms, of course, because he looks upon all the enumerated difficulties as tendencies toward that which is bad. But if we examine these tendencies regardless of their moral value or immorality and look upon them as various instinctual drives which are common to man in his individual and social life, we cannot help but be impressed with Fr. Montcheuil's extraordinary insight into the actual psychological processes which make up the energy of human behavior.

As I have said, it so happens that in the scheme of the drives which make up man's life and living in relation to his own corporal self and to his own environment, no important or sufficiently intense drive can be consciously suppressed or unconsciously repressed without this drive's breaking down into its more primitive infantile components and either producing psychogenic symptoms or offering some other outlet for the repressed or suppressed drives. The outlet on such occasion will be of inferior, more infantile nature; therefore, the whole process is considered to be first a breaking-down of a synthe-

[12] *Ibid.*, p. 137.

A Psychiatric Consideration of the Ascetic Ideal

sized drive into its component parts and, second, a regression to the level of these components, to an earlier, infantile level. Thus, a repression of genitality would produce a regression to a sadistic level, which socially might express itself in the form of an intensified drive for power or an intensified avariciousness, which in turn would lead to that dubious ideal of accumulating a great amount of money as soon as possible so as to be able to retire as young as possible and thus be able "to enjoy life," to do nothing, like a foetus living at the expense of its mother's metabolism—an ideal of highly socialized parasitism.

It is, therefore, particularly noteworthy that the ascetic ideal of Caritas gives up corporeal genitality and, as if knowing (or because of knowing) the danger, also cuts off the paths to which such a suppressed genitality may lead—power and riches. What the obscure psychological processes are by means of which psychological genitality in the highest sense of the word is preserved, thus making human beings function in a manner both serene and healthy, is a question which even modern psychology, with all its exploratory capacity to enter the deeper layer of the unconscious, is as yet unable to answer scientifically. Perhaps it never will be able to give the answer, any more than biology, which knows so much about life and its attributes and manifestations and is yet unable to say what life is.

Sigmund Freud

THROUGHOUT his psychoanalytic work, Freud lays stress on the ever-present conflicts between the individual and civilization. There seems always to be in Freud a lurking desire to save the individual from his own civilization, both for the individual's sake and for the sake of his civilization. These are the obscure corners of psychoanalysis. Cultural anthropology, which has developed during the last two decades or so, has not yet developed sufficiently to offer more light on the subject. On the other hand, the trend toward utilizing psychoanalysis for purposes of political and sociological reforms—such as preventing wars or revolutions or "producing" a special type of "mature" statesman—all this may be looked upon more as a fad and a sign of the times than a true development of scientific psychoanalysis. There is nothing in the Freudian system to suggest that values, individual and social, are direct results of mental health, and that therefore psychoanalysis by itself is capable of producing or generating the values which are to be found in our social ideals, philosophies, utopias and religions.

First published in 1951. Reprinted with the permission of Charles Scribner's Sons from *Sigmund Freud: His Exploration of the Mind of Man*, copyright © 1951 by Charles Scribner's Sons.

Freud seems to have felt that values are not for science to judge or manufacture. In this he was right, of course. But it is also in this that he was most misunderstood.

Freud must have felt very keenly the need to keep himself on the level of purely scientific observations. That is why he seems to have to justify his claim to speak of love as a factor against war and says that psychoanalysis should never be ashamed to speak about love for humanity. "Does not religion preach love of one's neighbor?" he reminds us. This would seem a very naïve reminder indeed, if we did not keep in mind Freud's great emphasis on the need to use reason, without inner effort or outside restriction, to observe and analyze what man does. Again, what Freud wants is to *know*. His aspiration for Logos is so great that he is compelled to set the field of Ethos completely aside. In the process, as we might foresee, he exposes himself to a danger he had always wanted to avoid: he comes at times dangerously close to confusing a mechanism in accordance with which a given phenomenon functions, with the phenomenon itself.

In this respect, one of the best examples of what I have in mind is his magnificent description of the formation of the superego. Having noted that "in its judicial functions the super-ego manifests itself as conscience," he proceeded to identify superego and conscience completely—so much so that when he described the neurotic sense of guilt and the murderous superego, the uninitiated misread him as saying that every and any sense of guilt is neurotic, and that it is better never to feel guilty of anything. This is not even a caricature of Freud's thought; it is rather a hostile misrepresentation of something by people who failed to understand, but did not fail to be afraid.

If Freud had remained on the scientific platform he chose to occupy, without making excursions into fields in which scientific measurements and analysis are not valid, he might have escaped certain errors. But I doubt whether he would have escaped the animosity of those who, coming from the other end of the road, committed an error similar to his: that of trying to assess a scientific truth by moral criteria. At any rate, when Freud traced the derivation of the superego from the very long childhood and dependence of the human animal, and when he dropped a hint that certain animals with equally long dependence might also develop a superego, he was probably right as far as this particular ingredient or element of the psychic apparatus is concerned. But when he equated superego and conscience, he touched definitely on a problem of moral philosophy and possibly religion. As if to assert his scientific position, he thus made a momentary excursion or raid into a field which lies totally outside psychoanalysis.

"The super-ego is," he says, "in fact the heir to the Oedipus complex and only arises after that complex has been disposed of. For that reason its excessive severity does not follow a real prototype but corresponds to the strength which is used in fending off the temptation of the Oedipus complex. Some suspicion of this state of things lies, no doubt, at the bottom of the assertion made by philosophers and believers that the moral sense is not instilled into men by education or acquired by them in the course of social life, but is implanted in them from a higher source."[1]

The same tendency leads Freud to consider religion as "an historical but not material truth." The believer and the philosopher might say that here Freud enters the field of that which transcends science, and he enters it with a plow fit only for material soil. Freud might say that he does not know how to use any other instrument except the scientific plow, and that he does not understand—as he once said—what the "oceanic feeling" is (apparently religious feeling, to which one of Freud's correspondents referred in a letter), for he has never

[1] *Outline*, pp. 121, 122.

Sigmund Freud

experienced it. These mutually contradicting attitudes are essentially of no real significance, for the transcendentalist certainly has no means of verifying Freud's scientific findings, and Freud has no means of checking on the assertions of the transcendentalist.

In this respect the whole situation is not exceptional at all. It has been so from the beginning of science and from the beginning of religious faith. If this were thoroughly understood, Freud's excursions into the field of values (even if these excursions were inferentially antireligious) could not be really dangerous to religion or philosophy, for since a scalpel cannot dissect the essence of morals, it cannot work to the detriment of morals. On the other hand, he who in the name of established moral values combats a scientific truth does a great injustice to the moral value, for he then combats knowledge, and knowledge is virtue, and to combat virtue cannot be moral.

All this seems rather simple and self-evident. It is so self-evident that the point has been missed by many keen minds. Thus, in a search to utilize the essential data of modern psychology, more than one authority on religion has turned away from Freud in favor of Jung. I do not speak here of those passionate opponents of Freud who in defense of their faith impute to Freud things he never did or said. I have more in mind such enlightened writers as the Dominican Father Victor White of Oxford, or the Jesuit Father M. C. d'Arcy, who took Jung's divagations about religion as supporting religion, in contradistinction to the views of Freud, who opposed it. It is therefore of special interest and value to find in Erich Fromm's *Psychoanalysis and Religion* (his 1949 Terry Lectures at Yale University) an excellent analysis of the findings and propositions of Freud and Jung from the standpoint of religious trends, and a convincing statement that Freud's findings are more conducive to religious attitudes than those of Jung's psychological cosmology.[2]

Fromm is not a follower of Freudian orthodoxy, but his conclusions alone would suggest that at least as far as religious attitudes are concerned one cannot reject Freud lock, stock and barrel simply because Freud himself considered religion a neurosis and an illusion. Freud considered religion a temporary institution and a provisional manner of seeing things, for he thought that as the primacy of reason comes to assert itself, the need for religious faith will disappear, will undergo a sort of atrophy of disuse.

There have been many scientists who somehow felt that religious faith must be disposed of, as if this act of disposing of it were a necessary prerequisite for science to occupy its rightful place in this world. Why those scientists have found it necessary to do so is a more important question than whether they are right or not. It could never be proved whether they are right or not, for the nonbeliever will find the scientific arguments against religious faith as sufficient and satisfying as the believer will find them wanting and unsatisfying. On the other hand, the psychological need of certain scientists to cap, as it were, their life's work with a refutation of religious faith is of the greatest interest to scientific psychology. Why should it be so? Why should it be so in the case of Freud? This is an unanswerable question, for the answer to it lies deep in the personal psychology of the creator of psychoanalysis.

In a general way, one might point out the fact that as a rule scientists dealing with biological and physical science have been found to be more often than not religious, whereas those scientific workers whose field is closer to "the humanities"—like sociology or psychology—show a corresponding decrease

[2] Erich Fromm, *Psychoanalysis and Religion*. New Haven, Yale University Press, 1950.

in religious interest. It is as if the more these workers seem to learn about man as he is, the more they feel that man by and of himself can become master of his own fate—as if the more they know about man, the less they wish to hear about God. All this is very paradoxical and obscure—but there it is, a bit of telling empirical evidence[3] to guide us; in actuality, we know almost nothing about the problem.

There is more than presumptive psychological evidence trickling in, so to speak, from various sources—clinical, literary, philosophical and scientific—that our evaluation of our human selves, of our abilities and capacities, is influenced by the degree of narcissism which we acquire or develop under certain conditions. Our narcissism, our unconscious self-adulation, develops in us a tendency toward a kind of megalomania (an unconscious one, of course). No one of us is ever free of this tendency. In the deepest layers of our unconscious, we are all potential self-worshipers and cheerfully grandiose fellows.

Science—i.e., the study of nature—inevitably and invariably keeps the scientist aware of the immensity of nature and its powers, and of the littleness of man who is privileged to gain but a fleeting vision of the true strength and mystery of nature. Consequently, the scientist (I mean the true scientist and not the technologist, the engineer, who are but craftsmen), standing before the gigantic panorama of nature, finds little that would stimulate his unconscious megalomanic trends, that is to say, the leftovers of his infantile, unconsciously fantasied sense of omnipotence.

In the case of the political or social scientist, or the psychologist, or the practical politician, the psychological situation is entirely different. As man studies various social sciences and humanities, he not only studies but beholds what appears to him his own handiwork, as it were: banks, theatres, museums, tanks, peace treaties and declarations of independ-

[3] Cf. Ft. Note 14, *The Psychoanalytic Quarterly*, Vol. X, 1941, p. 205.

ence, declarations of war and orders for execution and grants of reprieve, skyscrapers and atomic bombs. All this immensity, these vast expanses of intellectual horizons and achievements of life's instrumentation, are very impressive to man who created them. He cannot help but be impressed with his own capacities and insights, and the depths which reveal themselves to him through his own magic ingenuity. His narcissism becomes therefore reinforced instead of weakened; it is not his littleness but his own greatness that he seems to behold in the mirror which he himself produced. In other words, his unconscious, infantile sense of omnipotence, instead of being not a little jolted as is the case with so many scientific workers, is constantly reawakened, nurtured and regalvanized. As a result, he feels that he "could do and control everything" in his social and political functioning, in conquering disease, in extending man's life to untold length—in short, in everything to conquer nature and promote constant and eternal progress. True, every now and then there creeps in that universal anxiety of which no one is free: the fear of death. But in the hurly-burly of constant activity and preoccupation with one's own accomplishments (deep down they mean one's own even if they are labeled as accomplishments of humanity as a whole), in the rush of living and with the unsensed but potent help of our biological adaptability by way of "brushing off" the unpleasant or even fully forgetting it, we don't think of death, which in our unconscious megalomania we seem to conquer. In this state (unconscious) of megalomanic omnipotence, and our not unconscious conviction of our ultimate omniscience, an individual as a rule cannot feel much inclined toward the contemplation of his very little place in this very big universe. He cannot therefore be much given to religious contemplation or humble consideration of the existence of God.

Therefore, few in our age escape fully the narcissistic worship of progress or of Logos. And the greater and more original the genius of the individual, the more apt is this individual to escape or to avoid religious orientation, even in times of war, when death anxiety is so intense and so widespread. Masses of people may not escape this intensification of death anxiety in times of war, but the humanistic scientist may sometimes, like Freud, remain above the mêlée, above the anxiety, and above that which he would consider a weakness—religious faith.

However, the above considerations are only hypothetical, even though highly plausible in the light of psychoanalytic psychology. There is much yet to be learned about the religious reactions of scientists and scholars. Yet we know enough to be convinced that the solution of the problems which arise between science and religion does not lie in that type of vituperative, mutual recrimination which, if voiced by scientists, is of man and not of God.

We also know enough to set aside as of little true scientific and even less religious significance those attempts to "reconcile" Freud with religion which try to enhance some practical aspects of certain religious trends (Joshua Liebman's *Peace of Mind*). Such utilitarian attempts are bound to lead only to the satisfaction of those who, by way of conceptual agility, would make God a celestial banker and the Archangel Gabriel a certified public accountant. Such attempts may even lead to a cynicism which at one blow mars both science and the loftiest spiritual strivings of man.

Reuben Osborn published a book on Freud and Marx[4] some years ago, which was a perfect illustration of where a systematic, utilitarian point of view in such matters can lead. Osborn, having decided to reconcile Freud and Marx, proceeded to prove how Freud could be made useful for the revolutionary Marxian. For instance, Freud described the formation of

---
[4] Reuben Osborn, *Freud and Marx: A Dialectical Study*. New York, Equinox Co-operative Press, Inc., (no date).

the superego and demonstrated how powerful an agency it is in the psychic apparatus and therefore in the behavior of man; therefore, concludes Osborn, let us concentrate on our children and "give" them a Marxian superego. Things would then be considerably simplified for the march of the world revolution (*sic!*). Yes, Freud pointed out the role of the father figure, the father image in the behavior of crowds;[5] Osborn thought we could cultivate this image and thus establish a proper following for the proper leadership in the business of attaining the Marxian utopia.

Such naïve utilitarianism would not be of sufficient import to be dwelt on, were it not that the utilitarian spirit of our age is so strong, so deeply cultivated, and so richly fertilized with the acquisitive, aggressive instincts that cognizance must be taken of this rather nefarious tendency to put even tentative data of a given science into the service of our aggressive instincts, and as soon as possible. In the general stream of psychological interests, which have been stimulated to a particularly high degree by psychoanalysis, we make a utilitarian tool of psychology and we "build morale," or at least we claim to know how.

We try (this quite unwittingly, but nonetheless foolishly) to extend the concept of neurosis even to that war situation in which a man frequently breaks down because he is unable to face the murder of his fellow man by his own hand, and his own death at the hand of his fellow man whom he does not even know personally.

Freud was more emphatic about being a pacifist. He also placed considerable emphasis on the fact that civilization restricts the outward expression of our aggressive, destructive drives and internalizes them. This process, he said, has its dangers (for the individual), but it is useful for civilization.

[5] *Group Psychology and the Analysis of the Ego.* London, The International Psycho-Analytical Press, 1922.

Sigmund Freud

Putting this into the simplest language, this would mean that civilized man, by virtue of his being civilized, has learned not to kill and learned inwardly to prefer his own death to murdering his neighbor. But modern military psychopathology would utilize Freud to avoid what is called "combat fatigue" (the old "war neurosis") by various psychotherapeutic methods, so that man should learn not to be afraid to kill and to die. Should our youth really and successfully learn to kill and to die without fear, it would not serve Freud very well, and civilization and humanity still less. Yet this is how the "practical" among us seek to draw "material" from whatever science they may find, in order to fulfill a goal which is just the opposite of the goals of reason, morality, civilization and science.

The above statement, correct as it is in my opinion, is yet not entirely just, because it appears to lay the responsibility for the misuse of certain data of science at the door of the practical man. This is not quite just, because one could not expect from the practical man anything else. That is why he is called a practical man; he is always on the lookout for something to use. The atom can be fissioned? Let us make an atomic bomb. The superego is powerful? Let us "make it" and use it for a Communist revolution, or for an intensification of the acquisitive instinct. Sex is important? Let us put on a new type of "Freudian" strip-tease. Being practical seldom involves Eros in its integrated functioning, for loving thy neighbor as thyself is very "impractical." Being practical most frequently involves the destructive drives and a host of their minor aides in our intellectual life, from infantile sexuality (*partial* erotic drives) to narcissistic impulses.

As I have said, it is not entirely just to blame the "practical" man for his abuse of Freud. Yet Freud himself, in *The Future of an Illusion*,[6] suggested a methodological device which

[6] Freud, *The Future of an Illusion*, London, Horace Liveright and the Institute of Psycho-Analysis, 1928.

played into the hands of the overzealous utilitarian. In this monograph Freud considered religion an illusion, a form of neurosis. While he did not insist on a specific clinical diagnosis of this neurosis, he did seem to consider it allied to the compulsion neuroses. He insisted once or twice in this monograph that he was not questioning the truth of the claims made by religion; he nevertheless expressed his ultimate belief that religion will finally outlive its usefulness and be substituted by Logos, knowledge, reason.

This claim that one might consider not only an individual but a whole community neurotic, and that a whole community may suffer from a severe neurosis while the individual members comprising this community may not necessarily suffer personally from a neurosis, produced considerable confusion. For if we do not take Freud's statement merely as a manner of speaking, and if we take him (as so many did) quite literally, confusion by and of "practical" men becomes inevitable. So many practical people at once proceeded to make all sorts of diagnoses on all sorts of communities, nations, and states—and if you can diagnose a pathological condition, you may even be able to treat it and, who knows, cure it! It is thus that a variety of "cures" were formulated, to cure nations of anti-Semitism, of Communism, of fascism, of deviations from democracy, of reactionary attitudes, and of radical attitudes. In short, a vitiation of the psychoanalytic method was introduced, and it was a vitiation traceable directly to Freud's misunderstood metaphor, or his misconceived parallelism between that which is individual and that which is social. Social science, cultural anthropology (in certain quarters), social psychology and its ramifications of pseudo-psychoanalytical influence, and other activities in this direction have mushroomed since World War II. Here and there within psychoanalysis itself, particularly among the French-speaking psychoanalysts, the question of the place of values in the scheme of psychoanalytic methodology began to be discussed with increasing frequency and in ever greater detail, again particularly since the end of the last World War.

Many questions arise out of Freud's excursions into the field of religious psychology and the problems of conscience, through his equation of the superego and conscience. These questions are serious and complex, and many of them have tormented men's spirit from time immemorial. One of the first of these questions is that of knowledge and reason. It would seem that knowledge by itself carries no inference as to what is good or evil. When it comes to reason, the problem becomes very difficult and obscure. Reason alone, so-called "pure reason," is unthinkable within man. Reason by itself, not integrated with the rest of the personality, does not exist in any personality. Why then should Freud feel that reason, integrated into the personality and pervaded with object-libidinous, genital maturity, leads away from evil and toward that which is good? One wonders whether Freud did not implicitly, though not explicitly, assume the existence of values which find their way into man's psychic apparatus by means of the various psychological mechanisms he described so well, and perhaps by way of the biological and cultural paths which he again traced so well. And one wonders why Freud, having tacitly assumed the presence of those values, was able to express so much trust, so much confidence, in reason pure and simple. Freud never stated such an assumption directly or indirectly, but it does seem that either this assumption was implicit in his conclusions as to the future of our cultural development, or that he equated clear, objective thinking with ethical thinking—which is possible, of course, but hardly tenable. Throughout his writings, from the earliest to the latest, Freud seems to use the term "reason" in a rather undetermined sense. At times, he seems to think of it as "reason" (the *ratio* of traditional philosophers); at times, it seems to mean "intellect" (the *intellectus* of the philosophers).

At any rate, there is no justification for our expecting, still less for our demanding, that Freud should give us clear-cut and incontrovertible answers to the questions of moral values and the interplay of the latter with human reason. Freud was not a philosopher. He never claimed to be one. He did not even have much knowledge of philosophy, and his philosophical excursions and the obscurities of some of his conclusions are inevitable in that penumbra of human psychic activity which lies on the borderline between science and philosophy. A man who penetrated so deeply into so many layers of the heretofore unknown in the mental and affective activity of man could not avoid stumbling and touching upon some of those shadowy pitfalls which shift hither and yon in the twilight area of human psychobiological functioning.

This is said not to justify Freud, and still less to plead his cause—which incidentally is not clear enough anyway in this particular respect. It is underscored here more to remind the enthusiasts of His Majesty's opposition that arrogant discontent with Freud on the score of moral philosophy is out of place, since Freud never formulated and never attempted to formulate a moral philosophy. He was a scientist, and in his field he has not as yet been surpassed. But as far as the problems under consideration are concerned, Freud, as a person, led a truly good life of work and love, and like all of us wandered and wondered and blundered in an uncertain search for moral truth.

Those who seem disconcerted by Freud's apparent inability to answer the major question about moral values are more frustrated than right, and more angry than truly righteous. There were many questions of this kind that Freud touched upon, and many remarks which the ill-disposed reader could mistake for arrogant statements on the part of Freud. Moreover, the German language permits of some confusion as to what Freud thought of the soul. The simple answer is that he never told us anything about the soul, and there is no reason why he should have. Theology was as foreign to him as the insight into human emotions is foreign to blood chemistry. In the German language, "psyche," "spirit," "soul," and "mind" are frequently designated, and were so designated by Freud quite often, by one and the same word. Freud frequently used the terms "psyche" ("die Psyche") and "soul" ("die Seele") in the sense of the psychic apparatus—the id, the ego, and the superego.

If Freud's attitude toward the problem of moral values created considerable controversy, his attitude toward religious faith proper aroused a greater number of emotional conflicts among his own adherents as well as between the Freudians and the clerical world. There is little more to be said, although a great deal has been said, about Freud's attitude toward belief in God and in prayer, and the need to belong to a church as an institution. What has been said about Freud in this connection is mostly uncharitable, as if Freud's attitude as an unbeliever is more conclusive than his discoveries of fact. There are many religious people who would dismiss psychoanalysis as an evil and would wish psychopathology, particularly that of the neuroses, to be completely abandoned in favor of purely religious consolation and religious practices. It must be noted that the authority of psychoanalysis as a body of facts cannot be easily dismissed, and those who would invoke religion as a cure for neuroses, counteracting psychoanalytic curative efforts, are definitely in the minority. But the voice of this minority, if not authoritative scientifically, is rather loud, and it commands a moral authority which in this case is misapplied directly to stifle a body of facts about the nature of man which it would seem to be the moral duty of the religious teacher to know and to respect as a source of great knowledge of man and a possible amelioration of man's earthly existence.

The voice of this minority is harsh, and as in the cases of all passionate controversies a great deal is said which is not true to fact or fair to those involved. Whenever the voice is not controversial, even true piety and devotion often do not save it from a considerable naïveté.

One of the many examples that could be cited is a recent book by a Franciscan Father Alan Keenan, entitled *Neuroses and Sacraments*.[7] The book betrays a complete lack of knowledge of psychopathology and obviously confuses the religious, spiritual consolation the believer derives from the sacraments with true medicopsychological treatment, which is a different thing entirely. To claim that severe obsessional, compulsion neurotic symptoms or depressions can be *cured* by the administration of sacraments means to claim something that even the *Malleus Maleficarum* (*The Witches' Hammer*), which was published in 1489, never claimed. The nearly five centuries which have elapsed since the appearance of this book have produced considerable changes in the Christian Church with regard to neuroses. The old, oft-repeated untruth that psychoanalysis wants to take the place of confession has been denied by Freud himself and refuted by Catholic authorities, and it is based more on animosity to, than comprehension of, Freud.

Yet the prejudice against psychoanalysis on the part of religion, particularly the Christian religion, is so great that when it is not vociferous and intolerant it is at least singular. In the preface to a thesis for a Doctorate of Philosophy written by the Rev. R. S. Lee, the Vicar of St. Mary the Virgin of the University Church of Oxford, England (published separately in the series, "Theology for Modern Men"), an apparently devout editor writes: "A careful reading of this book will pro-

[7] New York, Sheed and Ward, 1950.

voke both *Christians and psychoanalysts* [italics mine] to think again, if only because it provides criteria by which more healthy forms of the Christian religion may be discriminated from less worthy varieties."[8] We used to hear of Jews and Christians, of Moslems and Christians; it is not a little amusing to read of "Christians and psychoanalysts"—as if psychoanalysis were the name of an apostate or heretic sect, or a pagan doctrine, and not a scientific discipline. At any rate, there stands the undeniable fact that the doctoral thesis, which was duly accepted and published (and the degree was duly conferred upon the Vicar of St. Mary the Virgin, Oxford, University Church), was entitled *Freud and Christianity*.

Its basic thesis is that Freud's ethico-religious conclusions are not fully acceptable to the Christian believer, but that Freud's scientific findings support the Christian doctrine, without injury or injustice done thereby to psychoanalysis or religion. There are many very telling and instructive passages in this rather penetrating book. It is at times perhaps a little too utilitarian and "concordistic," as it were, but it follows Freud with accuracy and the articles of faith with fidelity.

Perhaps, since this thesis is written by an Anglican (i.e., not a Roman Catholic) the following passage will prove of special interest: "Psychoanalysts tell us that in dreams a church is a common symbol of the mother, and there is no doubt too that the abstract idea of the church is readily made a substitute for the mother.... Those Christians who manifest a strong emotional anti-Papal bias, or who think of the Church of Rome as the 'scarlet woman,' betray the unconscious mother-identification by their negative reaction. They resist the idea of the Father (the Pope) having power over the mother (the Church). Their 'Protestantism' is a reaction formation. Their reaction is against their repressed Oedipus Complex wishes and their

[8] R. S. Lee, *Freud and Christianity*, London, James Clarke & Co., Ltd., 1948, p. 7.

intense emotional bias draws its strength from unconscious sources."[9] Here is another significant passage: "The value of psychoanalysis is that it reveals this danger [of pure fantasy life] to us and enables us to lay more emphasis on the positive reality-principle factors which support Christianity, assuming, that is, that religion is more properly a function of the Ego than of the unconscious and the Id."[10] This is an extraordinary and almost revolutionary thought! But it is probably close to the truth. It has not yet been sufficiently tested, for those whose religious faith could be supplemented by a thorough knowledge of psychoanalysis and who therefore could alone be capable of verifying and confirming this truth have until recently shied away from psychoanalysis in anxious diffidence or defiant animosity.

"It is not enough therefore to put on the surface mask of righteousness. We must have deeper harmony than that. That is why in studying religion we need to distinguish what is a real sublimation from a [mere] displacement, for in the latter we find, as it were, wolves masquerading in sheep's clothing. In a sublimation, however, the whole body is 'full of light.' "[11]

As one of the first practical outcomes of a more tolerant and enlightened attitude toward psychoanalysis on the part of religion, the following may be cited: There is a phenomenon called "scrupulosity." The average psychoanalyst almost never sees it. It is found mostly among those who study for the priesthood, or who are already ordained priests—although it is also found among lay believers. Before the days of psychoanalysis, it presented a well-nigh insoluble problem, for behind the manifestations of the depressive, ruminative, religious anxiety there often lay concealed serious mental illnesses. Today there are some seminaries and monasteries where scrupulosity is

[9] *Ibid.*, pp. 117, 118.
[10] *Ibid.*, p. 93.
[11] *Idem.*

Sigmund Freud

quickly recognized for what it is, and proper curative measures can be undertaken.

The enlightened influence of psychoanalysis is found today both in Protestant and Catholic institutions. There are some Catholic universities in which extensive courses on psychoanalysis are given.

But these immediately practical advantages of the application of psychoanalysis, significant as they are, are by no means the most valuable ones.

There are a number of earnest religious thinkers who are preoccupied with problems vital to religious life and the life of religion: aggression, ambivalence (the constant clash between love and hate), ascetic dedication, the contemplative life, moral issues in personal, social and public life, and the relation of emotions to the problem of will and reason. A number of devout scholars are busy restudying all these problems with the utmost care, intellectual honesty, and profound faith. The aid of the added insight with which psychoanalysis provides them proves invaluable both to the further development of religious scholarship and the deeper understanding of the faithful.

In recent years a group of Carmelite priests, in association with several clinical psychoanalysts, published an excellent volume of the *Etudes Carmelitaines,* in which many of the above-mentioned problems were treated with considerable sagacity and intellectual depth. Several studies on religious life and ideals have appeared in *La Vie Spirituelle* and its *Suppléments,* which are published by a group of Dominicans in Paris. Problems of monastic poverty, problems of neurotic religious needs and their differentiation from healthy ones, problems of obedience, humility and love in its protean, instinctual and higher moral manifestations—all these problems are seriously and sympathetically considered in the light of psychoanalysis, and all this is done, not merely by means of some sort of drawing of parallels and inferences which Freud never made, but on the basis of the psychoanalytic theory of instincts and Freudian metapsychology, which are studied and critically tested and accepted. There is a meticulous and assiduous effort being made—and it is truly a gigantic effort—to bring together Catholic scholarship and inspiration in the study of the *Summa Theologica* of St. Thomas Aquinas in the light of the data provided by psychoanalysis. There is a great deal in Thomas Aquinas' treatises "On Passions" and "On Truth" alone to warrant a thorough review and to provide a possible synthesis with the discoveries of Freud.

Such a synthesis is possible only if the usual error is avoided into which so many psychoanalysts and nonanalysts, sympathizers and adversaries, fall so frequently—almost chronically. It is the error of thinking that once you discover that you have an unconscious motive for doing something, you may conclude: (1) that the motive is invalid; or (2) that it disappears; or (3) that you lose the desire to do what you want to do "because you know the unconscious reason why"; or (4), what is even worse, that an unconscious motive is neurotic by very virtue of the fact that it is unconscious.

All this is preeminently untrue. Man is not a disorderly mass of obscure though set "Freudian" mechanisms, which if brought into the open fall apart and disappear. This is a fantasy which would never permit one to pursue the study of psychoanalysis lest the preposterous conclusion prove to be true that with the imagined "falling apart" of the mechanisms man himself would fall apart. This superficial viewpoint is widespread in many confused and confusing guises.

Even as widespread are the major objections raised against psychoanalysis for its alleged pansexualism, and Freud's atheism. That Freud explained the workings of the psychic apparatus in terms of psychological mechanisms moved some critics to raise added objections on the ground of his being purely mechanistic and deterministic. The last objection I consider of secondary importance—in truth an artefact. Is not all science mechanistic and deterministic? How could it be anything else? Within the sum total of its data, which are empirical, it tries to understand how things work (mechanisms) and what conditions (determinants), inner and outer, make them work the way they do. This is a characteristic, and an accepted one, of the *closed system* with which empirical science is concerned. The severest and the most austere theologian could not quarrel with this. The quarrel begins only when the scientist wants to "determine" God and the theologian tries to explain the third law of thermodynamics by means of transcendentalist hypotheses of revelation. Such quarrels are as old as they are futile.

These quarrels will probably continue in many fields and to the end of time and with the same futility, for they are not quarrels about facts and truth, but rather about mental attitudes which we guard with intense anxiety lest they be touched by new facts. In other words, it is not the wicked espousal of ignorance that causes these quarrels, but the fear lest in the light of a newly discovered fact we prove wrong. It is insecurity and a fundamental lack of confidence in our own beliefs that make us shy away so bitterly, so aggressively from the facts, which impose upon us the responsibility of fitting them into the scheme of life. It is easier to turn away from facts than to accept the burden of freedom from prejudice. It is the striving for freedom, the combativeness against prejudice in the intellectual as well as the emotional field, the aspiration to be fearlessly conscious of that of which man prefers to remain unconscious, that distinguishes Freud from among all his predecessors in the field of human psychology.

Perhaps these distinguishing characteristics of Freud would justify our assumption that Freud was not truly a man of our twentieth century. As the individualist, as the introspective rediscoverer of the value and the greatness of the individual and as the proponent of his autonomy, Freud seems rather to have belonged to the nineteenth century. There is something Spencerian in his Olympian bitterness against society and against society's attempt to encroach upon the freedom of the individual. He cared not for utopias, for social crusades. Man, he thought, should stand independent and free, and as a free agent learn to love his neighbor and develop ever more those emotions which bind people together. But Freud was doubtful whether this utopian process would ever be successfully completed, and he fell back on his one and only ideal: man, free, individualistic to the last, but not egotistic. Add to this his study of the turmoil of the unconscious, and his glance into the primitive past of man, and we come to recognize the picture of not a little romantic individualism of the latter part of the nineteenth century.

To this may also be added (and this would complete the picture) Freud's unshakable scientism: That which is scientific is true; there is no other truth; the unknown that is not accessible to science, even potentially, is unknown because it does not exist and not because of our human limitations. Man is to be reared and brought up to have a strong ego. This is uncomfortable to man, but without it man's primitive impulses would destroy his fellow men; he might destroy himself, of course, if his superego were too strong and offered him no opportunity to destroy anything else legitimately. In terms of values then—and values there are, according to Freud, but only in terms of the superego—there is more than a hint of austerity about Freud and his conception of man. It does seem that for some reason Freud felt the need to assert his scientific credo with an emphasis greater than was warranted, as if he had to assure his audience and his followers (and, who knows, perhaps himself) that all there is is science and scientific knowledge. The rest, whatever it is, is fantasy and illusion.

Thus, Freud brought about a recrudescence of the controversy which he thought he would settle, and in doing so he mobilized a great deal of emotion against himself and psychoanalysis—emotion which essentially had nothing to do with psychoanalysis, but rather with Freud's need to reassert repeatedly that science is supreme.

In this light, it is not surprising to find truly religious people who yet are Freudians without feeling the necessity of agreeing with him on matters philosophical. This would explain the almost pained exclamation of Karl Stern: "Freud's atheistic philosophy is a tragic historical accident, but it *is* an accident."[12] This also moves Stern to remind us that "there is no scientist who does not try to fit his findings, which are by their very nature fragmentary, into the jigsaw puzzle of some universal idea."[13] And: "However, the fact remains that psychoanalysis, like all great discoveries of the human intellect, can be used to make ammunition for nihilists or to provide balm for the wounds of mankind. . . . I presume that de Broglie is a Christian and that Planck was a Christian. Pascal and Newton were Christians. It is possible that they were Christians *besides* being Scientists, or *on account* of being Scientists, but why should they have been Christians *in spite* of being Scientists?"[14]

The ultimate and the deepest in Freud is, of course, that which offers us the opportunity to add to our total picture *and* vision of man—to put it in Freudian terms, that which would offer us a synthesis between the reality principle and our ego-ideal, which visualizes our human ideal ego—that is to say, that which we hope we (man) will ultimately become.

What Freud provided as a new method for the investigation of man cannot be replaced. His influence on the various and

12 Karl Stern, *The Pillar of Fire*, New York, Harcourt Brace, 1951, p. 279.
13 *Ibid.*, pp. 281, 282.
14 *Ibid.*, pp. 279, 280.

many branches of psychological science and medicopsychological endeavor stands uncontested. Even the die-hards who still try to throw Freud out of court are found to be using Freudian terminology. However, as for the question of a possible synthesis of man as he is with man as we want him to become and as he might become—this will have to await its day. The bigot and the overanxious man, the fanatic and the self-righteous and even the religious person—all, if they are too uncertain of themselves, combine to retard the attainment of such a synthesis.

Yet so strong and so telling and so convincing is the psychological system of Freud, that even in its most conspicuous controversy psychoanalysis wins in a very paradoxical way. By overcoming the anxiety which made the religious person rise in opposition to Freud, man finds it unnecessary to share with Freud his distrust of religion, which Freud was unable to recognize because he was unable to know it.

The whole process of a new religious synthesis is still in its earliest beginnings. No one has expressed it more trenchantly and more decisively than the above-quoted Karl Stern, himself a well-trained neuropathologist and practicing psychiatrist. Stern had been moving toward his conversion to Catholicism through many years of suffering and anguish, in the atmosphere of Nazi concentration camps, of war, hatred, expatriation, while searching in the Synagogue, the Old Testament, the Talmud, the New Testament, the laboratory, and Karl Marx.

Soon after he was received into the church, Stern wrote a letter to his brother, whose head had been shaven by the Nazis to mark him as a prisoner of Buchenwald, and who at the time lived already in the land of Israel. There is this passage in Stern's letter:

"Looking at the history of the human spirit at long range, it is a tremendous thing that psychoanalysis has rediscovered

Sigmund Freud

the primary position of love in Man's world. This discovery was made from a materialist platform, as it were. What else could we expect from a genius who is a child of the nineteenth century? Lop a few of the accidental ornaments off and you have a psychology which reaffirms and enriches the Christian idea of Man."[15]

---

[15] *Ibid.*, p. 278.

Scientific Psychopathology
and Religious Issues

FREUD'S official attitude toward religion is well known. His book *The Future of an Illusion* ends with a positive denial that there can be any knowledge outside science: "Science is no illusion. But it would be an illusion to suppose that we could get anywhere else what it cannot give us."[1] Yet the same Freud asserts: "One would like to count oneself among the believers, in order to admonish the philosophers who try to preserve the God of religion by substituting for him an impersonal, shadowy, abstract principle, and to say: 'Thou shalt not take the name of the Lord, thy God, in vain.' "[2] It is almost self-evident that Freud was far from having solved the problem for himself. There is no reason to expect a solution of this problem from Freud; he was imbued with the faith that only scientific knowledge is true knowledge, and yet in his scientific work he relied upon myths, sagas, folklore, dreams, fantasies, the greatest and the humblest flights of human imagination. In other words, Freud stood in his own way, so to

First published in *Theological Studies*, 1953. Reprinted by permission of The Newman Press.
[1] Sigmund Freud, *The Future of an Illusion*, New York, Horace Liveright and the Institute of Psycho-Analysis, 1928, p. 98.
[2] Freud, *Civilization and Its Discontents*, New York, Jonathan Cape and Harrison Smith, 1930, p. 24.

speak, since he elevated to the majesty of final causes the psychological mechanisms which he was privileged to discover.

In this respect Freud was a typical example of the scientist who confuses the mechanics of natural phenomena with the causation and purpose of natural phenomena. Someone aptly called this attitude the elevation of science to the level of unshakable dogma; it is scientism, not scientific. Yet even Freud, who gave himself fully to scientism, does offer a suggestion in numerous passages of his writings that he was not entirely unaware of his own inner struggle between dogmatic scientism and that something which is beyond conventional science. It is important in this respect not to forget that it was Freud who elevated the most unscientific of all tools, human intuition, to the dignity of a keen instrument for investigation of human psychology.

W. T. Stace is inclined to believe that the conflict between science and religion was established and deepened by the scientific revolution of the seventeenth century. He thinks that naturalism sought to establish itself as a dogma and consequently aligned itself against religion with all the power of conviction which the formulation of natural laws offers. This is quite true, but only to the extent that the scientist would insist that there is no truth outside science. ". . . No scientific argument—by which I mean an argument drawn from the phenomena of nature—can ever have the slightest tendency either to prove or to disprove the existence of God, in short . . . science is irrelevant to religion."[3]

This point of view is not new. However, it is not complete; it fails to give us a synthesis of that which religion and science have to offer, each in its respective way. This point of view, taken without further ado, might even suggest that we return to the Cartesian dichotomy in which the "natural" man would

[3] W. T. Stace, *Religion and the Modern Mind,* Philadelphia and New York, Lippincott, 1952, p. 76.

be considered an autonomous machine and the spiritual one a being apart. This dichotomy proved untenable to many, even in the days of Descartes, and it appears even more untenable to those who, whether they be religious or naturalists, take the human individual as an indivisible whole which cannot be cleaved into parts by subtleties of formal logical arguments.

Contemporary psychology does not visualize the individual as an arithmetical sum of various parts, but rather as a unified synthesis of all the ingredients which seem to make up man. In accordance with modern psychology, man is not made up of animal part and human part; man is both human *and* animal, rational *and* irrational, material *and* spiritual; he is one and all of those things at one and the same time. He is always confronted by the great problem which is most simply denoted as the problem of making a choice—a choice of being at any given practical moment an animal or a human being, a material or spiritual agent, a logical or paralogical mind.

All this presents more and more complicated problems, which cannot be solved by being either purely scientific or purely religious. As Stace puts it: "The key to the solution of this problem lies in the consideration that men's minds do not usually work in the way that logicians say they should."[4] This is really the crux of the problem, and we ought to dwell on this in greater detail, if possible. The suggestion that human minds do not necessarily or always, or perhaps ever, function in accordance with the precepts laid down by the logicians is one with which the contemporary psychopathologist will not find it difficult to agree, since he knows that affective factors more unconscious than conscious dominate our thinking more than it appears and more than we are willing to admit.

The problem then appears to be a psychological one. It is a

[4] *Ibid.*, p. 85.

problem of uncovering the manner of our confusion on the question of science and religion. I do not think that the present-day confusion can be easily cleared up yet. So many emotions, passions, insecurities, and intolerances activate our contentions on the subject that all one can do is to proceed with caution and diffidence and humble hope.

Embarking cautiously on this path of search, I would remind you first of all of the words of Liston Pope, who so aptly and concisely summarized the situation of the contemporary mind: "Scientism, not to be confused with science itself, is the faith that science is the only way to truth or knowledge and that science provides the only hope for man's salvation. Scientism is the dogma of science. Science the Searcher is transformed by Scientism into Science the Savior." And further: "Science the Servant will become Science the Master of mankind; having learned to control the physical world, it will learn to control human relations as well and to release the mind and spirit of man from all bondage except to science itself." And further still: "When science is made into a religion, becoming an object of worship and a system of ultimate truth, it invariably becomes a bad religion, teaching man to worship the achievement of the human mind. By the same token, it becomes bad science and tends to harden into a dogma."[5]

Here we have again a telling allusion to the fact that science, when it is permitted to develop into scientism, leads to the worship of the human mind. This is another way of saying that the center of attention and interest becomes not truth, universal or particular, not knowledge of man or God, but rather a self-contained preoccupation with the adoration of the human mind—a psychological condition of utmost importance from the standpoint of modern psychology. In its

[5] Liston Pope, "Christianity and the Social Sciences," in *Christianity in an Age of Science*, Canadian Broadcasting Corporation, n.d., pp. 24–25.

most direct form it is narcissism, and in its consequences it does not even lead to self-knowledge. Still less would it lead to a synthesis, the demand for which becomes louder and louder as our contemplation of human problems deepens.

Thus we are again led a step closer to the recognition that the problem we are dealing with is a psychological one. Its origins are not in scientific logic or truth or in theological or religious truth. Rather it is a problem of the psychological functioning of man. This functioning must be understood, if man's mind is not to stand in man's own way and thus prevent him from understanding that which he can and ought to understand clearly.

Let us observe that the intensity of the apparent conflict between science and religion seems to be fed cooperatively by science and religion in a very singular way. The scientist, as was pointed out, tends to try to answer questions of ultimate truth and ultimate knowledge. However, these are not scientific questions at all. As Etienne Gilson so well puts it, they are religious questions:

> If they [the scientists] don't ask religious questions, scientists will never be offered religious answers. Nor will these religious answers ever pretend to be scientific ones. Religious wisdom tells us that in the beginning God created heaven and earth, but it does not pretend to give us any scientific account of the progressive formation of the world. As Thomas Aquinas aptly says, precisely about this very text, there were things which Moses could not express to an ignorant people without using images which they could understand.[6]

One could hardly find a more authoritative and more lucid statement than the above. For Gilson is a profound scholar, a

[6] Etienne Gilson, "Religious Wisdom and Scientific Knowledge," in *Christianity in an Age of Science*, p. 21; cf. *Summa Theologica*, I, q. 66, a. 1, ad 1 m.

Scientific Psychopathology and Religious Issues

great student of Thomas Aquinas, and a man of an immense philosophical perspective which is as great as his lucidity and intellectual tolerance. He calls our attention to the changing conceptions of the universe from Newton through Einstein to de Broglie and Heisenberg. He is impressed with the "decreasing longevity" of the various scientific conceptions of the universe. The system of Ptolemy lived fourteen centuries; the Copernican system lasted only three centuries; that of Einstein less than a quarter of a century, to be replaced by the newer conceptions of Heisenberg and other contributors to microphysics. Gilson concludes that, while the progress of science continues at a steady pace, ". . . the fact remains that, by reason of its accelerated progress, modern science is exhibiting an always decreasing stability."[7] As for the scientists themselves:

> Confronted with their own amazing discoveries, they entertain no doubt about their truth, but they are beginning to wonder about their very possibility. "What is most incomprehensible about nature," Einstein says, "is it comprehensibility." As to Louis de Broglie, in one of the most remarkable chapters of his book on physics and microphysics, he makes this almost identical remark: "What is most marvelous about the progress of science, is that it has revealed to us a certain concordance between our thought and things, a certain possibility for us to grasp, through the resources of our intelligence and the rules of our reason, the deep seated relations that obtain between phenomena. We do not wonder enough about the fact that some scientific knowledge is possible."[8]

Gilson comments: "This remarkable statement clearly shows that nothing equals the ignorance of modern philos-

[7] Gilson, *op. cit.*, p. 17.
[8] *Ibid.*, p. 18.

ophers in matters of science, except the ignorance of modern scientists in matters of philosophy."[9] And he explains: "The question of the possibility of science is not itself a scientific question. Any attempt to answer it in a scientific way results in a vicious circle, since a scientific demonstration of the possibility of science implies the existence of science whose possibility it tries to demonstrate."[10]

Let us then agree with Gilson in the only possible conclusion:

Since the only way for us to account for the intelligibility of the world is to resort to a cause whose nature and operation made it to be, and to be intelligible, the answer to the problem must needs be found in the crowning part of metaphysics, that is, in that part of it which deals with the first principle and the highest cause. If there is such a cause, its name is God. In short, the only discipline that can answer this question is divinity, or theology. Now I quite agree that, to many scientists, philosophical or theological answers do not sound serious. But this is beside the point; for indeed it would not be serious to give metaphysical or theological answers to scientific questions; but the question asked by these scientists is not a scientific one; science never worries about its own possibility: were science not possible it could not exist; that is all. What is now happening is that on the basis of their scientific knowledge some scientists are beginning to ask metaphysical and theological questions. And they are welcome to do it; but if they do, they will have to look for metaphysical and theological answers.[11]

In other words, science keeps on attempting to give scientific answers to theological and metaphysical questions, and in

[9] *Loc. cit.*
[10] *Ibid.*, p. 19.
[11] *Loc. cit.*

Scientific Psychopathology and Religious Issues

doing so it does not even notice that it strays from the path of science. One wonders why. I have repeatedly asked this question on these pages, in one way or another. Let us now attempt a tentative answer. First of all, let us recall what was said about the ever-changing conception of the universe from Ptolemy to de Broglie. As Gilson put it: "Like the Patriarchs of the Old Testament, they seem to obey a law of diminishing longevity."[12] The whole aspect of physical determinism and scientific previsibility has changed. We live more and more in a world of "innumerable elementary indeterminations." This means, says Gilson, "that the strictly determined mechanical world of dialectical materialism, which Marxists still mistake for the world of science, died twenty-five years ago. They don't seem to know it yet."[13] They don't seem to know it yet because scientists who misconceive their explanation of the mechanics of a phenomenon for an ultimate explanation of the phenomenon itself, cannot give up their mistaken metaphysical position without giving up that worship of the human mind of which mention was made above.

The issue then is not one's attitude toward theology or metaphysics or religion or science itself. The issue is the attitude of man toward his own mind, which is charged with utmost narcissistic cathexes. The theologians, who since the beginning of the Jewish faith and throughout the Christian era have considered the human mind and its power of reason and understanding to be the very essence of man, believed that this power of reason and understanding, which can explore the very depths of nature and man and even reach to the Creator Himself, is man's endowment because he is made in the image of God. This image of God has no anthropomorphic, corporeal, or material meaning. The anthropomorphic idea of God is born out of the limitations of man's

---

[12] *Ibid.*, p. 17.
[13] *Loc. cit.*

narcissism; it is a human creation. But the image of God in man, as traditionally conceived, is a result of an act of divine generosity; it is of divine creation. And for centuries men who were both humble and wise in their self-knowledge understood that they were to worship, not the image, but its Exemplar.

This religious attitude is essentially different from the narcissism which is displayed by scientism toward the human mind. The scientistic orientation is of a special psychological brand, particularly when it concerns social sciences and psychology. For here we deal with man's persistent even though illusory conviction that he alone, by the processes of science and out of the neutral knowledge thus gathered, can reach the knowledge of the ultimate purpose of mankind's living and acquire the power to transform man into that image of man which science in its simple, technical unwisdom and skillful sagacity believes it knows and understands. This is the true difficulty of present-day scientific psychopathology, as it is the difficulty of all kinds of scientism; for, after all, this is a difficulty arising out of the over-estimation of man's own self-contained importance. It is a form of megalomania which is inevitable in all cases of severe narcissism; it is a fantasy of a power and wisdom which do not exist in man.

Since present-day scientific psychopathology, even more than physics, seeks to take a dominant place in the hierarchy of human endeavors and a leading role in the business of human relations, it is naturally confronted with the grim truth that as a science it possesses no more wisdom or charity than the physicists who split the atom and made the bombs and became stunned by the horror of their handiwork.

The problem is acute, and potentially very dangerous. For, after all, for centuries religion was the one and only human activity which concerned itself with man's relation to God, to eternity, to salvation. It was the only inner spiritual discipline

Scientific Psychopathology and Religious Issues 113

which conceived of, and understood, the deep interdependence among men, the great yearning for a mankind which would become a real brotherhood of men. It cannot surrender these concerns and aspirations to scientific psychology and sociology, because it cannot give up the very essence of what it is, the deep respect and concern for the human person as a person, as a unique creation which is both so very individual and yet so completely one with his brethren and the world as a whole.

That which modern psychology would designate as an unconscious sense of guilt is not sufficient to cover the sense of the individual's responsibility for his fellow men and his sense of communal duty in relation to each living individual. Scientific psychopathology, like any science, is unable to understand this ethico-religious sense of guilt which transcends the usual unconscious mechanisms, producing what Freud called the precipitate of the oedipus complex and the neurotic sense of guilt. It is unable to understand this sense of guilt even though it may be able to descibe the psychological mechanisms of the sense of religious responsibility and of sinfulness. However, as D. R. G. Owen has said, "To expose the psychological or sociological origin of a belief is not at all the same thing as proving it false. To suppose that it is, is to adopt the attitude of Ebenezer Bulver's wife, who when her husband insisted that two sides of a triangle were together greater than the third, replied, 'You only say that because you're a man.' "[14]

Yet how much contention and intolerance burn around the assertion that, as scientific psychopathology and sociology become more and more scientific, a more crying need is felt to recognize that the megalomania of the self-adoring human mind is by no means a sign of its true greatness. Only by the

[14] D. R. G. Owen, "Science, Scientism and Religion," in *Christianity in an Age of Science,* p. 13.

recognition of the value of the individual as a person will this contention be disposed of. It is this, I am sure, that Einstein had in mind when he said that "Science without religion is lame, and religion without science is blind."[15] To avoid this blindness and this lameness, it is necessary to accept the truth of John Donne's trenchant words: "No man is an iland, intire of itselfe; every man is a peece of the Continent, a part of the Maine; if a Clod bee washed away by the Sea, Europe is the lesse, as well as if a Promontorie were, as well as if a Mannor of thy friends or of thine owne were: any mans death diminishes me, because I am involved in Mankinde. And therefore never send to know for whom the bell tolls; it tolls for thee."[16]

The melancholy but uplifting truth of these words serves to underscore the singular character of the psychological origin of the conflict between present-day scientific psychopathology and religion. When I say psychological origin, I mean to say that there is no real conflict between these two aspects of truth, science and religion, each of which, in its own specific ways, is a revelation of God. I mean: scientism involves man with himself and yet drowns his individuality in statistical averages; but man cannot be abolished, and therefore he cannot help but strive to remain alive. If he strives to save himself by devotion to scientism, he gets dissolved in the freakish light of his delusion of megalomania, and like the schizophrenic who fills his world with delusions he dies while staying physiologically alive. If, on the other hand, he seeks salvation away from life, he again achieves but living perdition, because he who abandons scientism so often throws out with it science itself, and then his apparently religious views are bound to be distorted, since one cannot accept and submit oneself to the will of God while rejecting one of His greater

[15] Cf. C. A. Coulson, "The Unity of Science and Faith," in *Christianity in an Age of Science*, p. 42.
[16] Quoted by Stace, *op. cit.*, p. 273.

Scientific Psychopathology and Religious Issues

creations—science, the true knowledge and partial mastery of Nature.

I might seem to have left out of consideration the contentious arguments which are always teeming around such issues as the soul as the psychologist sees it and as religion views it. This I have done deliberately; for it must be clear by now that I cannot admit that the scientific psychologist *qua* psychologist and *qua* scientist is ever able to learn anything about the soul. If he claims to give a scientific description of it, he merely deludes himself by mistaking the manifestations of a phenomenon for the phenomenon itself. If he senses and knows what a human soul is, he perceives it with humble awe and he would never attempt to make a scientific analysis of it, anymore than he would attempt to make a scientific analysis of beauty, or greatness, or sacrifice, or a sense of responsibility.

Perhaps the best way of bringing this statement to a fitting close is to cite the words of the Lutheran theologian, Paul Tillich, in an essay on "Jewish Influences on Contemporary Christian Theology." He recalls the contribution of the contemporary Jewish religious philosopher Martin Buber, and says that because of scientism (he does not use this word) we get lost as persons and become engulfed in a conflict for which there should be no place in the life and functioning of the contemporary scientific mind. There ought not to be any conflict, if we allow ourselves to understand the nature of what we lose by trying to gain the illusion of complete mastery by means of scientism. For, under influence of the latter, science does become lame, because

> Men become things, living beings become mechanisms, thinking in universals replaces the encounter with individuals. Men are made into objects of calculation and management, of research and test, into means instead of ends. The I-Thou relation, the person-to-person encounter is lost. God himself becomes a moral

ideal or a philosophical concept or a being whose existence or non-existence can be argued for. But a God who is an object is not God at all.[17]

These words underscore, more than any other recent statement that I know, the essential inner conflict of contemporary man—a conflict which is mistaken for an objective, true, factual conflict between scientific psychopathology and religion. This conflict is best illustrated by the development of Freud's own thought and psychoanalysis. On one hand the author of psychoanalysis wished to remain a biologist, a positivist, a devotee of scientism. On the other he made the greatest contribution toward the rejection of disindividualized scientism; for the method of psychoanalysis is the method of the ever-deepening study and recognition of man as a person, not man merely as a statistical datum. In other words, psychoanalysis, like all the other sciences of man and Nature during the last half-century, reflects the same, almost eternal, and truly tragic conflict between man's striving to become the engineer of a world in which there would be vast populations but not a single self-conscious individual, and man's yearning to preserve his being in complete unity with the One in whose image he was created.

---

[17] Paul Tillich, "Jewish Influences on Contemporary Christian Theology," *Cross Currents*, II, no. 3 (Spring, 1952), p. 38.

Love in Freudian Psychoanalysis

THERE is a general tendency which has become quite habitual during the past few years—the tendency to employ various devices of argument which give the impression of methodological approaches but which in actuality are but logical or quasi-logical *démarches* based on preconceived attitudes on the part of proponents as well as opponents of psychoanalysis.

There are among psychoanalysts truly religious, devout men, practising Catholics, Protestants and Jews—very few, to be sure. Their presence is as a rule overlooked in psychoanalytic circles and most, if not all, psychoanalysts—with the exception of the few true believers—take it always for granted that religious belief is excluded from the system of psychoanalysis, and that God and the Soul are not subjects to be discussed but conceptions to be treated as the not unusual fantasies of the common, universal neuroses of the common man.

On the whole, the same attitude may be found toward conscience in its ethico-religious aspects, since it is taken silently for granted that Freud's superego suffices for the understand-

First published in 1953 in *La Vie Spirituelle*. Reprinted by permission of Sheed & Ward.

ing of the moral and religious drives of men, and that moral theology and religious faith—not being scientific—have nothing to contribute to the psychology of the superego. The few contributions on the subject which seem to prove that the superego is not conscience, even though conscience may and does at times utilize the psychological agency of the superego —these few contributions (by Odier, Nodet and myself) are isolated instances; they are generally regarded without any curiosity, or disregarded with self-contentment by the overwhelming majority of psychoanalysts.

The scientific mind—and there are a great many honest scientific minds among Freudian psychoanalysts—suffers as much as many others from the state of being prejudiced in favor of raising to the level of incontestable postulates certain rigid, quasi-philosophic artefacts of the speculative thinking of Freud himself, or of some of his pupils who feel that if they accept the clinical discoveries which Freud really made they are obliged to accept Freud's pseudo-philosophy, which Freud himself merely sketched without making it an integral part of his clinical psychological system.

Justice and need for scientific accuracy demand that we recognize that some of the violent opponents of psychoanalysis in psychological medicine and religious circles are hardly free from that *parti pris* with which psychoanalysts treat religion. The majority of the opponents of Freud tried to refute him by means of the same inconclusive devices of doubtful logic as those with which the proponents of Freud tried to "refute" religious faith; namely: they would take Freud's rather shaky philosophical speculations and proceed to disprove their validity—which is not difficult. And since a philosophical refutation of Freud's philosophy proves such an easy task, it is then assumed that the whole mass of Freudian clinical findings and his purely psychological working hypotheses are equally false, are not worthy of consideration, and even require wholesale condemnation.

In this controversy, as in all others, there are of course many middle-of-the-roaders of various types. There are those who remind one of the German professor who started his course in the history of religion aware that there might be among his students representatives of many orientations. He did not want to displease the truly faithful nor did he want to offend the agnostics; therefore, he started his first lecture by saying: "Gentlemen, some people believe in God, others do not; in this course we shall adopt an intermediate position."

For reasons which are too obvious I shall disregard the just-mentioned type of the middle-of-the-roader. He cannot contribute anything to our subject. But there are other types which may not pass without notice. There are those who try to reconcile the controversial issues by assuming the existence of a dichotomized person. The psychological or biopsychological sides of man are then considered the domain of the scientific medical psychologist, and the religious needs are left to the spiritual religious guide. This formula in itself contains nothing wrong, except that what it does in actuality is this: having left the religious needs to the special department of religion (everything is specialized nowadays), the psychologist or psychoanalyst feels free to consider man as a whole not only as if there were no God or soul or religious morality, but independently of the existence of God, the soul and religious morality. The result of this sharp dichotomy is anything but natural or salutary. One may imagine a psychoanalyst, neutral as far as religious belief but respectful of the faith of his patients, saying: "I think your belief in God is a neurosis, but if you insist on persevering in your neurotic faith you may consult your priest, while I try to analyse for you this illusion." This paradox is not based on bad faith, as some assume, or on the stupidity of all concerned. It is rather the result of the formalistic specialism which pervades our age. It is a result of emotional prejudices which we wish to keep and preserve at all costs, for it is obvious that neither true psychological science, nor religion, nor the patient who happens to be sandwiched in between, can benefit from this type of formalistic, logical, yet so unrealistic compromise between science and religion. As to a true hypothesis between the two, this seems quite impossible as long as the personality of the individual is cut in two by means of a purely formalistic dichotomy.

As a result of these difficulties, psychoanalysis and religion have stood far apart from the very outset. If in the course of recent years we do see some signs of *rapprochement* between the two, this *rapprochement* is due not to verbal compromises but (1) to the fact that moral consciousness has become a matter of serious attention among certain psychoanalysts in Switzerland and France; and (2) to the religious thinkers who began to consider the findings of Freud independently of Freud's atheistic excursions. In other words, Freud's superego began to be a subject of serious scrutiny, and it was found not to be identical with conscience. And it also became clear to some thinkers that Freud's philosophical excursions could be set aside from his psychoanalytical, clinical data, to the same extent as Boyle's and Newton's chemistry and physics could be considered quite independently of their theological excursions.

Yet the task of synthesis remains very difficult. For, after all, when two people actively don't know one another for fifty years, and actively oppose one another during half a century, they will inevitably find it very difficult indeed to understand one another. It is not a question of mere semantics; it is a question of emotional connotations. When a Freudian says "Eros" it not only connotes (for some) sex impure and simple, but it arouses all the emotional intensity

Love in Freudian Psychoanalysis

of opposition with which the disciplined religious and ascetic mind is accustomed to view unrestricted sensuality of any kind. As soon as an ascetic, dedicated person says the word "love" to a psychoanalyst who is suspicious of religion, the psychoanalyst at once sees a neurotic, inhibited sort of abstract benevolence devoid of that human quality of loving which the psychoanalyst supposedly considers as something that only he understands, that he would be able to approve only under the condition that it be fundamentally sexual, essentially carnal.

It is because of this emotional and methodological confusion that I seem to approach the whole problem anew, even if to do so I have to deal with some quite elementary aspects of the problem.

First of all, we shall have to agree that we have still a great deal to learn about the general terms which seem to have acquired the right of citizenship in our vocabulary—in our psychological jargon, I am tempted to say.

Take as an example the term "sublimation." I find that both psychoanalysts and non-analysts use this term as if it meant a *conscious* substitution of one forbidden activity by another socially acceptable one. This is not the real meaning of sublimation. Sublimation is an *unconscious* shift from an activity which is morally or conventionally unacceptable to an activity which is acceptable. Acceptable—to whom? Acceptable not only to society or the prevailing code of morals, but emotionally acceptable to the individual himself. Sublimation, therefore, is a result of the developmental, psychological, cultural process; it is not something that occurs suddenly; it is something that "grows on you," very gradually. Therefore, it is nonsensical to ask a person why he does not "sublimate" his aggression, or to admonish him to play a hard game of tennis instead of neurotically quarreling with people. Yet more often than not one finds people who overlook the unconscious, integrative nature of sublimation and who seem to believe that it can be achieved by conscious manipulations of one's own activities. It is extremely important, from the educational and moral point of view, to understand both the unconscious dynamics and the psychogenesis of given sublimations. Without such an understanding, it is difficult to understand our patients, and it is impossible to effect in them a lasting change in such symptoms as sexual perversions, trends toward delinquency, and criminality in general. As you see, the symptoms just enumerated are of particular importance to the spiritual adviser, and they have a special bearing on problems of moral behavior and religious faith.

The illustrative symptoms which I have just cited belong to a special class. They are symptoms of behavior and not symptoms of a purely subjective nature like a neurotic headache, or hysterical paralysis, or psychogenic gastrointestinal disturbances. These symptoms, purely subjectively experienced, are autoplastic—which means that the unconscious neurotic conflict ultimately finds autoplastic expression which in turn may cover a wide range of conditions: from depressive or anxiety states to neurotic vomiting. These symptoms are *symptoms,* that is to say, they are expressions of an illness; therefore they are not subject to moral or religious condemnation; a headache is not a sin, and a depression is not a sacrilege.

It is the alloplastic symptom—which means a symptom manifesting itself in human actions—that preoccupies the attention of the one to whom moral issues are not dead issues, and it is in the field of these alloplastic reactions of unconscious origin that most of the misunderstandings and quarrels about psychoanalysis take place. It is here in the domain of seemingly voluntary, or at any rate seemingly non-impulsive, behavior that clarity is lacking and ill-feelings run high. The moral philosopher has a great deal to say about unbridled sensuality and laxity of will, while the doctrinaire psychoanalyst insists on his neutrality and seems to assume a permissive attitude toward all sorts of behavior from regular adultery to other forms of sensuality or various forms of anti- or nonsocial behavior.

As was pointed out by André Snoeck, S.J., in his judicious and serene "Moral Reflections on Psychiatric Abreaction,"[1] Christian morality takes a serious view of certain forms of abreaction. Yet, in order to evaluate adequately the phenomenon and the dynamics of abreaction, it is necessary to have a clear conception of what the psychoanalyst understands by this term, what kind of phenomenon he denotes by it. Unfortunately, the prevailing psychoanalytic terminology is not always precise, and both the student within and without (*en dehors*) psychoanalysis are frequently exposed to considerable misapprehensions. It is not surprising, therefore, that even such an accurate student as Father André Snoeck uses the term "abreaction" more in the purely etymological sense than in its strict psychoanalytic meaning. Abreaction, derived from the German *abreagieren,* denotes a spontaneous, even impulsive, purely emotional reaction; it is mostly an autoplastic discharge of affect (tears, anger); it seldom if ever involves *agieren,* i.e. actually behaving, doing something. It is true that in psychoanalytic therapy we meet with both phenomena, but one must bear in mind that abreaction must frequently, if not always, mean a spontaneous discharge of affect without its true ideational content's being known in advance either to the patient or to the psychoanalyst, whereas acting out (*agieren, agir*) presents a rather infrequent reaction.

At any rate, even the references to the subdued light in the analyst's office are misconceptions. True psychoanalysis does not resort to stage management; it is carried out in broad daylight, both in the psychological and spiritual sense. This is the reason why the analyst's passivity is not the passivity of

[1] *Theological Studies,* June, 1952, xiii, no. 2.

an impassive, indifferent onlooker; he watches the patient carefully and does interfere, as Father Snoeck suggests that he should, with those aspects of the patient's *agieren* which are apt to do him, or society, harm. This interference with the patient's activities is not limited merely to preventing the patient from committing suicide or murder. From the very outset of analysis, the patient is admonished not to change his career or civil status (marriage or divorce) while under treatment. The process of psychoanalysis is not a series of lessons in self-indulgence; in this connection one should never forget Freud's own dictum that the whole course of psychoanalytic treatment must be carried out in an atmosphere of abnegation (*Versagung*). Next to this admonition that abnegation is the actual climate of psychoanalytic treatment, Freud's demand of tolerance and of an object-libidinous attitude toward the patient is the most important. By object-libidinous attitude, Freud means an attitude devoid of severe condemnatory judgment of the patient, as well as of that purely personal prejudice or bias which is commonly called love, or rather being in love—which is to Freud but an overestimation of one's object of sexual interest. In other words, Freud demands a rather high quality of love for the patient; it is something akin to paternal or maternal protectiveness, tolerance and reserve, which is combined with forgiveness and sympathy. It is a form of charity, the nature and role of which in psychoanalysis still remains obscured by contentious argumentativeness and suspiciousness.

While Freud did view the sexual instinct as the biological basis of man's emotional psychology, he never considered the gratification of the sexual instinct in its gross sensual sense as the ideal of man's life. "It is certainly true," says Freud, "in a general way that the importance of an instinctual desire is mentally increased by the frustration of it . . . But is it also true, conversely, that the mental value of an instinct invariably sinks with the gratification of it?" And Freud goes on: "However strange it may sound, I think the possibility must be considered that something in the nature of the sexual instinct itself is unfavourable to the achievement of absolute gratification."[2] While Freud insists that a too strict and too inhibitory attitude toward the sexual instinct is undesirable, he insists on this point primarily because this too strict and inhibitory attitude toward the sexual drives only serves to enhance the subjective value of these drives. As a matter of fact, love in the wider sense suffers when there are but few barriers in the way of sexual gratification. "In times," says Freud, "during which no obstacles to sexual satisfaction existed, such as, maybe, during the decline of the civilization of antiquity, love became worthless, life became empty, and strong reaction-formations were necessary before the indispensable emotional value of love could be recovered. In this context, it may be stated that the ascetic tendency of Christianity had the effect of raising the psychical value of love in a way that heathen antiquity could never achieve; it developed greatest significance in the lives of ascetic monks, which were almost entirely occupied with struggles against libidinous temptations."[3]

"Love alone," Freud insisted, "acts as the civilizing factor in the sense that it brings a change from egoism to altruism."[4] And further, Freud says: "We are of the opinion, then, that language has carried out an entirely justifiable piece of unification in creating the word 'love' with its numerous uses, and that we cannot do better than take it as the basis of our scientific discussions and expositions as well. By coming to this

[2] Freud, *Coll. Papers* (1912), iv, "Contributions to the Psychology of Love," p. 214.
[3] *Ibid.*, p. 213.
[4] Freud, *Group Psychology and the Analysis of the Ego*, London, the International Psycho-Analytical Press, 1921, p. 38.

decision, psychoanalysis has let loose a storm of indignation, as though it had been guilty of an act of outrageous innovation. Yet psychoanalysis has done nothing original in taking love in this wider sense. In its origin, function and relation to sexual love the 'Eros' of Plato coincides exactly with the love force, the libido of psychoanalysis, and when the Apostle Paul in his famous [sic] Epistle to the Corinthians, prizes love above all else, he certainly understands it in the same 'wider' sense."[5]

It should be noted that recent studies of early patristic literature by H. Graef[6] seem to corroborate to no small extent Freud's claim as to the origin and meaning of the usage of the term "love." It is love in this (what Freud called "wider") sense that he visualized as the highest developmental goal of man's psychological growth, and as the very substance of the professional relationship between the psychoanalyst and the patient. I know that this my statement might not be taken as reflecting the true Freudian position. Those who are inclined to be skeptical about the above statement are so apparently for two reasons. First, they doubt whether such heights of truly Christian tolerance and charity are possible to achieve in psychoanalysis; and second, considering the sexology with which Freudian psychoanalysis is filled, it would appear doubtful to many that Freud actually thought in terms of St. Paul's Caritas.

To respond to the first doubt: It is true of course that clinically, in actual professional relationships, in so far as they are relationships between human beings, there are many pitfalls, many dangers, many errors, and many failures in professional rectitude. However, I have in mind the aspirations, the rules, the demands and the Freudian principles of the relationship between therapist and patient. These are based on what is

[5] *Ibid.*, pp. 38–39.
[6] "Eros et Agapé," *La Vie Spirituelle* (February 15, 1950), Supplement no. 12.

Love in Freudian Psychoanalysis

known as an object-libidinous attitude, a term—like Eros—quite misleading if understood colloquially and etymologically, but actually denoting love in the "wider" sense—in the sense of charitable tolerance and true benevolence.

As to the second doubt: The manifestations which are purely sexual-sensual, erotic in the narrow sense of the word, are of course of paramount importance in the course of psychoanalytic treatment; but the major, the most important factor in Freudian psychoanalytic procedure is not the sexological aspect as such but the direction the sexual instinct takes, the transformations it undergoes, the degree of integration with the total life of the individual as a person and as a member of society. In other words, the trends of the libidinous drives must be more on objects and less on one's own ego. To put it in Freudian language, the more ego-libido the less object-libido. The more egocentric or egotistic the interests, the less altruistic they are. Freud speaks of the ultimate departure from narcissism, and the ultimate gratification of love is displaced on the ego ideal.

Basing his conclusions on strict clinical observations, Freud does not consider truly object-libidinous a person (man or woman) who falls in love many times and gets married and divorced as many times. "Object-libidinous" though such "love" appears, it is more a product of Hollywood than of psychoanalysis. Such pseudo object-libidinous trends are considered by Freud infantile, narcissistic and pathological choices of object.

I have already quoted what Freud had to say about the purely sensual aspects of the sexual instinct, as not being fundamentally able to provide true gratification. We may now recall Freud's libido theory, his working hypothesis as to the transformation of instincts, his hypothesis as to phylo- as well as onto-genetic development of sexuality from its purely biological sensual forms (infantile) toward what Freud himself calls a higher form of expression, which is found in sublimation and libidinization of the higher intellectual functions of man. If we also recall that Freud considered that the healthy path of sexuality and purely sexual love is in the direction of parenthood, of the active healthy wish for children and the psychological capacity for being a parent, and not merely the sexual companionship of a person of the opposite sex; if we also recall Freud's simple and direct answer as to what he considers the ideally normal person (he said that it would be a person whose life consisted of work and love [*arbeiten und lieben*]); if we recall all these things, we will note that whatever period of the development or whatever aspect of Freudian psychoanalysis we wish to look into, we find that Freud's clinical findings (I don't speak here of his philosophical theories) led him invariably to the conclusion that the ultimate, the ideal of human psychological health was, to use purely Freudian terminology, the ever-increasing libidinization of the higher human activities such as parental, filial and friendly love in general, at the expense of the purely sensual-erotic and aggressive-destructive drives. As a matter of fact, this transformation is the goal of psychoanalytic therapy, and the chief measure of this transformation is the degree to which the libido is directed toward objects and integrated in the totality of human functioning among and with other fellow human beings. The libidinization of this functioning, and the libidinization of rational realistic thinking—in these Freud saw the ultimate liberation of man from the slavery in which his own instinctual impulses, his unconscious, nondomesticated drives always hold him unless he achieves the highest degree of object-libidinous relationship to people and the world as a whole.

However, it must not be forgotten that Freud was rather pessimistic about the ultimate liberation of man. In this he remained a more or less consistently dour, skeptical, even pessimistic person. He thus represented a striking paradox in his personality: On the one hand he found himself so close to finding a true psychobiological, empirical foundation for the Christian ideal of what man is and ought to be; and on the other he remained a perseverant, rather pessimistic materialistic determinist in his attitude and methodology. This attitude bears the hallmarks of a certain stubbornness, of a silent, adamant unwillingness to admit that his own clinical findings led him beyond the purely mechanistic, rather shaky philosophizing with which he seemed to want to buttress his wondering about the nature of man, into whom he had gained such extraordinary insight.

As one reads Freud's writings and as one gains clinical experience, the question arises time and again: How did it happen that Freud, who almost independently arrived at the conclusion that love, Caritas in the Pauline sense, is the highest form of human functioning, yet refused to go beyond merely pointing out the psychological mechanisms underlying religious beliefs? How is it that Freud seems to have assumed not only a refractory but an almost combative attitude toward religion?

There have been in the history of social and psychological sciences a great many agnostics and atheists, but few of them have deemed it necessary to make their agnosticism or atheism a part of their scientific thought. To some extent Freud is no exception in an age of ever-growing scientism. And it is not to be denied that Freud's faith in the Logos of the psychoanalysed individual contains an element of modern scientism. Freud was quite consistent in his Platonic attitude toward man. He did not think that man *per se* is good; he was not very optimistic about human nature. Yet such materialistic philosophies as the Marxian doctrine he rejected without hesitation, primarily because Freud was a true humanist, which Marx was not. A certain pessimism overlays the Freudian thought—a depressive haze, an undertone of a life-long gloominess. These depressive undertones are particularly patent in his *Civilization and Its Discontents*, in his *Future of an Illusion*, in his correspondence with Albert Einstein on the problem of war and peace, in his famous warning that psychoanalysts are able only to relieve patients of their symptoms but not make them happy, since unhappiness is the lot of mankind. In his "Analysis Terminable or Unterminable," Freud even reaches the point of seriously questioning the efficacy of psychoanalysis in situations which he himself, and particularly his followers, had considered theretofore promising and encouraging.

In addition to this overcast of melancholy which makes itself felt in Freud's writing, and in his personality as it is reflected in these writings, another characteristic seems to stand out. He seems to shy away from anything that might bring him closer to that side of the nature of man which science is unable to know and understand scientifically. When a scientist wrote him about his feeling of oneness with the world, of the "oceanic feeling," Freud disposed of it almost sharply by saying that he himself never experienced this feeling and never felt the need for it. However, he proceeds to make a tentative suggestion as to the psychological mechanisms which are at play in the formation of the "oceanic feeling." Freud, not unlike so many modern scientists, seems to commit the error of confusing the mechanisms (physiological, or mechanical) with the substance of the phenomenon in which the mechanisms are at play. This, one must say, Freud does not very convincingly but quite persistently—although he does it more by way of formal implication than positive assertion.

Again and again, the puzzling paradox that is Freud appears to raise more questions than it answers.

If one divorces oneself from Freud's philosophic generalizations, one will have to admit that his empirical clinical system is in many respects at variance with what he chose to establish as a socio-ethical philosophical super-structure of psychoanalysis. If one bears in mind that love in the Freudian sense is not cohabitation; superego, despite some of the Freudian equations, not conscience; and the psychic apparatus not the soul—one could accept *in toto* Freudian psychoanalysis without agreeing with him on any of his mild attempts to invade the field of morality and religion. More than that; in the light of what has become known very recently about Freud and his early life, I would venture to say that were it not for certain of Freud's own traumatic experiences of childhood, either he might have left the field of values and religion without attempting to invade it, or he might have taken a different attitude toward those problems.

I am fully aware that this assertion may sound too bold to many and rather impertinent to others. I do not intend it to be either, and I make it in full humility, with all the meekness one must have when confronted with a complex scientific problem, and with all the respect due to a genius whose insight into the working of the human mind has surpassed the understanding of generations of psychologists. But his few scientific mannerisms and philosophic errors isolated him from the mainstreams of Christian thought, to which I believe the totality of Freudian psychology is not foreign and with which Freud was in sympathy in more than one point, whether he knew it or not and whether he was willing to admit it or not.

Two conclusions, or at least suppositions, impose themselves on the practicing psychoanalyst who studies Freud carefully but without dogmatic literalness. First of all, Freud's innermost attitude toward religion seems never to have been clear to Freud himself, and therefore was never made clear by Freud to others. He merely used the scalpel of the psychology of the unconscious to dissect our manner of feeling and thinking, regardless of the anxiety this awakens in man as regards his own relation to God and God's relation to him; thus, Vesalius—a good believer and tormented soul—dissecting human cadavers and cutting them into small parts *propriis manibus,* regardless of how taxing and anxiety-producing this type of inquiry must have been to his own faith in or conception of immortality and the ultimate rise from the dead.

The second supposition which suggests itself is this: There was great austerity in Freud's devotion to scientific inquiry, which makes many a man sacrifice broader and deeper perspectives on man to the immediate task of ploughing the limited field of his own specialty. This inevitably has the effect of narrowing the base of observations as well as the breadth of one's horizon. This is probably the major reason why so many physicists would feel that everything can be explained in terms of physics; why so many chemists would explain every life-problem in terms of chemistry; and why of recent years the tendency has become quite pronounced to explain every aspect of personal and social and religious life in terms of psychological mechanisms. These psychological mechanisms are of immense importance for the understanding of the dynamic forces involved in unconscious human behavior. They offer us a heretofore undreamed-of opportunity for a deeper understanding of the *inner phenomenology* of man's psychology. But the ultimate, the essential, the eternal enigma and revelation that is man cannot be understood by means of the finest methods of analytical chemistry, nor by the finest methods of analytical psychology. Yet it is often the way of the scientific mind to try to understand man by these methods, particularly when that mind is not fertilized by the inner faith and love which makes science not only human but humanistic.

As far as Freud is concerned, his humanism, his aspiration toward, I almost said faith in, the ultimate ideal of St. Paul's

Caritas, would make one suppose that the error of equating an assembly of psychological mechanisms with the essence of the phenomenon studied (like equating religion with an illusion) is not really the result of the Freudian system of investigation and of the body of empirical data which his method brought to light, but rather of some personal equation to be found in Freud's life and personal psychology.

For a number of years many thought that it would be profitable to gain some insight into Freud's own personal psychology. For obvious reasons it would have been impossible, and perhaps even unseemly, to attempt a "psychoanalysis" of Freud himself in his lifetime. A few biographical attempts to assess Freud from the standpoint of his own psychological idiosyncracies turned out to be more or less failures: to begin with, not enough supporting data were available; moreover, the writers were not able to free themselves of the trend to be contentious. The result was either a sentimental over-admiration, or a quasi-formalistic attack on the personality of Freud.

Since Freud's death, some of his followers have felt a little freer to look into some of the recesses of Freudian thought and not overlook the leads into some of the unconscious reactions of Freud himself. Then, too, new material on Freud's life and work has come to light, such as Freud's correspondence with Fliess, to whom Freud owed so much of his scientific inspiration. What became available and was published was only a number of letters from Freud to Fliess; the latter's letters to Freud were not found.

As a result, a number of established psychoanalysts and followers of Freud do not hesitate today to point out that Freud seems to have suffered from a life-long depression; that he always, even in his days of affluence, feared becoming improvident; that Freud was fascinated by the hero-conquerors of the past—Alexander of Macedonia, Hannibal, Julius Caesar, Oliver Cromwell; and that Freud never really kept a

K

sustained friendship, or rather that a number of his seemingly deeper friendships would sooner or later end in a rift. For instance, as one follows his correspondence with Fliess (from 1887–1902), one can see almost clearly how Freud somehow turned away from if not against Fliess, without apparent good reason, and thus brought to ruin what appeared to be an intimate, warm, deep friendship.

It is therefore not an exaggeration to say that Freud's depressive neurosis was responsible for a number of his difficulties with certain personalities whose statures were sufficiently great first to awaken his admiration. Freud's visualization of the ideal of charity and humanism seems to have been an aspiration which he was unable properly to attain in a number of relationships—although he was an exemplary *pater familias,* a kindly, tolerant husband, and a thoughtful, industrious worker. He was also a man who could stand an enormous amount of physical pain in the manner of an almost devotional, stoic ascetic; he suffered severe physical pain for many years and continued to work almost to the day of his death. In other words, Freud loved more than hated throughout his life; his hates, one might say, became transformed into depressive states, his loves remained humble, simple and unobtrusive.

All these characteristics are not very consistent, and at times they are quite puzzling. Among Freud's followers who have entered upon the study of Freud's personality since he died, and particularly since the correspondence with Fliess was published, the work of Siegfried Bernfeld and his wife Susanne Cassirer-Bernfeld may be briefly mentioned, in the hope that some light will be shed on Freud's inner struggle with himself throughout his creative years. I shall draw primarily on the short Bernfeld essays which were published during the past eight years or so: "Freud's Early Childhood";[7] "Freud and

[7] *Bulletin of the Menninger Clinic,* July 1944.

Archaeology";[8] and "Freud's First Year in Practice."[9] It goes without saying that in trying to gain some insight, or a little light, into Freud's problem, we shall employ Freud's own method of observation and research.

Let us first observe a certain *Fehlleistung* (*action manquée*) of Freud. Freud was a well-trained biologist, and he had great respect for factual truth. He would not knowingly, still less deliberately, misquote or misrepresent. As a rule, he checked on his source of information quite carefully. It is striking to find that in all quotations from others which he made throughout his many years of writing, Freud made *one* misquotation. Quoting from Shakespeare's *Henry IV*, part 1, act 5, Freud cites: "Thou owest Nature a death." The actual text reads "Thou owest God a death." Evidently Freud not only repressed the word "God," but he repressed it so well that it did not occur to him that he might be inaccurate, and he did not take the pains of verifying the quotation. Such repressions, as Freud taught us, are a result of unconscious emotional conflicts, of an inability to face consciously the affective content of the repressed. Here Freud, apparently as a result of a complicated anxiety and of other emotions, felt the need to substitute the word "Nature" for "God," even though it was of God that Shakespeare spoke. This is very revealing in so far as it suggests, be it ever so mildly and vaguely, that Freud himself quite unwittingly felt the need of substituting for Him (God) "an impersonal, shadowy, abstract principle." Such a substitution, it will be remembered, he once decried.

I should say that there is no doubt that there was in Freud some deeply-seated emotional tension—if not problem—in connection with this topic. There are some other allusions available in the same direction. In a letter of April 12, 1936 (Freud was eighty at the time) he wrote: "Easter Monday sig-

[8] *American Imago* (1951), no. 2.
[9] *Bulletin of the Menninger Clinic*, March 1952.

nifies to me the fiftieth anniversary of taking up my medical practice"; but Freud made the announcement of the opening of his office in May 1886, and Easter Sunday on that year fell on April 25th. Easter Sunday seems to have had a particular emotional meaning to Freud. In his letters to Fliess between 1896 and 1901, Freud mentions Easter in one connection or another twenty-two times, and when he planned a long-awaited meeting with Fliess, Freud said that such a meeting, if it could be arranged in Rome on Easter Sunday, "would be the greatest happiness" for him. This meeting never took place. The two men drifted away from one another before the plan could be carried out.

Another interesting thing which by itself may not mean much, but is of interest in the general context of Freud's trend, is this: when writing about one of his observations he wishes to say *crucial experiment,* and instead uses the Latin expression *experimentum crucis.*

In her essay "Freud and Archaeology," Susanne Cassirer-Bernfeld says this: "When he [Freud] was three years old his family moved away from their home town, Freiberg in Moravia, and after a year's stay in Leipzig settled in Vienna. This simple geographic change was a catastrophe for Freud, and he spent the next forty years of his life trying to undo it."[10] It is well known how Freud tried and succeeded in undoing this catastrophe. He turned to a meticulous study of the most obscure and self-contradictory trends in his personality; this study was actually a self-analysis, a depressive self-revelation which actually resulted in the conception and completion of his *Interpretation of Dreams* and the foundation of psychoanalysis. In this process of self-revelation he was confronted with many aspects of his personality which he did not particularly enjoy finding—such as his bitterness, his incestuous trends, his vain-glory. Among the neurotic symptoms we find

[10] P. 9.

a phobia for travelling in trains. One wonders whether this had anything to do not only with his oedipus complex which he found in himself, but also with his having emigrated from his native Freiberg at the age of three.

Partly through his letters to Fliess, partly through some of his dreams which he cites in his *Interpretation of Dreams,* Freud raises a little the curtain which hid his early childhood.

The three-year-old Freud was a lonely boy who had already suffered the pangs of self-torment when his little brother, whom he wanted out of the way, actually died. Freud stated that ever since that death of his little brother, when Freud himself was not yet two years old, he had a tendency to "self-reproaches."

Freud was attached at this time to a nurse, a simple Moravian peasant woman who, as Freud stated, treated him as if he were her own child. She is the "prehistoric old woman" of one of Freud's later dreams. In a letter to Fliess of October 1897, Freud relates that this plain woman, apparently a devout Catholic, told him about God and hell. It was she who consoled him that his little brother who died would live again. Freud tells us that this woman carried him into all the five Catholic churches of Freiberg, and it is also recalled that the little Freud would come home with her on a Sunday and would speak of God and hell.

It was from this woman that Freud was forcibly separated when he was three years old. It was a sort of double separation: First his adult half-brother caused her to be arrested by the police for some kind of theft. Freud had small understanding, if any, of what theft was, but his half-brother announced cheerfully and colloquially that the old nurse had been "put away in a box"—which meant put in jail. Freud tried to find her in a cupboard. Susanne Bernfeld quite neatly puts together Freud's disbelief that his old nurse was gone, for the dead to him were not really dead, and was not Easter Sunday the greatest day of testimony to the resurrection from the dead?

But this disappearance of the nurse from the house in Freiberg was not all. The whole family soon left Freiberg, never to see it again, as Freud never saw his old nurse again.

Thus, the first true love of Freud, which he experienced in the arms of a warm-hearted, loving nurse, was a love which was somehow vaguely but intimately interwoven with the sense of God and five churches and consolation and promise of life eternal. And this first true love ended as if by an act of fate, and Freud was destined to live the rest of his life in Vienna, more conscious of being a little Jewish boy than of the feeling of belonging when his Moravian nurse carried him "into all the five churches of Freiberg."

I would say that Freud devoted not only forty years, but a life-time, to trying to undo the catastrophe that befell him in his childhood. That catastrophe, like all events of this sort, could not actually ever be undone—but it is the trying, the perseverance to undo such catastrophes that absorbs the energies of man. This absorption may take the form of a sterile autoplastic neurosis, of a restless and not less sterile alloplastic neurosis, or—on very rare occasions—it may take the form of creative work. This last form was the choice made by Freud—an unconscious choice in the beginning of course, and later on a deliberate and perseverant one.

The choice led him to a fascinating truth, a truth both in psychological science and religion, namely this: The highest form of love is the highest form of living. The feeling of being in love, in so far as it springs from purely sexual sources, is but "an overestimation of the sexual object"; true love is as complete a departure from narcissism as is given to any person, and it is also a displacement of the love-affect onto the ego-ideal. The highest form of gratification is derived from the attainment of this ideal.

It seems that Freud was able to touch the depth of this eternal truth, despite the handicap which his childhood experiences presented at the hands of his family and fate, and despite the fact that in order to retain his hold on this truth about man he felt that within himself he had to relegate to the realm of illusions the "prehistoric woman" and the five churches of the little town of Freiberg in Moravia. Was it not all a true illusion as far as Freud was concerned? A promise unfilled, and a love that disappeared without even an affectionate gesture of farewell?

It is highly probable and quite plausible that Freud's scientific findings about the psychology of man are the product of his great aspiration to attain a lofty ego-ideal, while his attempts to produce what amounts to a really pessimistic sociology, and his thrusts at religious faith, may then appear but a tribute paid to—or penalties paid for—a tragic and bewildering childhood experience. As such they are not products of scientific endeavor but mere speculations, no matter how brilliant and deep, of a mind which lived under the spell of the scientism of the last one hundred years.

Some Denials and Assertions of Religious Faith

DISCUSSING certain aspects of spiritual direction, Thomas Merton in his *Ascent to Truth* cites St. Teresa of Avila and says:

> It is interesting to see what she gives as an example of stupid direction. A married woman is attracted to a life of prayer. Her confessor, instead of telling her how to carry out her household duties in a spirit of prayer, tells her to drop her work and to pray when she ought to be doing the dishes. Her life of prayer at once becomes an obstacle to her happiness as a wife, and her marriage, at the same time, erects a barrier between herself and God.[1]

The foregoing makes it obvious that the relation between pastoral psychology—or what is sometimes called today marriage counseling—and the so-called realities of life presented a real problem even in the middle of the sixteenth century. It still is a formidable problem. Of course things have changed somewhat in the last four hundred years, but mainly

---

First published in 1955. Reprinted from *Faith, Reason and Modern Psychiatry*, edited by Francis J. Braceland, M.D. Reprinted by permission of the publishers; copyright © 1955 by P. J. Kenedy & Sons.

[1] Thomas Merton, *The Ascent to Truth*, New York, 1951, p. 80.

Some Denials and Assertions of Religious Faith

in so far as our superficial frame of reference is concerned. They have changed very little with regard to the formidable struggle between man's spiritual aspirations and his desire to free himself from these very aspirations and become the one and only master of the universe and his own fate. There seems to be a real psychological connection by contrast, between the scriptural deluge and our experiments with A and H bombs. The deluge was ordained from on high, and man submitted to this higher order; the H bomb is the creation of the scientific and technological man, and he is ready to destroy the world to assert his mastery over it. Noah was told how to save animal and human life so that they might flourish after the deluge. The creator of the A and H bomb, or rather its potential user, must visualize universal devastation, but he goes on "improving" the destructive power of the instrument of his alleged mastery over the natural world.

In other words, the fundamental contradiction between charity and animosity, between moral values and "purely" technological progress, between free obedience to the will of God and to reason and constant aspiration to become Man-God despite reason, between religious faith and egocentric science, between principles and practical formalism—this struggle continues as fresh and as violent and as painful today as it was centuries ago.

Traditionally it is called the struggle between theology and science (or vice versa); it is called more often than not the struggle between religion and modern psychology. But it is really none of these things. In actuality it is the old struggle between man's respecting the will of God and man's seeking to abolish it in favor of the exclusive supremacy of a given scientific discovery.

It would be idle to try to review the course of the struggle between the two extremes of religious and scientific exclusiveness. Such reviews have been made before, and always with the same results: the fanatic, whether religious or scientific, remained a fanatic, eloquent or not, but always unconvinced by his opponent and always satisfied with his own arguments.

It is one of the most unfortunate aspects of our human activity, this displacement of our own human egocentricity onto the finest expressions of the human spirit: faith, and the search for the knowledge of nature. Very few indeed are endowed with that humility which makes both their religious and their scientific aspirations but one flood of inspired efforts toward the achievement of detachment and serene contemplation of life. Very few indeed can speak the way George Sarton speaks, a man who has devoted his life to the study of the history of science.

Every scientist (as every artist or saint) [says Sarton] who is sufficiently absorbed in his task reaches sooner or later that stage of ecstasy (unfortunately impermanent), when the thought of self has vanished, and he can think of naught else but the work at hand, his own vision of beauty or truth, the ideal world which he is creating. In comparison with such heavenly ecstasy, all other rewards—such as money and honors—become strangely futile and incongruous. Looking at it from that point of view, science is the best school of objectivity and disinterestedness, and the devoted men working in laboratories are very close indeed (though they hardly realize it themselves) to the monks and nuns mortifying their flesh in the cloisters. One can truly speak of the sanctity of science, as well as of its humanity, but it is better not to speak too much of it, for it is a subject far too confidential and too precious for expression. Also it is better not to encourage the constitution of a new class of hypocrites. If there be sanctity it will flourish best in secrecy; nobody should ever know of it, except perhaps much later.[2]

[2] "Science and Morality," in *Moral Principles of Action*, ed. Ruth Nanda Anshen, New York, 1952, p. 451.

Some Denials and Assertions of Religious Faith

This admonition of Sarton's reflects a rare attitude. Here the quest for scientific knowledge, and the labor and ardor involved in this quest, seem to be blended into a search for unity with the totality of life, a search which in a singular manner brings about or springs from humility and dedication. This is a far cry from the self-serving egocentric and exclusivistic theologian who despises science, and from the exclusivistic, intellectualistic, egocentric scientist who has only contempt for theology and hopes to rule the world by means of a few spectacular gadgets. Sarton's words demonstrate better than any argument that science and theology (the science of the knowledge of God) have a great deal in common, and that neither has a right to seek exclusive dominion over man's knowledge, since fundamentally they are one and spring from one source and mystery.

It is not necessary here to labor this point any further. Suffice it to recall that even such methodical thinkers as David Hume, and from Hume to Whitehead many other philosophers, pointed out the *a priori* nature of the major scientific premises, and that science at its source is essentially *irrational*. This word is not mine. Whitehead himself uses it in agreement with the many philosophers who were occupied with the problem of scientific knowledge. He couples this term with the term "instincts," from which he sees stem both science and religion, each in its own way.

We may recall in this connection Jacques Maritain's view on the primary role of intuition in our approaches to God, and it will really not be difficult to see that the conflict between science and religion is not a true one but an artifice, a dangerous and cruel artifice to be sure, a sort of perennial artefact of human existence. The conflict is not between science and religion as it appears to be but between what man wants to do with science, and what he wants to do with religion. Make either of them purely utilitarian, power-seeking, an instrument for man's self-assertion and actions only in his own behalf, and the conflict becomes not only inevitable but intolerant and intolerable—for the dedication, the sacrificial humility, the charity of either or both are set aside in favor of what is mistakenly called the self-expression of the individual.

What I have said thus far is rather commonplace, even trite. Yet as one begins to contemplate the issues involved and the problems that arise from the interplay of science and religion, one is almost forced to reiterate the trite, self-evident assertion that science and religion are one, that true knowledge of man and God are one. Yet it is an almost staggering fact that man seems to be as afraid of this oneness as he yearns to achieve it, and therefore he becomes divisive within himself and with his fellow men. In this divisiveness, however, he struggles less within himself than he fights with his fellow men. This perennial combat, as we look at it through the quieting mist of centuries, may even sometimes appear amusing. An example, one of many which to a contemporary appear a bit entertaining rather than serious: Rambert de' Primadizzi of Bologna was a Dominican Father, a disciple of St. Thomas Aquinas (whom he knew personally); he was one of the first Thomists; he wrote the *Apologeticum veritatis contra corruptorium*. This word *corruptorium* was an obvious expression of contempt for the opposition raised against the philosophy of St. Thomas. One of the earliest representatives of this opposition was William de la Mare. This English Franciscan wrote a critique of St. Thomas and he gently called it *Correctorium;* but that which was for a gentle Franciscan a *correctorium* was for a passionate Dominican a *corruptorium*.

Apparently the struggle for the attainment of truth, as long as it is a human struggle, is bound to be accompanied by all the weaknesses that are of man. It is bound at times to acquire the aspect of a struggle for recognition of one's being the exclusive possessor of the truth, rather than be what it should ideally be, a common effort for the attainment of truth—for truth is always something that belongs to all as soon as it is attained by one. Thus we could pass centuries in review and always find a *correctorium* called a *corruptorium*, a St. Teresa of Avila discovering how stupid spiritual directors might guide a believer away from God through what appear to be means of achieving communion with God. Such paradoxes are not only frequent but appear to be the rule in our ways of searching for the infinite and the laws of nature.

If I have cited an example or two of such paradoxes as I have found in the field of religious thought or activity, we must not assume that these paradoxes are confined only to religious thinking and struggling. What could be more paradoxical than the intellectual activity of a man like Fechner? His name is known to every physicist and psychologist; he hoped to establish a psychology on an experimental, scientific, materialistic basis, and he remains known to us almost exclusively as such. Few ever think of Fechner as of a religious person who was preoccupied throughout the greater part of his adult and scientific life with problems of religion and religious knowledge.[3]

Paradoxical as it may seem, then, I am always drawn to the conclusion that the agelong conflict between science and religion is not based on anything inherent in science or in religion, but rather in the scientists and representatives of religion who claim exclusive knowledge of something of which they do not know much and are lost between the *correctorium* and *corruptorium,* so to speak. Yet despite, or perhaps because

[3] Gustav Theodor Fechner (1801–87), *Religion of a Scientist,* trans. Walter Lourie, New York, 1946.

of, these lessons of history, which at times were tragic and had to be paid for with hundreds of thousands of human lives, the struggle between psychology or psychiatry, for instance, on the one hand, and religious faith on the other appears to have become in the course of the last few years both sharpened and more nonsensical at the same time.

An enormous literature has accumulated on the subject, a literature produced by psychiatrists as well as theologians. I have in mind the earnest literature and not the glib, presumptuous productions which demand a pan-religionist orientation or assume a pan-psychological attitude. Such intellectually "imperialistic" attitudes really lead nowhere. Numerous examples of such attitudes are always available. We all know the self-assertive assumption that religious faith is an infantile reaction, that totalitarianism is neurotic, etc. We may cite in this connection the very extreme example of Kenji Otsuki, editor of the *Tokyo Journal of Psychoanalysis,* who wrote some remarks under the title "Christianity and Communism as Brothers." Condemning both in the same breath, he finally concluded:

As for myself, however, I believe that the world peace may not be finally realized, till the Westerners will outgrow Christianity, and Easterners the Buddhism by means of psychoanalysis.[4]

Since psychoanalysis has influenced contemporary psychology and psychiatry to an enormous extent, it might not be at all unreasonable to conceive of a psychoanalytic imperialism that seems to claim omniscience and omnipotent sagacity. We know, of course, that Freud made no such claims. We also know that Freud put at the center of his psychological system the individual's capacity to love. Freud stressed love of one's neighbor more than mere hedonistic sexual love. Yet because

[4] Vol. XII, No. 3, March, 1954.

Some Denials and Assertions of Religious Faith

of the constant veering between the *correctorium* and the *corruptorium* to which we seem to be addicted, Freud stands out in the minds of men as being only a pansexualist, only an atheist, just as Fechner stands out in our minds as only a physicist.

If we divest ourselves of this addiction to "onlyness," we might look upon present-day psychopathology with less anxiety and therefore, with eyes less jaundiced, might recognize with Allport that there are infantile atheists and mature believers, and that the quasi-philosophical and pseudo-theological excursions of psychoanalysts—from Freud to many of his disciples—are but artefacts on a solid body of empirical knowledge which cannot be neglected and which threatens religion as little as does the Copernican system. The fact that the discoverers of this solid body of empirical facts want to enter the field of theology and cut it up with the positivistic knives of psychophysical parallelism should in no way disturb the true student of human psychology. The fact that they rush into a field they do not know, with their banners of the *corruptorium* raised high, should not deter us from simple and dispassionate examination of what there is of scientific value in the given body of knowledge. An arrogant scientist may remain an arrogant person, but the science he represents is not his own property and it is never arrogant.

Considered from this point of view, the body of knowledge about the psychological nature of man which psychoanalysis has accumulated is valuable knowledge, but it has nothing to do with religious faith or atheism, nothing to do with problems of morality. For it is a body of knowledge which if true would correspond to and could be utilized by religious faith and moral teachings and, if false, would be of no interest to anybody, would wither away gradually from the tree of knowledge and disappear. One must therefore consider it rather regrettable that various psychological schools, and particularly certain so-called schools of psychoanalysis, choose to assert that psychoanalysis *proves* or *disproves* the existence of God, or enables us to know God better. Nothing could be further from the truth. Such attempts as C. G. Jung makes to engage the interest and sympathy of religious people by his references to God are bound to confuse more than to enlighten. I say this not out of partisanship but rather as a result of such experiences as one goes through when reading Jung's own Terry Lectures (Yale University), or especially when studying Victor White, O.P., in his *God and the Unconscious*,[5] to which Jung himself wrote a foreword.

Perhaps the simplest way of stating my misgivings on this point would be to recall the critique made by Augustin Léonard, O.P., a convinced Thomist and a man deeply and extensively versed in philosophy and contemporary psychology. When White seems to agree with Jung that the "suprarational" manifests itself to us through the "infrarational," and to hold that Jung's "undifferentiated libido" corresponds to Aquinas' *naturale desiderium*, Léonard observes that this way of thinking is rather obscure, and reminiscent of psychophysical associationism. More than that, with considerable spiritual and intellectual authority Père Léonard states, in a spirit of terse tolerance, that the Divine Quaternity postulated by Jung is a result of confused deductions, and that, consequently,

> those who christen the psychology of Jung a *mystic psychology* are certainly not entirely wrong. In comparison, and because his method is more strict, Freud is less dangerous (from the religious point of view). That which Jung calls religion, that which he honestly believes to be religion, is not religion at all; *even from*

[5] London, 1952.

the empirical point of view, it appears to be only a very incidental manifestation.[6]

It may be added here that since World War II there has grown up an enormous literature on religious psychology and on the relation between psychology and religion. The number of worthy and scholarly works on this general subject has reached by now several hundred if not over a thousand, and a great number of these books are not written by theologians or philosophers but by scientific psychologists and psychiatrists. To do nothing but to enumerate these contributions would take many pages; to make even brief references to them would certainly take more than two hundred pages. Suffice it therefore to say that I know of no better review and synthesis of the problems involved in the relations between religion and psychology than the various articles of Père Léonard, who, besides reviewing the whole literature from William James and McDougall to Scheler and Jaspers and the more poignant existentialist literature bearing on the subject, has contributed a thoughtful and succinct analysis of what he has read without the slightest tendency to fall into dogmatism or formalism. Especially as regards Freudian psychoanalysis, to the writings of Léonard one should add the writings of Père Albert Plé ,O.P., editor of *La Vie Spirituelle* and author of many searching studies, among them "Saint Thomas Aquinas and the Psychology of Freud," which may be read in English translation in *Dominican Studies,* Vol. V (1952).

The consensus of opinion of those to whom religion is not a neurosis to be cured, and psychology not a devilish concatenation to run away from, tends to the conclusion that while psychology can throw a great deal of *psychological* light on religious experiences, and religious faith may enrich one's

[6] "Incertitudes et perspectives en psychologie réligieuse," Supplément 25, *La Vie Spirituelle,* 1953, pp. 220–21.

psychological functioning, *psychology as a scientific discipline can shed no light whatsoever on the relations between man and God.* To put it again in the words of Léonard:

> The religious act is an intentional act and is related to an object which is situated beyond the reach of our [practical] experience. Consequently, an empirical study of the relationship between man and God can never reach the second member of this relationship. What we are apt to observe is only the reaction of a person, without our knowing the nature of the Stimulus that originated this reaction.[7]

The above conclusion seems to be so simple, so true and so unassailable, yet the conflict between religion and psychology does seem to continue, and does seem to serve to obscure old issues and befog new ones. The question of why this should be so remains actually unanswered. Perhaps some day, someone sufficiently inspired and dedicated will be able to enlighten us on the psychology of this conflict.

Some contemporary thinkers seem to sense the answer. They seem even to touch the root of the problem, but unfortunately the problem stands. Etienne Gilson is one of the few perspicacious thinkers who put his finger on the very basis of the issue when he said that scientists, when they begin their queries into the depths of their fields, seem to ask metaphysical questions and yet expect nonmetaphysical answers to their questions. This is an attitude as untenable as it is revealing: untenable, because whoever enters metaphysics should not object to metaphysical thinking in that field; revealing, because the greatest majority of scientists sooner or later come to the borderline of that which is scientifically unknowable, and most of them refuse to acknowledge their position and begin to treat the unknowable either with a faith and devotion

[7] *Ibid.,* p. 215.

that transcends science, or with an intellectual contempt that rejects not only the ultimate solution but a solution to the very problem they themselves had posed or come upon.

In other words, there is more than a mere suspicion that the scientist who comes to ask metaphysical questions and turns away from metaphysical answers may be afraid of those answers, and that *his* science—i.e., his scientific exclusiveness—may be a real "defense neurosis." Let me emphasize that while I am ready to stand by the above statement, I do not in any way wish to say that science is a "neurosis of mankind." What I want to say is that even good and fruitful scientific work may at times be utilized by the scientist to avoid that anxiety which man must experience at his first contact with a spiritual value that lies and always will lie beyond his scientific knowledge.

Freud never understood this, of course; he saw in religion only a neurosis. Yet the truly religious know how to differentiate a religious attitude from that sensitive scrupulosity which is a neurosis. Because the scientific psychologist knows or may know a great deal about the psychology of spirituality, it does not mean that he necessarily knows anything about spirituality itself. Conversely, because the religious thinker may attain some really important psychological truths, it does not mean that religion should reject psychiatry as unnecessary.

The religious man who wants to go a hundred miles away from his monastery to conduct a retreat must *go;* he must use a horse, a car, a train, or a plane. He would not attempt to get transported there merely by means of prayer and meditation. Science and technology require a solution in space and time. The spiritual director who tries to solve a scientific and technological question by means purely spiritual takes a position that is both untenable and revealing. It is untenable for obvious reasons; it is revealing because he who would deny nature and science in matters natural and practical is apparently afraid, anxious, lest a confession to the scientific achievements of man be a violation of his religious faith. In other words, his faith seems weaker than he thinks, because he insists on making it appear stronger than is necessary.

It is self-evident, then, that one can call religion a neurosis only with the same right and on the same basis as one could call science a neurosis; in doing so, one never goes beyond captious name-calling—whichever side one happens to be on. It is almost frightening to think that so long ago as the thirteenth century there were already men like St. Albert the Great who, even before his subject Thomas Aquinas, felt objections to the separation of nature (science) and religion—yet this was seven hundred years ago.

The conclusion imposes itself, despite the perseverance of prejudice to the contrary, that Nature and Supernature cannot be opposed to each other since they derive from one and the same source, and that scientists and theologians must share equally the onus for their separation.[8]

Just because they are inseparable partners, the scientist frequently touches on many issues that are purely moral, and he may not refuse, as Darwin tried to do, to solve moral issues on the basis of the teaching of morality and take refuge in some sort of utilitarian ethics which is both nonscientific and nonmoral. On the other hand, psychology and psychopathology have not yet been fully delineated as truly separate disciplines, and therefore both the experimental laboratory and speculative theology are apt to claim these branches as their own. Thus psychology, especially psychopathology, remains suspended between scientific empiricism and purely religious thinking. As a matter of fact, the delineation of psychopathology and of psychology as an independent branch of human knowledge became possible only less than three decades ago, when Freud introduced the concept of the psychic apparatus.

[8] See Charles E. Raven, *Science and Religion*, Cambridge, 1953.

This semi-empirical finding made it possible definitely to separate the concept of the psychic apparatus from the soul. It also made possible a host of psychological investigations which theretofore had been impossible either because the muscle-nerve preparations of the frog prohibited us from visualizing the psychic apparatus, or because traditional theological thinking would seem to refuse consideration of a psychic apparatus, since the latter was outside the tradition of faculty psychology or was imagined to contradict the very existence of the soul.

At any rate, we are at present only beginning to familiarize ourselves with the concept of the psychic apparatus, and to find that it stands in no way in contradiction to the theological conception of the soul. This explains why scientific psychologists can indulge in flights away from metaphysics into some sort of utilitarian psychology, and why certain theologians are yet able to speak profound scientific psychological truth in terms of moral theology. An excellent example of this latter can be found in an article by Thomas Gilby, O.P.:

. . . in the following pages will emerge the spectres of the god-like man, the purely spiritual man, and the perfect citizen man, to haunt us with what we can never be. When regrets turn to anxiety, there is illness; when they turn to humility, there is health.[9]

It would be really impossible to contest this statement. The strictest and "purest" psychologist would have to admit that the nonpsychological phraseology of the above statement expresses a scientifically sound psychological truth.

Such direct correspondence of theological with clinical psychological insight is, however, rare in the history of theology,

[9] "The Origins of Guilt," *Proceedings of the International Conference on Medical Psychotherapy*, Vol. III, *Proceedings of the International Congress on Mental Health*, London, 1948, London–New York, 1948, p. 13.

and still rarer in the history of psychology. Why it should be so is not at all difficult to see. Theology has always considered itself as the discipline based on religious faith. Its postulates have always been recognized as postulates of faith. Psychology, on the other hand, for reasons too complex and too difficult to restate here, has always claimed a certain independence from faith. It had to become dehumanized and mechanistic in order to assert its scientific freedom from that irrational element which is found, nevertheless, at the root of each science, and which such men as David Hume freely recognized.

Psychology, in order to become humanized again, seemed to be forced by the very nature of its subject matter into channels that were not purely empirical, purely utilitarian. Thus, even the perseverant atheist that Freud claimed to be had to introduce the concept of Eros, which he himself stated was not so much Plato's Eros as St. Paul's Caritas. More than that: In order to deepen this process of the humanization of the psychology of man, it became necessary for Freud to demonstrate the "naturalness" of religion—which he chose to call an illusion. To what extent it was an illusion or not, Freud really never demonstrated.

He never was able to demonstrate it satisfactorily, because the two fundamental problems that he had to resolve he never did resolve. First of all, Freud never was free from a potent gravitation toward the very religious attitude he was at so much pains to deny *urbi et orbi*. He therefore chose the least characteristic and most fluid traits of religion—its ritual aspects—and by way of singular concordism chose to equate the established rituals of religion with the sclerosed repetitiousness of the "ritual" of the compulsion neurotic. He thought that he had thus disposed of religious *faith,* and particularly the Christian faith to which he seemed to gravitate so intensely and which he wished to deny just as intensely. All this was a part of Freud's unconscious conflicts, of which more

Some Denials and Assertions of Religious Faith

evidence has come to light within the last few years, and into which Freud seems to have had rather scant insight.

The second problem that Freud had to solve in this connection, but failed to solve, is that of the relation between reason and faith and fear of death. Faith meant to him the denial of reason and the establishment of the primacy of the irrational. In this respect, one may frankly consider Freud really ignorant despite his enormous erudition and cultural sagacity. This was Freud's blind spot, as it is the blind spot of many scientists; in conformity with the scientific tradition of his age, Freud equated faith with the rejection of reason. One wonders how surprised Freud would have been if he had learned of the place St. Thomas Aquinas assigns to reason, to intelligence (Freud's Logos) in his theology. How much more surprised Freud would have been if he had learned that Thomas Aquinas was opposed to that knowledge of God which was based on authorities only, and if he had learned how much the deep mysticism and contemplative functioning of the mystics such as the Carmelites (according to one of the greatest of them, St. John of the Cross) had to be based on reason, intellect, and rational knowledge.

Thus Freud himself, and the great majority of his followers, fell into the error of what I would call mechanistic concordism, or psychomechanistic parallelism. That is to say: If two emotional or behavioral phenomena are found to be functionally similar as far as their psychological mechanisms are concerned, then those two phenomena are presumed to be psychologically identical. Religion thus became an illusion, the practice of a given religion a compulsion neurosis. Consequently one could assume, as Freud assumed rather tentatively and not without pessimism, and as the Japanese psychoanalyst assumed more boldly: Since neuroses must be cured, let us get together, mobilize our psychoanalytic skills, and cure the world of Christianity and Buddhism and be done with the matter.

While, as we can easily see, there lurks behind this type of thinking a megalomanic sort of patriotism in favor of one's own scientific inventions, this attitude seems to have taken the religious thinkers unawares. Instead of discovering with comparative ease that the antireligious attitude of Freud was a purely personal problem of Freud himself, and that the very unconscious psychological mechanisms that he discovered, far from leading toward the denial of God, at times not only preserve the tenets of religious faith but confirm them in a very unique way—instead of grasping all this and subjecting it to proper scrutiny, many theologians and religious thinkers chose to accept and take on faith Freud's method of investigation, to accept his conclusion that religion *is* an illusion, if——, and then to reject the whole scientific wealth of psychoanalysis because it allegedly contradicts the principles of religious faith.

It seems very strange that the authority of this manner of thinking most frequently invoked is Freud himself. Now, if it is true that Freud's thinking was correct but his conclusions wrong, would it not be more scientific and logical and correct to say: We cannot disagree with the clinical experience of half a century of psychoanalytic workers and reject this total experience only to avoid being led by Freud to his own conclusions in a field of which he knew very little, and which moreover seems to have been the very center of his inner conflicts, conflicts that remained active within him throughout his scientific lifetime and never were resolved—the field of religious faith.

There is a serious methodological and philosophical difficulty in all this. The difficulty does not stem from Freud; it is more or less traditional, and it could be traced to the seventeenth century, which misunderstood some aspects of the

Renaissance and assumed that science, in order to be scientific, must divorce itself entirely from purely deductive thinking and reject any aspect of thought which might suggest attitudes based on deductions. "Pure" science thus established for itself an attitude of being on guard and jealously protecting itself against any suspicion of leaning toward anything that might be characterized as metaphysical.

We might in this respect recall with profit Whitehead's suggestion that the renaissance of sciences was not a revolt against religious attitudes, Catholic or Protestant, but against the extreme formalism and therefore unrealistic rationalism into which medieval thought had begun to degenerate. Whitehead reminds us that the advent of scientific self-assertion took place in the spirit of what was actually a religious faith, since science insisted *in advance,* accepted *in advance,* that there *is* order in nature, that there *are* immutable laws of nature, and that it is the job of science to uncover these laws and to learn all that is possible to learn about them.

The period of *pietas literata* of the sixteenth century and that of Christian humanism would seem to lend considerable support to Whitehead's suggestion. Furthermore, Whitehead made a poignant statement which is very telling when he said:

Induction presupposes *Metaphysics.* In other words, it rests upon an antecedent rationalism. You cannot have a rational justification for your appeal to history till your metaphysics has assured you that there *is* a history to appeal to; and likewise your conjectures as to the future presuppose some basis of knowledge that there *is* a future already subjected to some determinations. The difficulty is to make sense of either of these ideas. But unless you have done so, you make nonsense of induction.[10]

[10] Alfred North Whitehead, "Science and the Modern World," *An Anthology* (New York, 1952), chap. 3: "The Century of a Genius," pp. 402-3.

The obvious is at hand: the extreme emphasis on science and the scientific method, particularly in matters of human psychology, "makes nonsense of induction" and thus leads one's own creative thinking astray. It is on the basis of the above that I have been led to the conviction that the major error committed by psychoanalysis is that it took too literally the correspondence of certain psychological (unconscious) mechanisms in apparently dissimilar psychological states (religious ritual and compulsion neurosis, for instance). Thus it overlooked some of the essential *psychologically* distinguishing features of the phenomena which many psychoanalysts, following Freud literally, chose to equate; they thus made nonsense out of their own valid and correct preliminary inductions. The field of social, and particularly religious, psychology offers innumerable examples of this error. I shall here limit myself to presenting one that I consider most significant and the most damaging so far as the method of what we might call psychomechanistic parallelism is concerned.

The extraordinary insight Freud had into the unconscious workings of the psychic apparatus made it possible for him to gain a psychological understanding of those pathological reactions (and some normal ones) which characterize the ebb and flow of the affective states commonly (albeit not entirely correctly) called manic-depressive reactions. Freud's studies of primitive attitudes toward the totem and various taboos,[11] and his studies of depressions[12] as well as of some aspects of mass psychology,[13] offer us an unusual insight into what has become commonly known as the psychodynamics of depressive states. According to Freud and Abraham, these states develop on the following psychological substratum: the object (father or mother or any other person standing in emotional

[11] *Totem and Taboo*, 1912-13.
[12] "Mourning and Melancholia," 1917, *Collected Papers*, IV.
[13] *Group Psychology and the Analysis of the Ego*, 1921.

Some Denials and Assertions of Religious Faith 159

proximity to the given individual) is both loved and hated. The love part of this particular state of ambivalence may remain unconscious, or may become conscious directly; the hatred part, however, remains repressed and comes to the surface mostly indirectly. The actual presence of the person toward whom the individual is ambivalent is not required for the individual in question to show the consequences, particularly the pathological consequences, of the ambivalence.

What happens is this: The object is unconsciously *incorporated* by the individual in question and there, inside this individual, the object is loved and hated with utmost intensity. The outward expression of the love and hatred of this *incorporated* person proceeds in a singular manner: The individual with the incorporated object within himself does not perceive the object as an object, but as something that is himself. Thus the imaginary individual in question loves the incorporated object as himself, and hates this object as himself. The clinical result of this psychological complexity is inordinate self-love, which is recognized as one of the most flagrant manifestations of narcissism; and the self-hatred expresses itself in self-reproaches and self-accusations that do not appear realistic at all and more often than not represent a reproach, once made or deserved in actual life, by the object which became incorporated and is now treated as the person (the patient) himself—as his own ego, which has been altered by this incorporation.

Should the unconscious hatred go to the point of the patient's unconsciously wishing to kill the incorporated object, the patient may try to kill himself. In other words, the unconscious psychological mechanism of *incorporation* produces the result of unconscious identification with the object; killing oneself then appears to be not so much the result of one's own rational sense of unworthiness and self-depreciation, as the result of the intense unconscious desire, which becomes an irrational need, to kill that object which was incorporated and with which the patient has identified himself (unconsciously). Suicide under these circumstances is only formally suicide; psychologically speaking, it is murder.

Since Stekel pointed out the equation "Suicide is murder," and since Freud and psychoanalysis in general accepted this point of view, it is assumed that the concept is one that was born out of psychoanalysis. This is not true, of course. Only the psychological mechanisms of this singular equation were discovered by psychoanalysis; the Judeo-Christian tradition of morality has always considered suicide a sin because it considered it an act of murder, and the term "suicide" itself is hardly one hundred and fifty years old. It was called "self-homicide," or *"homicide de soi-même,"* till the end of the eighteenth, and even into the nineteenth century. Esquirol still used this term in his writings on the problems of depression and of suicide.[14]

It will have been noted that the essential prerequisite of depressive and eventually suicidal trends is the severe ambivalence (unconscious) toward the incorporated object. Only the binom *love and hatred* would lead toward the act of *unconscious* incorporation. Let us make a note of this aspect of the problem for further reference and turn for a moment to another question.

We seem to accept the psychological act of incorporation without much elucidation. The legitimate question arises: By what means, by which psychological route, *how* is this process of incorporation carried out? It is not a voluntary, single, rational act—of this we are sure. In other words, it is not a result of conscious imitation of a given object; it is not a result of voluntarily subjecting oneself to the process of pathological transformation of one's own ego into a loved

[14] Jean Etienne Dominique Esquirol, *Des Maladies Mentales* (2 vols.; Bruxelles, 1838). See chap. "Du Suicide."

and hated incorporated object which in turn becomes totally absorbed into ones' own ego. Then how *does* this identification through incorporation take place? A very illuminating although still partial answer to this question was given by Freud and by Abraham. Since the whole process is unconscious, the mechanism of the act of incorporation is also unconscious. Freud pointed out the anthropological roots of this incorporation in the prohibition to eat the totem animal of a given person during the life of the person (father), and the totemistic feast and the mourning for the dead person Freud viewed as illustrative of the process of the mechanism of incorporation. In other words, the mechanism is that of the unconscious fantasy of eating, of swallowing the object. Freud demonstrated the pathological and more or less normal working of this mechanism in depressions and in mourning for the dead. Depression does appear to be a pathological form of mourning. At any rate Abraham, a little earlier than Freud, discovered the same mechanism of incorporation through the fantasy of swallowing in depressions. In the patient's dreams, free associations, general clinical demeanor, in the trends of their psychoses, ample evidence was found as to how universal the fantasy (and therefore the mechanism) of oral incorporation is; as a matter of fact, it would seem that this mechanism is *the* psychological means that permits us to attain our unconscious identifications.

Let us go a step further and say this: The unconscious fantasy of swallowing the object is a reflection of the universal human way of becoming something one wishes (consciously or unconsciously) to become; it is a form of our human way of doing things (consciously or unconsciously); it is our constitutional, *natural* manner of identifying ourselves with other people and things, in part or in whole. It is as natural for us to do this as it is for us to grasp objects with our hands and walk on our feet. The great mystery of how one and the same psychological mechanism may produce such an enormous variety of normal and pathological results is yet to be solved; this mystery, I think, will never be solved unless and until scientific, clinical psychodynamics occupies itself with the problems of value and of will.

I say "occupies itself" in a definite, positive sense; I have in mind not the method of parallelism or concordism, which is bound to be a sterile method, but the method of trying to find a true synthesis between moral and religious *values* and the functioning of the human ego in its purely automatic, unconscious responses within the psychic apparatus by way of what have become known as psychological mechanisms. In other words, both metaphysics and moral theology must be considered, in addition to what we already know from clinical psychoanalysis, in order to produce a proper synthesis. Even now, in the absence of such a synthesis, a great deal can be learned by way of dispassionate study of the so-called psychological mechanisms that happen to be utilized in a given religious act. We must never forget, however, that the most objective, dispassionate studies may involve an admixture of bias, or prejudice, or affective reaction of some kind so that a great part, and frequently an essential part, of that which the student is studying is totally overlooked.

Thus the psychologist studying a given religious act may remain objective throughout the study but, unless he also knows whether he is affected by his own religious or antireligious attitude, a whole host of phenomena within the purview of his study may escape him and his conclusions be vitiated. What I have in mind is not *discounting* one's religious bias, but *taking into account* one's religious bias. Without such taking into account, the psychological study we wish to envisage will fail of its goal, and, what is worse, its conclusions will represent a distorted picture of the truth.

This is exactly what has happened with many psycho-

Some Denials and Assertions of Religious Faith 163

analytic attempts to understand certain aspects of religious practices. It is not difficult to relegate religious practices and rituals, all in one heap, to the field of magic and superstition. Once a psychological mechanism is found to be operative in magic thinking, and a similar and even identical mechanism is found to be operative in a religious act of devotion, it is easy without further ado to equate magic and the religious act —if we agree to the unspoken postulate that the psychological mechanism is *the* determining factor in the nature of a given phenomenon. Well, the neuro-muscular mechanism of picking up a fork and a pen is the same, but eating is not writing. This is not a caricature of the purely mechanistic view; rather, I believe it is a good snapshot. Not all the details are in focus, not all the shadings are well shown, but it is a faithful snapshot.

We can now call attention to the many religious workers, some of whom have been referred to above, who in the course of the past two decades or so have devoted a great deal of time to study of the religious life in the light of modern psychopathology. It is from such studies that we may learn the true art of synthesis between religion and scientific psychology. With some of them[15] I have had the privilege of discussing in some detail the problems touched upon in these pages, and in particular the illustrative example that follows.

From the formalistic psychoanalytic point of view, the Sacrament of the Eucharist could be studied with regard to the psychological mechanisms involved. What would one then find in the sacramental act of communion? First, the fact that it is a sacrament could be looked upon as a manifestation of the "magic" aspects of the ritual—the magic elements being a survival of the primitive belief in magic. (It must be borne in mind that as a practicing psychoanalyst I am fully aware

---

[15] Bruno Jésus-Marie, O.C.D., editor of *Etudes Carmélitaines*, and Albert Plé, O.P., editor of *La Vie Spirituelle*.

of the simplification to which I resort here. I simplify the argument actually for the sake of brevity and succinctness, and not for the purpose of shading down any of the valid arguments that psychoanalysis has to offer.)

Let us now go a step further. There is magic, one could say, in the act of receiving the sacrament. What is happening in this act, it could be argued, is the usual natural recourse to oral incorporation of the symbolic body of Christ, with the resultant momentary and magic identification with Christ himself. In other words, it could be further argued, the ritual of communion intuitively utilizes the primitive and non-rational mechanism or mode of identification with Christ, and the communicant can thus proceed to live out his ambivalence toward Christ as does any person who identifies himself with an object by way of oral incorporation. It is, one might hear people say further, at once a totemistic feast and an act of identification with the crucified Son of God.

As a matter of fact, there would be little which a believer would be able to take exception to, in principle, in this tentative and condensed formulation that I have heard from many earnest students and practitioners of psychoanalysis. Yet even a cursory study of the religious act under consideration sheds a totally different light on the situation. The act of communion is not an unconscious act, but conscious and intentional, a self-conscious and voluntary procedure in which the act of identification with the Lord is in no way automatic, or dependent on the mechanism of incorporation alone; this latter, it seems, is but a culmination of a series of psychological steps that are far from being related to magic or to purely formalistic adherence to a magic ritual.

For the communicant may not go to the communion rail unless he is in the state of grace. What does this mean from the point of view of the major mechanisms as postulated by psychoanalysis? It means that the communicant may not receive the Eucharist (to identify himself with the Lord) unless he has cleansed himself of the burden of sin. This he must do by searching his own conscience, by confronting himself with the magnitude of his own transgressions, and by making an act of contrition; then and only then is the Sacrament of Penance considered valid, and then and only then is the penitent vouchsafed absolution. It is from this moment on that he can with a clear conscience kneel before the priest and receive the sacrament. (I deliberately leave aside any consideration of the supernatural and theological aspects of the problem; it is better to remain here on purely psychological grounds and see where our inquiry will lead us.)

Let us note that from the psychological, and particularly from the psychoanalytic, point of view it is rather remarkable that on the road from the beginning of the act of penance to the act of communion there is a steady, albeit intuitive, insistence that the sense of guilt be got rid of before, and not after, the act of incorporation. Furthermore, the self-reproaches and self-accusations are directed consciously against one's own self, and are accompanied by the full awareness that whatever sin one feels guilty of is a sin against God. In other words, it is a frank admission that one is aware of the source of the commandments imposed upon one's conscience, i.e., God the Father. It is not merely a sense of guilt, nurtured and whipped-up as it were by a cruel superego, which as such remains almost totally unconscious and beyond the control of reason and will.

The psychological result of the Sacrament of Penance is then the elimination of one's ambivalence, the reduction or sufficient attenuation of the sense of guilt which was due to sins of which one had taken cognizance, and the establishment of a sense of humble unworthiness on the part of the communicant which then permits him to perform the sacramental act of identification with the Lord. Thus the sacramental act, oral incorporation though it be, is not an unconscious performance by one's own ego in the service of the superego, but an incorporation vouchsafed by God the Father through the authorized priest.

All this may appear self-evident to the initiated, and trite and perhaps a little irritating to the traditionally agnostic or atheistic psychoanalyst. It must, however, be stated in order to emphasize the depth of the religious intuition, the depth of the psychological understanding which religious faith offers as it leads one from sin through penance and communion to an identification with Christ the Redeemer.

From the point of view of psychoanalytic psychology, there is no doubt that the Sacrament of the Eucharist, this culminating act of the Christian believer in his devotion and submission to the will of God, has been carefully prepared by means of a series of psychological steps which seem to eliminate entirely the usual psychological consequences of oral incorporation: namely, a manic state or a state of depression. Humility and simple serenity in which one would be hard put to find a trace of exaltation or depression are almost self-evident in the postcommunion state. As one considers the postcommunion prayers, one is impressed by their simple psychology of gratitude and awareness of one's sense of duty and striving for service. The well-known postcommunion prayer of St. Thomas Aquinas is most revealing in this respect.

There is therefore no need to quarrel with Freud, who did not wish to believe in God. There seems to be sufficient evidence, in what he himself has offered us, to the effect that his own religious feelings were intense enough to produce within him a serious counter-force that drove his faith into the underground of his unconscious. As I have pointed out elsewhere,[16] Easter Sunday and Rome had a particular fascina-

---

[16] Gregory Zilboorg, "L'Amour et Dieu chez Freud." See also Suzanne Cassirer Bernfeld, "Freud and Archeology," *American Imago*, VIII, 2.

Some Denials and Assertions of Religious Faith

tion for Freud; among his earliest memories are those of being carried to Mass "into all the five churches" of his native town by his devout Moravian nurse. And later on, in his *Psychopathology of Everyday Life,* he offered us an excellent example of how he had repressed everything that had to do with his consciousness of God. Thus he reports how he remembers relating to a fellow train passenger his profound impression of the frescoes in the Duomo of Orvieto. To his amazement, Freud was unable to tell at that moment either the subject matter of the frescoes or the name of the artist. By way of a series of free associations, he finally recalled the name of the master painter, Signorelli. By way of careful self-analysis, he concluded that he had repressed the name because of its first half, *Signor,* to which he arrived via a number of associations, one of them being the German word *Herr.*

It was a remarkable piece of self-analysis on the part of Freud. Yet what appears not less remarkable is that that piece of psychoanalysis done in 1898, almost thirty years before he wrote the *Future of an Illusion,* lacked the recognition of what now appears to be so obvious:[17] *Signor* is the Italian equivalent of *Lord* in Church language, as is the German word *Herr.* Freud saw mainly the formal connections in his associations; he failed to see some of the deeper content of the repressed. It is, for instance, of particular interest to observe that the subject matter of Signorelli's frescoes in the Orvieto Duomo is *The Last Judgment.*

In this bit of self-analysis Freud does reveal in his associations the Turks' (Islamic) idea of death and sexuality, but it is the Turk and not the Jew that he permitted to enter into his consciousness. Why it was that Freud, despite his astonishing

[17] I.e., since the publication of his correspondence with Dr. Fliess and the appearance of Ernest Jones' first volume of Freud's biography. See Ernest Jones, *The Life and Work of Sigmund Freud* (Vol. I; New York, 1953); and *The Origins of Psycho-Analysis, Letters to Wilhelm Fliess, Drafts and Notes, 1887-1902,* trans. Eric Mosbacher and James Strachey, New York, 1954.

candor with regard to himself and his revealing self-analysis, nevertheless struggled so hard to avoid recognizing his own religious trends, may never become known. Freud wrote an article on denial;[18] one may find there a clue for a possible answer. In any case, the fact of this intense unconscious struggle against the idea of God does not seem to impair in any way the positive aspects of Freud's psychological discoveries; these were made despite his conscious antireligious attitude, or perhaps because of his unconscious, intense, positive religious leanings.

[18] "Negation," 1925.

The Sense of Guilt

WE ARE all familiar with the amusing display of impatience on the part of the Queen in *Alice in Wonderland:* "Let us have the verdict first and the evidence afterwards." There is something more than mere impatience in the Queen's exclamation, and there is a great deal of her attitude in all of us—regardless of age, civil status, or vocation. We all want to "know the end" in advance of reading the details in the many pages preceding the dénouement of the story.

If this particular left-over of our childhood were the only form that impatience took, there would be considerable cause for amusement and almost none for concern. The trouble, however, with this little childishness of ours is that often it appears in many more earnest guises and is uttered in less obviously childish speech by people of considerable stature and prestige. Then issues become confused and exchange of opinions turns into argumentative sparring.

The topic, "The Sense of Guilt," is one of those which arouse impatience in us more often than not. It is a kind of prejudice, against which one ought always to be forewarned. Whenever the subject of the sense of guilt is discussed, we recall at once the modern psychological descriptions and

Written in 1956 and published here for the first time.

concepts which were offered us by Freud; we then almost automatically recall the apparent clash between "Freudian" guilt, and guilt as morality and religion traditionally know it. Then we pronounce the sentence that Freud, or psychoanalysis, or Jung, or Adler is doomed to the sea of errors. We proceed to examine the evidence which psychoanalysis has to offer, and the confutations which religious morality has to offer. This mode of "examining the evidence" cannot be very fruitful because, the verdict having been pronounced in advance, the *ex post facto* "examination" of evidence in the light of the previous verdict does not possess even academic value.

The process I have just described almost never manifests itself in the simple and crude form in which I have presented it. Our manners, intellectual gyrations, and emotional preoccupations express themselves in forms both more complex and more delicate, so that our prejudice remains frequently unnoticed either by the participants or by the observers of the argument.

The trouble is that we have not yet learned to study such official antagonists of religious faith as Freud. We listen to their empirical findings with that skepticism which is almost a form of anxiety, lest their findings might seduce us into following their positivistic or antireligious argument. I have always felt that this anxiety, so very well concealed under the cover of a sincere desire to keep one's faith, masks a not less sincere desire to defend oneself against one's own (perhaps unconscious) religious uncertainties and even doubts. It seems to me that it is this unconscious uneasiness that prevents us from reaching to the very core of the matter. The problem is a grim and obscure and confusing one, and I doubt whether I can succeed here in doing more than reformulating and restating the issue with a little less uneasiness and/or less insecurity than is often the case.

The Sense of Guilt

We must start with the usual seemingly simple and clear statement that there is a conscious and an unconscious sense of guilt. We can then proceed, as certain psychoanalysts do (and quite wrongly, I dare say), to state that conscious guilt is normal and unconscious guilt is abnormal—neurotic or psychotic, as the case may be. A closer glance into the meaning of this formulation will at once make us aware of some difficulty. A depressed, or let us say a sad, person may say that he is not a very successful person, that in his most recent conference with his business partner he was rude to him and offended him without any reason; that he does not know "what got into him," but he is not so kind as he ought to be to his employees.

If we proceed to examine the facts on which this person seems to base his self-reproaches, we may find *some* justification for his sense of guilt, but not enough to explain the keenness and the pain of it. The quality and the quantity of his sense of guilt seem too great as compared with the facts consciously seen and consciously presented. Thus, we have here a conscious sense of guilt, or a full awareness of the apparent causes of it, which is real enough, but not entirely sufficient for the emotional reaction described. In the light of modern psychology we are forced to assume if not to admit that there are other unconscious sources of guilt which have attached themselves to the consciously perceived and consciously stated factors as added psychological determinants, and have produced the intense sense of guilt which presents itself to our observation. In other words, in addition to the conscious determinants, we may safely state that unconscious determinants have played a definitive role in the sense of guilt in question.

So, we may say without hesitation that it is almost a postulate that our psychological reactions are always a result of a multiplicity of determinants—they are *over*determined. The psychic economy (i.e., the economy of the psychic apparatus) depends upon the nature of the determinants that produce a given reaction. Our reason and our will are always in danger of being partially or considerably or almost totally impeded —depending upon the number and the intensity of the unconscious determinants.

Thus, a person may constantly seek to destroy himself because, he says, he is no good at all, and because he is a murderer and a cannibal to boot, and because he has always been a bad son, a bad friend, a bad husband and a bad father. We may proceed to study the life history of this unfortunate man and to our surprise discover that he never killed anyone, that he never was a cannibal, that he never even liked meat, that, as a matter of fact, if on occasion he did take a piece of meat, he insisted that it be so well done that it looked and felt like leather. We shall, in other words, find that his ideas are delusions. Yet we shall also find that it was true that he was a bad son, a bad husband and a bad father. Suppose that we succeeded in consoling this man so that he felt at least easier in his conscience for having been a bad son, husband and father; his delusions would not seem diminished, and his intense horror of the monstrosities he had allegedly committed would continue to torment him unabated. Evidently there is something more to his avowed sense of guilt, no matter how conscious he is of it; the ideational content, in which the sense of guilt is rooted, seems buried in the unconscious and thus continues through its unconscious emotional connection to cloud his reasoning and impede the function of his will, and it does all this as efficiently as a drug or a brain lesion.

When the importance of the ideational content of the unconscious was first discovered, it was rather difficult for the psychologist or the layman to accept the idea that thought and ideas can be unconscious. Gradually it became easier to

The Sense of Guilt

speak of unconscious thoughts, as if we really knew what we were talking about. I say "as if," because I am not so sure that even now the most confirmed psychoanalysts and the most glib protagonists of what is routinely known as "dynamic psychology" really know what they are talking about in this connection. "Unconscious thought," "unconscious ideological content" as I put it when I spoke of the sense of guilt—these are empirical working concepts, but they are not really understandable, not as yet at any rate.

The unconscious by definition and description is subject to the primary process; that is to say, its elements and components are all mixed together so that it knows no time, space, causality, or contradiction. How does it happen that we yet recognize unconscious thought and ideas, and unconscious logic of emotions—how does it happen that the disorder contains within itself definite groups of order, that the absence of "because" and "despite" yet permits rather definite even though special unconscious syllogisms? Anyone might try to invent an explanation, but at the present state of our knowledge his explanation would be as good (or as bad) as mine. For we have no adequate explanation of this puzzle. What is more important, however, than taking notice of this our ignorance, is to note that this is not entirely a psychological question. There was a time when psychology was defined as the science of human behavior; today, this purely phenomenological, "external" definition will no longer hold. Moreover, no sooner do we try to probe a little deeper than the empirical crust of the newer psychology, than we find ourselves confronted with philosophical (particularly epistemological) questions, metaphysical (particularly metapsychological) and ontological problems which the most skillful and most scientific psychologist is unable to penetrate.

The above digression seems to me quite proper and even necessary, because during the past half century we have grown accustomed to take for granted the various extra-psychological, and I must say pseudo-philosophical, excursions of modern psychologists, and assume that these excursions were inseparable parts of the empirical systems which they represented or discovered. So much that is truly superficial, and untenable even on a superficial level, was silently considered as part and parcel of the sociological matrix of Alfred Adler's psychology that his true empirical contribution was lost in the mist of his "theory," which at best was an *ad hoc* semi-materialistic construction and at worst a superficial adaptation of an amateurish sociology. So much that is of an oriental-cosmological mysticism was added by Jung to his original empirical findings that the human being, the person in the individual sense, was almost lost in the Jungian system; when we speak of Jungian analytical psychology, we are either confronted with the embarrassment of the riches of the Universal and the Infinite, or with some inwardly self-contradictory, empirical metaphysics—a *contradictio in adjecto*.

When we now turn to the theory of Freud, we find that it is much less difficult to separate the empirical data of psychoanalysis from their purely theoretical superstructure. Freud's great advantage lies in the very disadvantage which he has as compared with Adler and Jung. He was a poor sociologist and a poorer philosopher, but somehow neither his sociological nor his metaphysical excursions seem to be really a part of his scientific empirical system. What happened to Freud was something rather unique and, I may say, fortunate: Freud was a clinician despite himself. A scientific empiricist by training and bent, he indulged his coldly contemplative, slightly speculative mind by pondering every now and then in a rather impersonal way on life, death, and God. But instead of allowing himself to follow his own spiritual trends, he preferred to depersonalize them, and thus to deny as illusions many of those things which in the light of recent publications

The Sense of Guilt

were part and parcel of his spiritual search and struggle. What happened as a result was this: The clinical, empirical system of Freud seems to stand very well the test of time and experience; his metaphysical excursions stand apart from his clinical findings as something personal which is of Freud, to be sure, but no more of psychoanalysis than Freud's purely personal and cherished possessions. To me Freud's *Moses*, or his *Future of an Illusion*, are as much of Freud as the Etruscan vase which he owned, or the Egyptian statuettes which he cherished. But that which is of Freud is not necessarily of Freudian psychoanalysis.

And yet all the above qualifications, even if fully accepted, leave our problem far from clarified. For it is not only that certain unconscious ideation seems to lead to a conscious sense of guilt and harsh self-accusations; the sense of guilt itself may become buried in the unconscious and from there affect our behavior in such a way that the whole gamut from neurosis to psychosis, or from total inability to act to recidivistic criminal activity, may be produced by various types of the unconscious sense of guilt. The problem is truly baffling.

Very early, in 1915, Freud observed a type of person whom he called "a criminal from a sense of guilt."[1] At that time it seemed to Freud that mostly, if not only, young people are afflicted with this trouble. Later, case studies by Franz Alexander[2] and Marie Bonaparte showed that a severe, complex, *unconscious* sense of guilt may lead to gruesome crimes, including murder. This is what Freud had to say in fact about the problem:

"In our analyses we discover that there are people in whom the faculties of self-criticism and conscience—mental activities, that is, that rank as exceptionally high ones—are un-

[1] Freud, *Coll. Papers*, Vol. IV, p. 343.
[2] Franz Alexander and Hugo Staub, *The Criminal, the Judge, and the Public: a psychological analysis*. New York, Macmillan, 1931.

conscious and unconsciously produce effects of the greatest importance; the example of resistances remaining unconscious during analysis is therefore by no means unique. But this new discovery, which compels us, in spite of our critical faculties, to speak of an 'unconscious sense of guilt' bewilders us far more than the other and sets for us fresh problems, especially when we gradually come to see that in a great number of neuroses this unconscious sense of guilt plays a decisive economic part and puts the most powerful obstacles in the way of recovery. If we come back once more to our scale of values, we shall have to say that not only what is lowest but also what is highest in the ego can be unconscious."[3]

To return for a moment to Freud's remark about "a criminal from a sense of guilt," the following lines of Freud are very instructive: "It was a surprise to find that exacerbation of this unconscious sense of guilt could turn people into criminals. But it is undoubtedly a fact. In many criminals, especially youthful ones, it is possible to detect a very powerful sense of guilt which existed before the crime, and is not therefore the result of it but its motive. It is as if it had been a relief to be able to fasten this unconscious sense of guilt on to something real and immediate."[4]

Please note that in the above quotation Freud uses once the term "sense of guilt" without qualifying it, and once he adds the adjective *unconscious*. This is a very important aspect of Freud's writing, as well as of the writings of the greatest majority of Freudian psychoanalysts; the concept of the unconscious is so familiar to them, they work with the unconscious so much more than with the conscious, and more often than not they concern themselves with the conscious only in so far as it reveals the unconscious—that as a

[3] *The Ego and the Id*, London, 1947; pp. 32–33. (First published in German in 1923.)
[4] *Ibid.*, p. 76.

The Sense of Guilt

result they frequently omit the qualifying term "unconscious" and speak merely of "the sense of guilt," of the wish to do this or that, of the thought concerning this or that. The uninitiated would not suspect at first that it is about the *unconscious* thought, the *unconscious* desire, the *unconscious* sense of guilt that they are speaking. The moralist and the theologian, like anyone else, are frequently and legitimately confused by the looseness of the language, and out of this confusion more than one problem arises which the moralist and theologian are hard put to resolve.

It is difficult, at first glance, to accept almost as a postulate that one should strive to reduce, limit or abolish entirely the sense of guilt in a given individual. The painful question always arises: How could anyone continue to live as a human being if he were relieved of his sense of guilt? However, we must recall that the sense of guilt in question is not the realistic, conscious feeling of guilt in relation to consciously perceived and willfully carried out acts which are immoral or legally forbidden, but the *unconscious sense of guilt* which literally may play havoc with our behavior *before* our reason and good will take cognizance of what has happened and try to correct, to make amends, or otherwise to compensate for the moral or legal transgression.

Yet, even with all these qualifications, our difficulties are far from alleviated. Unconscious sense of guilt may "drive" a person to suicide and to murder without the individual in question appearing at first too compromised intellectually, or emotionally. These are the most difficult cases to assess clinically; it is easy to imagine how much more difficult it would be to assess such cases in the confessional, or during talks with the spiritual director. The penitent's unconscious sense of guilt might be such that a given penance would only spur him on to want more and more penance. In other words, instead of being relieved by penance and absolution, the penitent might find himself feeling "just as badly," or "worse." In psychoanalytic practice such cases are known as showing the so-called "negative therapeutic reaction." A certain interpretation seems indicated at a certain point of psychoanalytic treatment; the patient seems psychologically ready to accept it; the interpretation is given; the patient accepts it; and next day some of his symptoms, instead of having disappeared, become accentuated, and a new symptom or two may even appear.

How can we recognize such cases? What can we do with them? In some such cases the task of the confessor might prove a little easier than that of the clinician.

It is necessary to recall in this connection St. Thomas Aquinas' simple but keen insight into the psychology of the sacrament of penance. The act of contrition, he points out, is accompanied by sadness (we could call it a mild depressive state, today) because the penitent is sad for having sinned, for having offended God. But penance is not accompanied by sadness, because penance is performed with hope of forgiveness. Here you have your differential diagnosis, so to speak. Whenever a sense of sadness is carried over into the period of penance, and whenever the penance prescribed appears insufficient to the penitent, we probably deal with an unconscious sense of guilt whose characteristic is a well-nigh insatiable desire for more and more punishment. In other words, we probably deal with a psychopathological problem which in its severer form has become known as masochism.

This is what led Freud to return to the problem when he discussed masochism in 1924 and said: "Patients do not easily believe what we tell them about an unconscious sense of guilt. They know well enough by what torments (pangs of conscience) a conscious feeling of guilt, the consciousness of guilt, can express itself, and so they cannot admit that they could harbour entirely analogous feelings in themselves

The Sense of Guilt

without observing a trace of them. I think we may meet their objection by abandoning the term 'unconscious feeling of guilt', which is in any case an incorrect one psychologically, and substitute for it a 'need for punishment' which describes the state of things observed just as aptly."[5]

Freud's suggestion is quite satisfactory from the standpoint of the formal clinical approach, but fundamentally it robs the problem of some of its psychological essentials. Freud, being a strict positivist, or rather trying all the time to be one, would be satisfied with the psychological economics of masochism, the crude formula of which might run approximately as follows: the stronger the need for punishment, the greater the demand for ever greater punishment. This "quantitative" point of view eliminates the whole question of values. And Freud refuted himself in this respect when, discussing the unconscious sense of guilt one year earlier in *The Ego and the Id*, he pointed out: "If anyone were inclined to put forward the paradoxical proposition that the normal man is not only far more immoral than he believes [himself to be] but also far more moral than he has any idea of, psycho-analysis, which is responsible for the first half of the assertion, would have no objection to raise against the second half."[6]

It is obvious, is it not, that Freud seemed to be quite reluctant to enter the area of morality. Immorality—yes, this he could dissect and expose to light in detail. In this he was like the pathologist who dissects a corpse to seek the cause of death and exposes to light the fatal wound; thus he serves science, forensic medicine, the law itself—but he is relieved of the necessity of passing on the morality of the murder, on the problem of life and death and immortality. Freud, it seems, almost deliberately avoided coming closer to the problem of values and morality. He merely limited himself there-

[5] "The Economic Problem in Masochism," *Coll. Papers*, Vol. II, p. 263.
[6] *The Ego and the Id*, pp. 75–76.

fore to the cool promise not to raise objections to the idea that man is more moral than he has any idea of.

This admission may appear at first a little amusing, but in actuality it is rather disturbing to the clinician and the pastor who seek a point of convergence and a line of contact and cooperation. It is disturbing, because Freud in making the admission stated an enormous truth and then stepped aside, as it were, refusing us the benefit of his extraordinary perspicacity. What Freud admitted here is what he stated more or less directly on other occasions, namely: ". . . not only what is lowest but also what is highest in the ego can be unconscious."

It is here that the pastoral problem comes up against a very difficult task: If our highest aspirations and hopes can be unconscious, how is it that they become unconscious? Are they repressed because we are ashamed of that which is highest in us? This is obviously not the case. The unconscious does not contain anything positive, or directly good; the unconscious is made up mostly of those matters which we prefer not to admit into our consciousness because they are not acceptable to our conscience, our morality. In other words, that which is highest within us, if it be unconscious, is not a higher aspiration but a sense of shame, a sense of guilt (unconscious) for not following that which we consciously avow or proclaim; it is the eternal *mea culpa* deeply buried so as to permit us not to think of ourselves as bad, as we would actually consciously be if we were freed of this (unconscious) sense of guilt.

The above considerations may appear somewhat enlightening to the professional psychologist and clinician, but actually they must carry with the little enlightenment that they contain a considerable degree of disappointment, if not a moderate amount of confusion. This I believe is as it should be, because the problem appears to become more complex instead of more simple as we develop what is commonly known as greater insight into the mechanics, or workings, or dynamics of the

The Sense of Guilt

human mind. Granted, one might say, that everything thus far described and discussed is correct, it would seem that the two fundamental questions which confronted us from the beginning will continue to confront us with the same tenacity and with rather little hope for an enlightening answer.

Question One: After all is said and done, how is it that a sense of guilt which seems to vary in intensity and scope even though it be unconscious may be responsible for the commission of both criminal and virtuous acts—that is to say (to use a purely positivistic terminology) for social or antisocial behavior, ethical or nonethical? Does the sense of guilt as it is understood by the present-day psychology of the unconscious represent something so paradoxical and strange that it just exists as a sense of guilt without any real moral content, so that neurotically or otherwise it might turn into something bad, even criminal, or something good, even virtuous—like, say, humbleness or readiness to serve one's neighbor? What manner of guilt is it then, that it seems suspended between right and wrong, being neither and embracing both? This leads us directly to

Question Two: Granted that clinical psychology is purely empirical, is it possible to proceed with it in any direction—investigative, therapeutic, or educational—without any set of values which are independent of the scientific hypotheses under which this psychology operates? By "independent" we do not necessarily mean in the sense of some superhuman and supernatural values which are beyond the scope and the ken of psychology, but independent in the sense of values not based on the scientific positivism of the given system but on a moral tradition the essence of which lies inevitably ouside science as such.

Let us try and find some plausible answer to Question One first. It is not an easy task. Freud sensed the difficulty more than he seems to have been fully aware of when he suggested that the unconscious sense of guilt is psychologically untenable, and when he suggested that the term "the need for punishment" be substituted for it. He pondered at that time the psychic economics of masochism. At one time he suggested that a sense of guilt is apt to develop in a person if a strong aggressive impulse remains thwarted even without entering consciousness, that is to say, if it undergoes repression without ever having become conscious, if it is thwarted, held back, damned up, so to speak, without ever having been permitted to enter consciousness except in the form of that vague sense of malaise which goes with any sense of guilt.

Let us note now what the criminal, or generally aggressive act, antisocial or not, represents from the standpoint of the economics of the psychic apparatus. It seems that such an act represents a breaking through of some damned-up aggression; and at the same time this antisocial act provokes social sanctions which produce a sense of suffering caused by the punishment. To put it very schematically, we deal here with a sort of devilish (unconscious) method for the establishment of an affective equilibrium, an equilibrium which hurts others, makes the individual himself suffer, and causes him to seek again and again the gratification of that singular thing which Freud called the "need for punishment."

Let us recall again for a moment *Alice in Wonderland*. We might be tempted now simply to pronounce some condemnatory verdict before the evidence is in, and be done with the problem. But we cannot afford this rejection, for it really is a matter of considerable importance, that "need for punishment." One cannot help but feel that there is something missing somewhere in this chain of psychological phenomena which, although hypothetical, do seem to be corroborated time and again by a wealth of clinical observations.

Let us accept Freuds' term "need for punishment" in its literal sense. This term might coincide with the colloquial

The Sense of Guilt

expression, "a glutton for punishment." What does it mean? To stick the label of masochism on it would explain very little indeed—if anything at all. In a general way these appellations imply that the individual who is burdened with the unconscious need for punishment might seek by way of murder or suicide (I deliberately choose extreme examples) to hurt his own self. This is obviously not an act of love, nor is it an act of justice, since: (1) it *is* unconscious; and (2) it is frequently performed by way of hurting someone else.

From the purely mechanistic point of view, what seems to be happening here is simply this: The hostile aggression, the drive to destroy, to annihilate, may come out and express itself momentarily in full force on something or someone outside the person who is the bearer of this destructive hatred, and murder or some similar act will ensue. However, we all know that for one reason or another this drive to destroy often becomes inhibited in us even before it shows overt signs of existence. What happens then is something akin to that which occurs to the man who for one reason or another is prevented from giving vent to his rage: He remains silent instead of breaking out in vituperations; he may even show tears in his eyes, his hateful glance fixed on the object of his hatred as he bites his own lips. Whether you call this biting of one's own lips a result of an unconscious sense of guilt or of a need for punishment, the fact remains that it is an automatic, almost reflex-like act which the psychophysiologically or mechanistically minded observer would and does speak of as "turning the aggression on one's own self."

So much for the purely mechanistic view, which would (at the suggestion of Freud himself) drop the term "unconscious sense of guilt." However, it is interesting that the term was retained in Freudian psychoanalytic literature. More than that: The term "need for punishment" gradually acquired the meaning of "need for punishment because of an unconscious sense of guilt." This view is not expressed exactly in these words as far as I know, but the whole trend of the psychoanalytic literature seems to be just this, particularly so since the development of ego psychology. It would seem that the simplest mechanism of defense against the pressure of accumulated aggression is the direct release of this aggression; for obvious reasons this creates untold dangers to the person involved, and as a result a self-punitive mechanism is brought into play which is called "the turning of aggression on one's own self."

Would it were all so simple, but innumerable problems arise here. How does the feeling, the knowledge—even though unconscious—of the wrongness of the aggressive impulse come about? And how is it that, even before the aggressive act is committed, it is treated unconsciously as an act already committed, and the punishment is at once (unconsciously) meted out? This is really sentence first and verdict afterwards; it is even more: execution first, with sentence and verdict trailing incomprehensibly in the shadows of the unconscious.

I have said before and, in order to understand both the inner psychological phenomena involved and the moral issues concerned, it is worth repeating, that the act of aggression which we are discussing, and the act of seeking punishment or the act of self-punishment, are suffused with hostility. Hostility is the quasi-respectable, quasi-scientific term meaning "hatred." And the mechanism of turning the aggression on one's own self is suffused with the same hatred, except that this hatred is directed onto one's own self instead of onto others. Again, as I have said, this is not a direct psychological mechanism; it is either a derivative of a number of others or it is combined with them. The whole thing hinges on the mechanism of unconscious, involuntary identification, and this identification with a person is seldom if ever based on love alone. It is always combined with either strong ambiva-

The Sense of Guilt

lence, which means a heavy admixture of hatred with whatever love exists, or it is based predominantly on hatred, in which case we deal with so-called hostile identification. This identification is in turn expressed in the unconscious by a rather constant, even though singular, fantasy that the object, i.e. the person with whom an identification is made, is swallowed and thus *incorporated* into the individual in question.

It is easily seen that the incorporated object, in so far as it was originally feared and hated, is also an agent of hatred within the human personality. Its psychological role seems to cause one a sense of guilt, or a sense of insecurity, and/or a need for punishment, direct or indirect—by way of various displacements, substitutions or distortions, or by way of mild neuroses or severe psychoses. It may therefore easily be seen that the incorporated thing is not a "kind" thing: It knows no charity; it acts in accordance with the primitive *lex talionis;* it always demands its pound of flesh. It is what is known as the superego.

This is the reason why those among psychoanalysts who recognize the existence of moral values as being independent of the psychological mechanisms described above are unable to accept the equation of the superego with conscience. Speaking on purely theoretical grounds, one is forced to say that the sense of guilt based only on superego pressure is not really a sense of guilt but a sense of fear of one's own superego. The so-called sadistic superego (there is never a permissive superego) frightens the individual into a sense of guilt in the same way as a strict and overdemanding father frightens a child; this fear appears as a sense of guilt and produces at times that intense insecurity the origin of which is betrayed by the popular expression, "being afraid of one's own shadow"—an expression that shows how we intuitively understand that which remains to us scientifically still obscure. My shadow is not myself, it is something that is thrown off me by the light of the day. If I have reasons to be afraid of something which I have within me, I begin to be afraid (by way of projection) of that which is outside myself, into which I read the danger that comes from within me.

It is at this point of our considerations that one feels the need of much more study than has been done. And one (almost hopelessly) wishes that psychoanalytic studies had learned to avoid passing on things so much beyond their scope as morality, charity and conscience, and that pastoral psychologists and moral theologians would refrain for a while from spending so much time and energy on pointing out the logical and theological errors of the psychoanalysts in matters of morality. The errors are obvious, and the more we try to understand the real psychogenetic nature of the psychoanalytic concepts in question, the more obvious those errors will become—by themselves, as it were.

What seems to be much more important in this state of confused issues is to appreciate the full value of the two orders of things: the psychological and the spiritual. Granted that the greatest number of present-day psychologists do not know what spiritual is, and deny its existence, and believe that the nonexistence of spiritual experiences can be proved by the translation of these terms into modern psychological terms. Let us grant all this. The error is too obvious; it is as if one would insist that if you can translate St. Paul's Epistles into Eskimo, it is *eo ipso* proven that St. Paul was an Eskimo. However, he who appreciates the order of things called spiritual will at once be struck with the fact that the empirical generalizations of the psychoanalyst are actually correct, and that, far from refuting the higher order of moral issues, these empirical generalizations actually confirm it. This is particularly true of such concepts as the superego and the (unconscious) sense of guilt—both psychological factors of unconscious

The Sense of Guilt

nature. I have said enough about both and alluded to some of their major characteristics to be justified now in offering the following general proposition.

The superego is not conscience for many reasons, but the major reasons are those we want now to put forward. The origin of the superego lies in the child's ambivalence and fear. And conscience is not made up of fear, but of regret for having done something wrong. The superego is by its nature unforgiving; it is the epitome of aggression and hatred. The superego cannot be quieted; it can only be pacified with direct or indirect "payment in kind," only to come up again and demand again and always the maximum penalty for acts conceived and perhaps never committed. Conscience is never nonrealistic, and it does not treat a fantasy, conscious or unconscious, as if it were a fact. Conscience does not condone indulgence in conscious fantasies at the expense of facts, and it will not accept fantasies for facts. Conscience *regrets*, where the superego is *angry*. Conscience glows with hope when its owner repents and makes amends. The superego never says: Go, and sin no more; it merely says: Wait until I get you next time, or, It is all right to be sorry, but you must pay for it time and again until the end of your earthly days. Conscience knows forgiveness and cedes its position to charity; the superego concedes nothing and cedes less.

As you see, we are dealing with an unusually difficult and complex problem. For the superego is an unconscious agent, and its language is action or depression; in order to express itself in human language, it resorts to the language of conscience. It is obvious that the psychoanalyst who equates superego with conscience cannot differentiate which voice it is that is talking the language of conscience at any given time. Only the one who knows and truly understands both the actions of the superego and the actions of conscience will be able to assess how much of each there is in each of the steps and manifestations of the sense of guilt. In this connection, we must recall that it would be wrong to say that there are two types of sense of guilt: conscious and unconscious, or irrational and realistic. There are endless gradations between the unconscious, irrational sense of guilt and the fully conscious, rational one.

These gradations depend upon a very striking psychological characteristic of the psychic apparatus: It does not react to a given situation realistically; it never really spontaneously evaluates any given situation as it is. Being a biopsychological apparatus, it is more or less automatic in its reactions; one might say that the psychic apparatus cerebrates but never really reasons. The ego, even the healthiest one, is to some extent a captive of the superego and the id, and unless the given reaction is fertilized as it were by free reason, all the experiences of the past, all the automatic neurotic reactions, including all gradations of the unconscious sense of guilt, are mobilized. Thus, a true reaction of conscience might be and usually is colored by a host of reactions from the past, ranging the whole gamut from mild insecurities (anxieties) to severe self-accusatory and self-destructive reactions. In other words, both the ideational content and the quantitative, affective intensity may present a great number of gradations and variations.

It is the differentiation in quality and quantity of these neurotic sources and reactions which are the chief problem of pastoral psychology. Therefore pastoral psychology must always be the fruit of the joint efforts of the psychiatrist and the priest.

Psychiatry's Moral Sphere

ON APRIL 10, 1958 Pope Pius XII received in audience the members of the 13th International Congress of Applied Psychology. On that occasion he delivered to the gathering a discourse on certain aspects of modern psychology—the third discourse the Holy Father has delivered since 1953 on what the *Osservatore Romano* called "this delicate and important philosophic discipline." Henri Piéron, professor emeritus of psychology in the Collège de France, expressed the warm gratitude of the congress for the reception with which the Holy Father had honored it, and especially for the moral direction he offered in his discourse.

At the congress and at the papal audience were representatives from all corners of the world; there were Catholics and non-Catholics, and not a few positivists and materialists. The president of the congress was Leandro Canestrelli, director of the Psychological Institute of the University of Rome. It is noteworthy that the pope referred to this eminent Catholic scholar in his discourse and called attention to Canestrelli's book (published in Italian in 1955), *Liberty and Responsibility in Psychological Research*—a topic to which almost no attention has been paid in this country.

First published in *America*, 1958.

189

Pope Pius XII's masterly address of April 13, 1953 to the fifth Congress of Catholic Psychotherapy and Clinical Psychology serves as a source of guiding principles for Catholic psychiatrists and psychoanalysts. But the practice of psychotherapy raises more questions than can be answered in any single discourse, and there remained a number of more or less moot points and obscurities. Hopes had been expressed that these would some day be cleared up by the teaching authority of the Church. From the standpoint of this hope, the discourse of April 10, on psychotherapy and some related matters, takes on particular importance.

It will be noted that applied psychology hardly belongs to the field of psychotherapy proper. Yet the fact that the pope chose to speak of some psychological tests *as well as* of psychotherapy is not due to any error or lack of clarity on his part. Rather it is an added assertion that the field of human mental functioning, though it seems fragmented, for theoretical or practical purposes, into many "specialties," is still a unitary field, for the human personality is unitary and indivisible. This fact imposes equally serious, and more or less similar, moral obligations on all those who occupy themselves with any field of psychology. The emphasis on the importance of the human person is what makes this audience and this discourse a truly memorable event.

While the pope, in this discourse, broke much new ground, he did not depart from the Church's tradition. In speaking of the rights of children and the extent to which public authorities must recognize these rights, he pointed out that the authority of the family and of the Church come first, and referred to Pope Pius XI's great encyclical on Christian education, *Divini Illius Magistri* (1929). He reminded his hearers that in an allocution of September 13, 1952 he had spoken on the moral limits of medical research and treatment, and that on September 3, 1954 he had pointed out that an order by the

Psychiatry's Moral Sphere

public authority does not necessarily make an act morally licit. He had stated then, he said, that public authorities must concede to certain physicians and psychologists rights that go beyond those which a physician usually possesses in relation to his patient.

It is of paramount importance to note here that the pope speaks of psychologists and physicians as if they are, or mostly are, the same persons. In the United States this is not the case, whereas in Italy the faculties of psychology and psychiatry (a purely medical discipline) are mostly headed by one and the same person. One should not, therefore, see in the pope's way of speaking an implied authorization for nonmedical men to treat the mentally ill. Concerned as he is with the moral issues at stake, the pope is not discussing the licensing of psychotherapists, for which conditions and rules vary from country to country.

This is of particular importance to bear in mind since the pope, in discussing the importance of the moral aspects of psychological work, points out that he is familiar with the "Ethical Standards for Psychologists" which were published by the American Psychological Association. This is not, of course, an endorsement of the claims of nonmedical psychologists, nor a refutation of the professional standards of the American Medical Association as regards psychiatry and psychoanalysis. Without necessarily endorsing the APA code, the pope praised the effort to frame it. "Even if this code contains some questionable assertions, one must approve the idea that inspired it: the recourse to serious and competent persons [7,500 members of the APA were canvassed] in order to discover and formulate moral norms."

One important point should be clearly understood: The pope does not want his words to be considered as a rejection of modern psychology. "No one would deny," says he, "that modern psychology, considered in its totality, deserves approval both from the moral and religious points of view. To learn more about human beings, to strive to cure the illnesses of the mentally ill," are laudable goals.

The methods used are another question. He who would treat a mentally sick person must himself be a person not only of scientific competence but of inner moral stature. Moreover—and this is one of the salient parts of the pope's discourse—the value of the human personality, and the fact that this personality may not be violated in its freedom or its integrity, must never be lost sight of. We are again reminded of the unity of the human personality:

The individual, in so far as he is a unity, an indivisible totality, presents a unique center of being and of action, an ego which possesses itself and disposes of itself. This ego is the same in all our psychic functions, and it remains the same despite the passage of time. The universality of the ego—in extension and time—is a principle that ought to be applied, particularly when we consider causal connections which tie a person to his spiritual activity.

It is the vision of a man free and choosing between good and evil that the pope draws before us, of a man who, particularly when he is a psychotherapist, must never lose sight of the ethics of his profession and the eternal destiny of the human person who comes to him for advice and help.

With this vision in mind, the pope proceeds to incorporate in his discourse certain theological and moral considerations, and also to answer some questions which the congress apparently had addressed to him with a request that he enlarge upon his previous statements.

The discourse is a very rich document. To summarize it would be no mean job; and, paradoxically, the summary would be longer than the address itself. In one place, for example, the pope points out where the theologian and the psychiatrist come to a parting of their ways, and yet he does not quite see why it should be so. His conviction, expressed rather directly, is that the problem is not insoluble, the obstacles not insurmountable. He sees no reason why psychologists and theologians cannot ultimately reach an understanding. He points out how much work there is to be done in common by both theologian and psychologist in cases of people whose "only constant trait is their inconstancy."

Another area of moral concern is the use of psychological tests. It is one thing for a doctor to use a test for scientific or medical investigation, and quite another for the police to use it in the detection of crime. Narcoanalysis and the use of lie detectors to extract confessions from suspects are illicit.

Around this point clusters a mass of juridical and moral problems to which only allusion—but definitive allusion—is made in the discourse. Psychological tests which, if the results were revealed, might lead to legal indictment, or perhaps even conviction, are illicit. No one has a right to violate or vitiate the freedom of a person to make a conscious choice. It might seem to some that in such cases the consent of the person tested or treated by psychotherapy would suffice to justify the means used. This is not so.

The pope points out that there are limits to a man's moral right to dispose of his own body; there are therefore limits to a person's rights as far as his inner, mental, life is concerned. The pope reminds us of his allocution of April 13, 1953, and more specifically points out that there are secrets which the possessor may never reveal to another person—even if that person happens to be the psychotherapist who treats him. Secrets learned by the priest in the confessional may never be revealed under any circumstances to any person—"even to one single prudent person." This principle is apt to give rise to considerable objection, particularly on the part of psychoanalysts. But one can find ways and means of achieving proper therapeutic and scientific results without violating the moral principle.

The pope also notes that many an aspect of one's inner life is actually inaccessible—an allusion to the apparent sense of omnipotence which some modern psychological techniques seem to suppose.

There is a wonderful paragraph dealing with "heroic altruism," i.e., with those who offer themselves as "guinea pigs." Many of these people, says the pope, are worthy of admiration and imitation, but "one must be on guard not to confuse the motive or goal of the act with its object, and thus to ascribe to the latter a moral value which does not belong to it."

On the whole, this discourse, far from putting restrictions on psychotherapy and applied psychology, delineates with greater clarity than ever before the moral sphere in which the psychiatrist must work. Thus it explicitly makes an appeal to modern scientific psychology and theology to find a common path in the reassertion of the freedom and unity of the human person.

Freud and Religion

WITHIN the short space of about six years (approximately between 1951 and 1957) Ernest Jones wrote a three-volume biography of Freud. Jones is the founder of psychoanalysis in England; for many years he presided over the International Psychoanalytic Association. He was a personal friend of Freud's, of thirty years' standing; he belonged to the intimate so-called "Committee of Seven" which unofficially but effectively dictated the policies of organized psychoanalysis for many years.

It is but natural that in completing a biography of the founder of psychoanalysis, a biography covering about fifteen hundred pages, Jones should restate a number of things which heretofore were familiar to professional psychoanalysts and to many cultivated readers. It is also natural that in doing so, Jones should bring into focus some of the most controversial aspects of psychoanalytic theories and also some of his own biases, personal and professional. Some of these controversial aspects have been illumined by a great deal of discussion, spoken and written. On the whole one may say that few of the so-called "Freudian principles" have failed to be properly

First published in 1958. Reprinted with permission of the publishers, The Newman Press; copyright © 1958 by Margaret Stone Zilboorg.

thrashed out and in a minor or greater degree synthesized with that body of knowledge which is known as psychopathology.

However, there is still an atmosphere of tension and readiness for contention with regard to the question of the relationship between psychoanalysis and religion. It is true that in some minds, about whose religious inwardness and directness of faith there is no doubt, there apparently exists no great conflict between religion and psychoanalysis as a body of new knowledge for which we are indebted to Sigmund Freud. Thus, the Vicar of the Anglican Church of St. Mary's at Oxford, R. S. Lee (*Freud and Christianity,* New York, 1948), and the Professor of Psychology, Father Peter Dempsey, O.F.M. Cap., University of Cork, Ireland (*Freud, Psychoanalysis and Catholicism,* Cork, 1956), bear sufficient witness to the possibility of a satisfactory synthesis between psychoanalysis and religion. These men believe that it is possible to make a synthesis without any injury to science or offense to religious faith.

But this possibility is far from being sufficiently and universally established. The discourse of Pius XII on April 15, 1953, on the occasion of the Catholic Congress of Psychotherapy and Clinical Psychology, points to the moral limitation of certain aspects of psychoanalysis, but the pope in that discourse assumed anything but an irreconcilable attitude toward psychoanalysis as a theory and as a method of psychotherapy. That in that discourse the pope should not even have raised the question of the "scientific atheism" of Freud is quite easy to understand. The pope spoke then to a Catholic organization; consequently, no one questioned the faith of this group, which included a great many priests and religious and whose honorary president was none other than the President of the Pontifical Academy of Science, the Rector of the University of the Sacred Heart in Milan, Father Agostino

Gemelli, O.F.M. Moreover, Freud's name was not mentioned in the papal discourse, and Freud's attitude toward God was not a matter under consideration.

Of recent years certain Thomists, like Father Noël Mailloux, O.P., in Canada, or Father Albert Plé, O.P., in France, or Father Augustin Léonard, O.P., in Belgium, have written extensively and exhaustively on the synthesis between the major psychological tenets of Freud and Thomistic philosophy. Father Léonard, in addition, made a significant contribution to the solution of the problems involved in several articles in the *Supplément de la Vie Spirituelle,* in which he reviewed systematically a great number of articles and books on present-day psychology, which almost always reflect the influence of one or another school of psychoanalysis. Father Léonard thus has not only brought to the Catholic reader a rich mass of material dealing with the problem, and—I may add—with judicious perspicacity, but has concluded that Freud as a person is not the same thing as the psychoanalysis which he created. Freud's atheism is not a *conditio sine qua non* for the practice of good psychoanalysis.

The contributions of Father Bruno Jésus-Marie, O.C.D., or Louis Beirnaert, S.J., are further examples of the same trend.

Yet the completion of Freud's biography by Jones brings into relief the old problem, which is far from being really solved. The average scholar, not to speak of the average man, remains under the impression that Freud's atheism is an essential component of psychoanalysis. Few, if any, suspect that Freud's atheism might have been of purely personal origin. Far from being one of the pillars supporting Freudian theories, the contrary might be true: that Freud utilized the premises of the psychoanalysis which he founded in order to justify his atheism, which seems to have presented for him a greater inner problem than one might at first suspect.

It is neither scientific nor just to enshroud the personality of Freud with untouchability regarding the unconscious, or emotional, sources of some of his ideas.

Thus Jones, noting that Freud's interest in Moses was a deep emotional preoccupation, has this to say in connection with Freud's thoughts on Michelangelo's Moses:

> The question over which Freud had then cudgelled his brains was this. Was Moses on descending from Sinai unable to control his anger, as the Bible related, or could he attain the heights of self-control which Freud maintained Michelangelo had depicted? We know that this preoccupation coincided with the time when he was suppressing his own indignation at the way his Swiss followers had suddenly repudiated his work, and that merely confirms what his intense preoccupation alone would have taught us: namely, that he had emotional reasons for identifying himself with his mighty predecessor.[1]

It is not clear why Freud in the emotional condition in which he found himself should have chosen just this "mighty predecessor." It is doubtful really whether Freud himself, even unconsciously, tended to consider himself the twentieth-century giver of the New Law, the august transmitter of some new scientific Ten Commandments. I say only that it is doubtful, because there is evidence that Freud was a man of heroic dimensions and of heroic, even though unostentatious, bent. It is doubtful whether there were many people in history who, like Freud, suffered the intensity of pain he suffered for the last sixteen years of his life. From the first operation on his jaw (cancer) onward, Freud was in constant pain, constant discomfort, his speech was impeded, and yet he worked and wrote to the very last.

[1] Ernest Jones, *The Life and Work of Sigmund Freud* (3 vols., New York, 1953-1957) 3, p. 368.

Freud and Religion

His *Moses* was written when he was eighty, deprived of his books and his home; yet he had lost none of his almost sardonic mastery over circumstances, and in personal defeat he dreamed of himself as a conqueror. Two instances can be cited in this connection:

1. As one of the conditions for his leaving Vienna legitimately, so to speak, the Nazi Gestapo asked him to sign a document stating that the Gestapo had treated him well as befitting his station of great scholar of international repute, etc. Freud was ready to sign the document but asked whether he might be allowed to add one sentence: "I can heartily recommend the Gestapo to anyone."[2]

2. On his way to London, Freud dreamed that he was going to land at Pevensey! He told this dream to his son, who was already in England and who had come to meet him on arrival in London. Freud added the explanation that Pevensey was the place where William the Conqueror landed in 1066.[3] A telling paradox: The expulsion of the old and pained Freud from the city where he had lived since childhood was transformed by him unconsciously into another Battle of Hastings. He did not come to England to seek refuge; he arrived to conquer.

Yet, Jones himself seems to doubt that what one might perhaps call "the flight into the heroic" was wholly responsible for Freud's apparently intense identification with Moses, and he states in a footnote: "I have idly wondered if Freud's little brother Julius's Jewish name could have been Moses, in which case Freud's identification with it [sic] would have the profound meaning of a reaction to hatred like Napoleon's with his brother Joseph. Unfortunately the Nazis destroyed all the relevant records."[4]

[2] *Ibid.* 3, p. 226.
[3] *Ibid.* 3, p. 228.
[4] *Ibid.* 3, p. 368, note.

The speculative reference to Freud's little brother Julius acquires here special significance. It does seem that Jones dipped into Freud's very early childhood in order to produce a conjecture on a mere phonetic basis, so to speak. It does seem that if Jones could find proof that the little boy Julius, who died at the age of eight months (when Freud himself was only nineteen months old), was named in Hebrew Moses, he would be justified in assuming that, by the circuitous route our emotions frequently take in the unconscious, Freud might have in later years identified himself with *the name* Moses (that is apparently the meaning of the strange "it" in Jones' footnote). It does not matter now whether Jones may prove right or not. What does matter is the fact that in this quite interesting hypothesis Jones seems to take for granted that the events in the life of a child at the age of nineteen months might prove to "have a profound meaning." This assumption is correct, even if it probably does not seem correct as far as it goes; for it is a little difficult to imagine why the little, not yet two-year-old Freud would have fixed in his heart and mind the name Moses—which apparently was not used in the family. Why did his brother's name not fix emotionally some deep attachment to Julius Caesar, since Freud loved Rome and admired many conquerors?

In the light of the above, it becomes especially significant to note that in the very first volume of his biography Jones stated that Freud was jealous of his little brother (Freud was eleven months old when Julius was born). In a letter to Fliess (1897) Freud admitted that he had wished his little brother would die, and that the fulfillment of that wish when Julius died at the age of eight months "aroused self-reproaches, a tendency which had remained [with Freud] ever since."[5] To this Jones adds two important observations: (1) "So we see that the infant Freud was early assailed by the great problems of

[5] *Ibid.* 1, p. 8.

birth, love, and death."[6] (2) "In the light of this confession it is astonishing that Freud should write twenty years later how almost impossible it is for a child to be jealous of a newcomer if he is *only* fifteen months old when the latter arrives."[7]

We seem justified, therefore, in assuming that the following is well established: Jones is a thorough believer in the influence which events and names, even in very early childhood, may exercise on the life of a person, and he believes that given certain circumstances these factors might many years later produce reactions and behavior of profound meaning.

There is another aspect or episode in Freud's childhood. He had a Catholic nurse who, as Freud himself wrote later on, "carried him into all five churches of Freiburg." This nurse took care of Freud till he was two-and-one-half years old. Admitting that upon his return from church the little Freud would speak of the church services and imitate some things he had seen at Mass, Jones attaches no significance whatsoever to these impressions. If his nurse threatened him on occasion with hell-fire, Jones assumes that the little Freud, who as an infant "was assailed by the great problems of birth, love, and death," remained rather impervious to these other early impressions by which he was admittedly affected. These impressions took place quite a while after the death of the little brother—that is, when Freud apparently spoke well and possessed some histrionic powers. Jones thinks that it would be erroneous "to attribute any lasting influence to Nannie's theological beliefs."

Jones further assumes that some writers attribute Freud's negative attitude toward Christianity to the fact that this Catholic nurse was discharged because she stole some money from the family—an act against the tenets of her religion. Jones rightly points out that Freud was told about the real

[6] *Ibid.*
[7] *Ibid.*, note.

cause of the disappearance of his nurse when he was forty-six years old, and that therefore Freud could not establish in his mind the immorality of the nurse as connected with her Catholicism. Jones concludes: "There is no limit to the fantastic whimsies writers will invent to further some adverse criticism of Freud." Is the adverse criticism here "the seeking of the emotional roots of certain attitudes in the childhood of the given individual"? Jones states unequivocally, with reference to little Freud's behavior upon his return from church: "My opinion about such behavior is that its significance was theatrical rather than theological."[8]

It is characteristic not only of the personality of Jones, but of a great many scientists, that they betray considerable intolerance whenever the "solidity" of their antireligious views is brought into question. The most scientifically oriented minds, once they take an antireligious bent, betray that emotional attitude which they seem to avoid so successfully in their own scientific work. They readily agree that being emotional means not being guided by reason, but they deny the emotional nature of their own attitude and frequently fall into the trap of their own unreasoning, the existence of which they deny repetitiously and with a perseverance that gives one the impression that they do protest too much. Actually, they reveal a great deal of their own prejudices to their readers or audiences.

It is this fervor, asserted so vigorously but denied as prejudice just as vigorously, that leads to rather singular arguments. We thus read in Jones' biography that Freud "went through his life from beginning to end as *a natural atheist*" and that this "needs no explanation"[9] (whatever this may mean). The family of Freud is depicted for the same purpose as rather lukewarm, if not indifferent, to religion. It is admitted that Freud's

[8] *Ibid.* 3, p. 349.
[9] *Ibid.* 3, p. 351; italics added.

father was fond of reading the Torah, and the astonishing observation is made that the Torah is "a book of Jewish philosophy rather than of religion"[10]—which is obviously not true at all. It is also pointed out that Freud " was of course obliged to attend occasional lessons in the synagogue during his school days." No evidence for this is cited. There is no doubt that there is some error in this statement, since the synagogue, particularly the Orthodox one, never had instruction classes for the young in the days when Freud was a youngster. Jones adds: "The memory of this seems to have faded in later years, otherwise he [Freud] would not have been uncertain of the name of the most prominent object there—the Menorah."[11] To this a psychologically trained reader has a rather skeptical reaction; first of all, the Menorah is not the most conspicuous object in the synagogue, and second, forgetting—according to Freud himself, and to Jones and to all psychoanalysts—is more often than not a mark of repression rather than a corroboration of the insignificance of the thing forgotten.

In addition, if one recalls how anxiously persistent Freud was in refusing to get married in accordance with the Orthodox Jewish rites, and how hard and how long he struggled against this (his fiancée and future wife was a practicing Orthodox Jewess), one is hardly able to avoid the impression that Freud, far from being a "natural atheist," was actually inwardly in turmoil about the whole problem of religious practices and religious faith. Religious problems seemed to arouse in him certain anxieties. When he published his study of Michelangelo's Moses, he, the founder and editor of *Imago*, where the article first appeared, concealed from its readers the real name of the author. If one recalls the various qualms Freud had through the years about publishing his further con-

[10] *Ibid.* 3, p. 350.
[11] *Ibid.*

siderations of Moses, one does begin to suspect that all was not peaceful in the soul of Freud with regard to religion. Whenever he dealt with the topic of religion, he rejected religion in its entirety, frequently confusing faith with superstition, ritual with magic, theology with illusion.

It is still too early to pronounce a final judgment as to the origin and meaning of Freud's rebellion against religion in general, and Christianity in particular. Yet, it is fairly certain that Freud was not entirely happy about his own trends regarding religion. He was simultaneously not quite certain as to his own opinions and yet truculent and even harshly provocative about his own convictions. To a man in Tufts College School of Religion Freud wrote: "At all events what you say is a striking proof that theology has not damaged your capacity for free thought."[12] At the same time he confided to Arnold Zweig that "we live here in an atmosphere of strict Catholic beliefs" and therefore he was loath to make public his thoughts about Moses (he referred to this book at first as "an historical novel"). He was afraid, he said, that the publication of *Moses* might invoke a banishment of psychoanalysts and the deprivation of their livelihood. He added: "There is also the consideration that my contribution does not seem to me well founded enough nor does it please me much."[13] Freud referred to the animosity which a certain Father Schmidt had expressed against psychoanalysis, although he admitted that the priest had raised no official complaint against *The Future of an Illusion,* the first of Freud's books in which he considered religion an illusion and expressed the hopeful belief that, with the growth of scientific knowledge, mankind might do away with religion entirely.

It must be added that the years of concern about his *Moses* were ominous and turbulent years. Hitler was already the

[12] *Ibid.* 3, p. 192.
[13] *Ibid.* 3, p. 193.

master of Germany, and the shadow of his domination had begun to darken Austria too. In one of his letters to Lou Salomé, with whom he corresponded often and to whom he confided his thoughts on religion, Freud concluded thus:

And now you see, Lou, one cannot publish this formula, which has quite fascinated me, in Austria today without running the risk of the Catholic authorities officially forbidding the practice of analysis. And only this Catholicism protects us against Naziism. Moreover, the historical basis of the Moses story is not solid enough to serve as a basis for my invaluable piece of insight. So I remain silent. It is enough that I myself can believe in the solution of the problem. *It has pursued me through my whole life.*[14]

To a student of Freud's writing, it becomes obvious quite early that, if not the questions regarding Moses, the problems of religious faith in the broadest possible sense preoccupied Freud throughout his life. Freud, as has already been said, both identified himself with the Jewish tradition (of which, according to Freud himself, Moses was the inspired founder) and at the same time somehow rose against this tradition. This is again shown by his flight from anything that had religious implication, and by such remarks as this (on the occasion of the decision that the psychoanalysts abandon Vienna): "After the destruction of the Temple in Jerusalem by Titus, Rabbi Jochanan ben Sakkai asked for permission to open a school at Jabneh for the study of the Torah. We are going to do the same."[15] Yet Freud seems to have felt that his psychoanalytic theories *in toto* were a sort of New Law which set religion totally aside and that religion, while it might be utilized in some cases, should be thoroughly refuted.

He thought that psychoanalysis was a system that ought to

[14] *Ibid.* 3, p. 194; italics added.
[15] *Ibid.* 3, p. 221.

stand by itself. Medicine, like many other disciplines, should be used as a background and not as the backbone of psychoanalysis. To put it in the words of Jones: "There should be a special college in which lectures would be given in the rudiments of anatomy, physiology, and pathology, in biology, embryology and evolution, in mythology and the psychology of religion, and in the classics of literature."[16] Be it remembered that by "psychology of religion" Freud did not understand human psychological processes by means of which religious belief might come to expression, but rather the refutation of religious faith. As far back as 1904, more than thirty-five years before the publication of *Moses and Monotheism*, Freud stated with sufficient emphasis so that it was printed in italics, that modern religion "is nothing other than psychological processes projected into the outer world."[17] Jones considers it an expression of tolerance on the part of Freud when the latter wrote to the Swiss Protestant minister, Oscar Pfister, saying: "In itself psychoanalysis is neither religious nor the opposite, but an impartial instrument which can serve the clergy as well as the laity when it is used only to free suffering people."[18] Perhaps Freud did thoroughly believe in this exquisite neutrality of psychoanalysis in questions of religious faith, yet it must be remembered that Freud considered the whole field of "myths of Paradise, the Fall of Man, of God, of Good and Evil, of Immortality and so on" as belonging to metaphysics, and he hoped "to resolve" these myths by "transforming metaphysics into metapsychology."[19]

It is obvious that there cannot be any doubt as to Freud's true opposition, if not overt hostility, to religious faith; for his bias in favor of his metapsychology is as incontestable as

[16] *Ibid.* 3, p. 289.
[17] *Ibid.* 3, p. 353.
[18] *Ibid.* 3, p. 352.
[19] *Ibid.* 3, p. 353.

it is clear from the concluding lines of *The Future of an Illusion*. It was science and the sensible world which carried conviction for Freud; religion, or that which he called religion, had to be replaced by scientifically established data. Neither Freud nor any of his disciples ever explained how his metapsychology, which is certainly not scientific in the conventional sense of the word, how this purely hypothetical construction, brilliant and profound though it is, could encroach upon the field of theology. Yet this was Freud's belief. He saw no contradiction in his equating prayer and genuflection with those compulsive, purely personal repetitive actions which are found in compulsion neurosis. Consequently, he saw no contradiction between actual *compulsive* psychopathological acts and the free exercise and practice of rites of worship. Freud, therefore, fell into the very unscientific attitude of making an equation between a person and a state, or nation, or race; to him a neurosis—heretofore such an intimate, personal reaction—became, particularly after he published his *Group Psychology and the Psychology of the Ego* (1921), an affliction that could affect the body politic without necessarily affecting individually each person comprising the given social group.

The possibility of such an equation could have been sensed at the time *Totem and Taboo* was published. As a matter of fact, even earlier (1910) in his little article on Leonardo da Vinci, Freud, as Jones puts it, "stated unequivocally his conclusions about the source of religious beliefs, which in a succinct fashion express what was [in Jones' opinion] undoubtedly his [Freud's] main contribution to the psychology of religion."[20] Jones then proceeds to cite the following words of Freud: "Psychoanalysis has made us aware of the intimate connection between the father complex and the belief in God, and has taught us that the personal God is *psychologically* nothing other than a magnified father; it shows us every day

[20] *Ibid.* 3, pp. 353–54.

how young people can lose their religious faith as soon as the father's authority collapses. We thus recognize the root of religious need as lying in the parental complex."[21]

It will be noted that the evolution of Freud's ideas as to the origin of religion shows no concern with any aspect of transcendence in the life of man. Transcendence seems to be taken for granted as nonexistent or as belonging to what Jones rather contemptuously calls "metaphysics." It seems very puzzling that those who accept Freud's views on religion also accept almost unquestioningly Freud's metapsychology, which has more aspects of transcendence of the human person than of the naturalism which Freud claims as his own. Like so many scientists of generations before, Freud possessed an intense curiosity about the nature of man, and he had profound respect for reason (unimpeded by emotions and unconscious difficulties). He looked for laws of nature but turned away from natural laws. The latter he seems to have disregarded in favor of a special type of parallelism which he considered, at least as far as religion and religious experiences are concerned, conclusive.

There are many ways of summarizing and expounding Freud's views on religion. Here we follow Jones rather closely, because among psychoanalysts there is no one living more qualified to present these views, (1) because he shares them so thoroughly, (2) because he knew Freud so intimately, and (3) because Freud did consider these views as part and parcel of the whole system of psychoanalytic theory.

Jones reminds us that in 1919, i.e., two years before *Group Psychology* appeared, Freud wrote a preface to a book by Reik (*Das Ritual*). Freud said that he arrived at "an unexpectedly precise conclusion: namely that God the Father once walked upon earth in bodily form and exercised his sovereignty as chieftain of the primal human horde until his sons united

[21] *Ibid.* 3, p. 354; italics added by Jones.

to slay him. ..." It is from this murderous act of liberation that the oldest form of religion was born—totemism. All future religions stem from this primal one, and "they are concerned with obliterating the traces of that crime or with expiating it...."[22]

Two things will now become clear. (1) At the beginning Freud thought religious beliefs *psychologically* true. This he expressed pre-eminently in *The Future of an Illusion*. (2) However, Freud did not feel fully satisfied with this partial solution; he seems to have yearned for cultural, anthropological, and historical bases on which to build his refutation of religion. The historical basis Freud seems to have intuited years before, and he brought his intuition to full expression in his *Moses and Monotheism*. In *The Future of an Illusion* (1927) Freud merely demonstrated the psychological mechanisms involved in some religious ideas, and concluded that these psychological mechanisms alone were not sufficient for him to accept religious beliefs. In other words, he actually never *refuted* the existence of God, nor the natural laws involved in the development of morality and other tenets of religion. He merely considered all these tenets not acceptable, because they seemed to express themselves (on the human plane) in the manner human beings express themselves as a rule, and Freud had described the processes—the psychological ones—so well and with such insight. Perhaps Freud himself, and undoubtedly most of his disciples, failed to notice that the psychological mechanisms themselves cannot serve as a measure of religious truth, nor of any truth for that matter.

As if sensing the weakness of his argument, Freud looked for the true historical roots of that religion which he wished to refute. These roots he found in another parallelism which is rather puzzling and, considering Freud's systematic rejection of the racial unconscious, rather striking. He conceived

[22] *Ibid.*

a parallelism between the individual unconscious experiences connected with the complex psychological constellation that has to do with what is usually covered by the term oedipus complex, and those experiences (apparently also unconscious) which the group, the race, mankind carries within itself as a group, a race, mankind *in toto*. These experiences have to do with the origin of totemism, with the primal horde (Freud's daring and intensely fascinating hypothesis), with the murder of the primordial, primeval father, the burden of the sense of guilt resulting from this murder, and the worship of the father who originally was so hated that the sons murdered him. The worship of the father becomes the worship of God; for according to Freud the personal God is no one else but the idealized (may we say, spiritualized?) father. How this complex consciousness is carried over from days lost in the mist of the past to the individual, personal, intimate experiences of our own believers of today, Freud is of course unable to tell.

Jones uses the old Jungian term, "archetype," at least once when discussing Freud's views as to the origin of religious beliefs. Resorting to the use of a Jungian term neither confirms nor refutes the correctness of Freud's views on religion. What it does seem to suggest is that Freud never was able to give a really satisfactory explanation for his inclusion of what has to be called, for want of any other term, the racial unconscious into a system of thought which is fundamentally individualistic, almost organic—naturalistic, at any rate.

The introduction of such concepts as racial unconscious or archetype introduces an extra-individual, nonorganic and non-naturalistic set of factors which belong to the order of metaphysics as much as to philosophy and anthropology. This set of conceptual factors may be very helpful indeed, although it is difficult for this writer to see how an unconscious can exist in a race. The unconscious and its affect as far as a person is concerned are not conceivable without that person's having a body, an organic, individualized unit which could serve as "the seat," or the tangible but mysterious, perceptible container of the unperceived, which the unconscious actually is.

This is one of the many questions which are left open, and some in a state of considerable unclarity, by many of Freud's daring excursions into fields which either do not fully belong to psychology, or transcend the sensible world of scientific endeavors. Yet, one cannot help but regret that Freud seems never to have grasped the deep intuition of many of the scriptural passages which might have stood him in very good stead.

Let us take but one example of the many hundreds which are available to those whose minds are not bent on denying (under the guise of scientific refutation) religion, but on examining many of its tenets in the light of those new observations which Freud disclosed to the world. Take the dictum that the sins of the fathers are visited upon the children. Whatever the interpretation of this dictum (as a punitive threat, a stern warning, a statement of an unavoidable fact), one can legitimately approach it in the spirit of respectful consideration. We may say then that it is true that sins of the fathers are visited upon the children, and stand before this truth tolerantly and patiently waiting till the time may come when our human, scientific knowledge of man offers us a factual explanation of this mysterious transmission of fathers' sins to innocent children. Would it not then be plausible, even inevitably reasonable, to say the following in the light of modern psychology and the psychological mechanism of identification which Freud described: Children always identify themselves with one or the other of their parents. The identification may be positive or negative or, to put it in other words, loving or hostile. In cases of positive, loving identification, the offspring takes over ("acquires") those character traits of the parent whom he loves and approves. As a rule (although far from always) no harm comes from such a positive, loving identification.

Be it remembered that when we speak of identification we always have in mind a series of unconscious psychological processes. Any conscious processes of the same kind are of necessity reasoned, voluntary, and belong to a later stage of the growth of the human individual—a period after the age of reason has been reached. Consequently, such an identification is a deliberate identification and ought to be properly called imitation. There is therefore an important difference, for instance, between the imitation of Christ which may ultimately lead to a healthy identification, and that pseudo-imitation of Christ which is but a search for martyrdom, a thin covering for a masochistic identification which is psychologically unhealthy, and fundamentally due to an unconscious hostile identification with someone, hidden behind a neurotic conception of Christ.

Identification, then, is an unconscious psychological process which begins rather early in one's life. It is made up of layers, so to speak, some of which are deposited even in very early childhood, and they always bear the earmarks of the impulsiveness of childhood and of *affective,* rather than rational, origin. In other words, the most noxious type of identification, the least rational, takes place in infancy, in a matrix of hostility borne by the child against the very person with whom the identification takes place. Thus the innocent child "inherits" the sins of his parents and bears the evil fruits of these sins. Thus an old scriptural truth turns out to be also a psychological truth which time and again finds its empirical and dynamic corroboration in the light of the most advanced clinical psychology of today.

Unfortunately, the above example, no matter how fleetingly sketched, is but an illustration of what Freud did not do in his approach to religious and moral issues. Instead, he turned

Freud and Religion

his study into an attack. This attack was in the nature of a double negative, one might say. Religion is an illusion, a fantasy, because it is not scientific. If it is unscientific, it is against science, and since we are for science, we are against all the enemies of science and therefore against its greatest enemy—religion. This rather sharp rendition of Freud's attitude borrows its sharpness from the knights in scientific armor, known throughout the history of scientific endeavor and literature. To us, witnesses of the beginning of the second half of the twentieth century, this attitude has been visible since the mid-Victorian period saw the Darwinian revolution shuffle onto the scene with a sedateness and plodding perseverance befitting the spirit of its day. Modern genetics and biology and physics (it is the Helmholtzian physics that was Freud's point of departure into the unchartered seas of the psychology of the unconscious) took up the traditional antireligious attitude which also characterizes the official Marxian attitude.

There is something remarkable about the secular struggles between the scientist, who insists on having all the answers, and the religious person who would turn away from science, or even turn it down wishing to supplant it by purely religious disciplines, offering theological answers in the place where scientific ones are sought. What has always been characteristic of this struggle is the passion, the considerable intolerance, the certain exclusivism which insists that "only our school," "only our system of thought" provides the best and the real answers. What is of particular interest to those living in the beginning of the second half of the twentieth century is that the climate of the argument seems to have changed. The change came imperceptibly, but it is no less thorough or fundamental. It is well exemplified by the words which Pius XII addressed to a group of pilgrim students of the University of Paris on Easter Sunday, 1949:

In your studies and scientific research, rest assured that no contradiction is possible between the certain truths of faith and established scientific facts. Nature, no less than revelation, proceeds from God, and God cannot contradict Himself. Do not be dismayed even if you hear the contrary affirmed insistently, even though research may have to wait for centuries to find the solution of the apparent opposition between science and faith.[23]

The dispassionate certainty and serene security of these words bespeak something more than a mere acknowledgment of the tolerant coexistence of science and theology. They bespeak rather a conviction of the unity of the universe and of the unitary endeavors of man to seek for an explanation, synthesis, and understanding of the mysteries of nature—human, social, material, and spiritual—which have such manifold ways of manifestation before the sensible and intellectual eye of man.

One must acknowledge with considerable regret that science, or scientists on the whole, have failed to achieve that state of equanimity and balanced security about themselves and the believer. Among them the battle seems to rage with all the earmarks of that passionate intensity which cannot easily be passed for objectivity. It would, therefore, be rather unfair to consider Freud, and the extremely competent representation of his views by Jones, as unique among scientists. Rather, they should be considered as expressions of the psycho-philosophical scotomatization characteristic of many, if not the majority, of those who espouse the strictly scientific faith. They depend on a rather refined subjectivity which is offered as objectivity. This objectivity is scientific, but the whole structure of present-day science is not only based, but is insistent upon being based, on the sensory apparatus of man which, next to

[23] *Acta apostolicæ sedis* 45 (1953) p. 277.

our passions, is probably the most faithful servant of our subjectivity.

A most recent expression of this spirit of a great part of modern science is that from the pen of a professor of biology, Dr. Leo Francis Koch, of the University of Illinois.[24] The passionate partisanship of Koch's article does not diminish his skillful competence as a representative of the fraternity to which he belongs, and to which he seems loyal above the demands of duty. Consequently, in discussing vitalism versus mechanism, he not only tries to defend the materialistic philosophy of modern science, but endeavors to offer an extension of the concept *machine* in accordance with the views of Bronowski whom he quotes as follows:

> A machine in science is a concept with definite properties which can be predicted. And we do not mean by this that its behavior is determined in every particular. . . . There is nothing in our concept of a machine to exclude from it a choice by tossing a penny or looking up a table of random numbers, or forecasting the future in a form which says that tomorrow will be fine three times out of ten.[25]

Koch appreciates the fact that "pure determinism" is not always able to stand the test of reality, and yet he would not go along with Heisenberg's suggestions as to indeterminism, and he rises rather energetically against Bergson's *élan vital* or DuNoüy's telefinalisms or Sinnott's telism. In common with many materialists of today, he wishes to create a sort of scientific humanism without telling us much about the sources of the values which the very concept of humanism requires. Koch chooses the following words of Frank to point up his views:

[24] Leo Francis Koch, "Vitalistic-Mechanistic Controversy," *Scientific Monthly* 85, no. 5 (November, 1957) pp. 245–55.
[25] Bronowski, in Koch, *ibid.,* p. 253.

"The most successful scientific investigation has generally involved treating phenomena as if they were purely materialistic, and rejecting any metaphysical hypothesis as long as a physical hypothesis seems possible. The method works."[26]

To the above Koch is prompted to add the following comment:

But to be realistic, the method to which Frank refers is most effective with inanimate matter, less effective with living matter, and least effective when treating events in which human purposes and motivation are of primary concern. So it is that further improvisation is necessary in applying that method to biological and social problems. Such improvisation must be based on inspiration and ingenuity.[27]

It will be noticed the word "ingenuity" reflects only partly a scientific attitude, while the word "inspiration" is definitely unscientific. As if to make clearer the unclarity, Koch here quotes as an example of such ingenuity and inspiration the above-cited words of Bronowski on his concept of a machine in science.

We can now return to Freud, who as Jones reminds us "was simply an unbeliever." Freud claimed that psychoanalysis is a science—which it isn't quite, but rather a uniquely profound and rich body of knowledge empirically arrived at by way of extraordinary intuitive work. After making the claim that psychoanalysis is a science, Freud states:

Religion is an attempt to get control over the sensory world, in which we are placed, by means of the wish-world, which we developed within as a result of biological and psychological neces-

[26] Frank, in Koch, *ibid.*
[27] *Ibid.*

sities. But it cannot achieve its end [as defined by Freud]. Its doctrines carry with them the stamp of the times in which they originated, the ignorant childhood days of the human race. Its consolations deserve no trust. Experience teaches us that the world is not a nursery. The ethical commands, to which religion seeks to lend its weight, require some other foundation instead, since human society cannot do without them, and it is dangerous to link up obedience to them with religious belief.[28]

This statement is followed by the well-known suggestion that there is a parallel between religion and neurosis. This position of Freud, as is easily seen, is an antireligious one not because religion is wrong in itself, but because it seems to him wrong insofar as it seems an unstable foundation for ethics. There is another reason, which is common among many materialistically oriented scholars. Opposition to religion appeared to Freud a necessity because religion, he believed, is opposed to science. This is indeed a vicious circle which almost strangles the most astute scientific minds. It is worth noting for further reference that this vicious circle seems to be made up, psychologically speaking, of two halves: One of them is a hostility against religion (as if to say: "We can get along without you"); the other might be called in psychological jargon a "defense" against religion, as if the strictly scientific, materialistic mind must always defend science because allegedly it is always being attacked by religion. To the psychologically initiated such a drive to defend one's own position is more a sign of insecurity than serene conviction. Only the man who is anxious and insecure finds it necessary to assure himself and others time and again of the validity of his position.

Freud did not prove an exception to this manner of thinking. To Freud, the believer fights to defend religion's losing battle "inch by inch, as if with a series of pitiable rearguard

[28] Jones, *op. cit.* 3, p. 359.

actions."²⁹ He even goes a bit too far in his own admission by saying: "At such cost—by the forcible imposition of mental infantilism and inducing a mass delusion—religion succeeds in saving many people from individual neuroses. But little more. . . . Nor can religion keep her promises either."³⁰ The argument in favor of a purely scientific world-view is cast in the characteristic defensive vein:

> An attempt has been made to discredit radically scientific endeavor on the ground that, bound as it is to the conditions of our own organization, it can yield nothing but subjective results, while the real nature of things outside us remains inaccessible to us. But this is to disregard several factors of decisive importance for the understanding of scientific work. Firstly, our organization, i.e., our mental apparatus, has been developed actually in the attempt to explore the outer world, and therefore it must have realized in its structure a certain measure of appropriateness; secondly, it itself is a constituent part of that world which we are to investigate, and which readily admits of such investigation; thirdly, the task of science is fully circumscribed if we confine it to showing how the world must appear to us in consequence of the particular character of our organization; fourthly, the ultimate findings of science, just because of the way in which they are attained, are conditioned not only by our organization but also by that which has affected this organization; and, finally, the problem of the *nature of the world irrespective of our perceptive apparatus is an empty abstraction without practical interest.*

No, science is no illusion. But it would be an illusion to suppose that we could get anywhere else what it cannot give us.³¹

In the long run nothing can withstand reason and experience,

²⁹ *Ibid.*
³⁰ *Ibid.*
³¹ *Ibid.* 3, p. 358; italics added.

and the contradiction religion offers to both is only too palpable.[32]

It must again be pointed out that in these pages we have limited ourselves almost entirely to using those lines from Freud's writings which were chosen by Jones himself; for only by doing this could one be reasonably assured that personal religious bias would not interfere with the choice of quotation. Freud's attitude toward religion could be studied from many an angle, and the many writings of Freud present a rich and very revealing source of insight into the multiplicity of Freud's hypotheses as well as the perseverance with which he both pursued and was pursued by religious problems. Rewarding as such studies would be, it is our belief that the summary of Freud's writings on the subject as it was made by Jones is the most authoritative and the most competent that has come heretofore from the pen of an experienced and in some respects very typical Freudian psychoanalyst. This being the case, it becomes doubly interesting and noteworthy to find whatever inner or outer contradictions are to be found in Freud's attitude toward religion in the very words and statements culled out from authentic sources by this cultivated psychoanalyst who has been steeped in psychoanalysis for almost half a century, i.e., almost since the very inception of psychoanalysis.

Thus we come across such trenchant and at times contradictory statements of Freud. "Psychoanalysis has . . . . . taught us that the personal God is *psychologically* nothing other than a magnified father,"[33] and: "An illusion is not the same as an error, it is indeed not necessarily an error. . . . We call a belief an illusion when wish-fulfillment is a prominent

[32] *Ibid.* 3, p. 357.
[33] *Ibid.* 3, p. 354; italicized by Jones.

factor in its motivation."[34] By motivation Freud means unconscious motivation, i.e., affective, emotional trends which dictate the formation of the illusion under consideration. Jones recalls in this connection a book by H. B. Acton, *The Illusion of the Epoch*, published in Toronto in 1955. Jones was impressed by Acton's reference to Ludwig Feuerbach, who fifteen years before Freud was born suggested that in psychopathological states and in the psychology of savages there often appears many a phenomenon that could serve to explain the normal life of man. Jones refers to Acton's reminding us of Feuerbach's statement to the effect that "Religion is the dream of walking consciousness; dreaming is the key to the mysteries of religion."[35]

It is rather doubtful, after what has been expounded, whether it is possible to rid oneself of the suspicion that, after all, it is not certain whether Freud and those who followed him in his thoughts on religion knew clearly what it was that he meant by religion, whether by religion Freud understood the same thing as do the believers in God. One will seek in vain any reference made by Freud to the many true believers like St. Ignatius of Loyola, or St. Francis de Sales, or St. John of the Cross. It seems that Freud, the bold but very careful student, studied little, or gave evidence of having studied little, of the writings and the psychology of the great men of the Church, or of the prophets, or of the Psalmist for that matter. The question, ludicrous though it may sound at this juncture, arises: What did Freud mean by religion? Answers Freud: "In my *Future of an Illusion* I was concerned much less with the deepest sources of religious feelings than with what the ordinary man understands by his religion."[36] To this Jones remarks:

[34] *Ibid.* 3, p. 356.
[35] *Ibid.* 3, p. 360.
[36] *Ibid.* 3, p. 358.

"He [Freud] added later that this is the only religion that ought to bear the name."[37]

This much is clear now. It would appear that the religion Freud had in mind was not really religion but the somewhat sentimental, somewhat anxious attitude toward God on the part of the man in the street. It is the anxious, cowering belief of the little man, who feels the burden of what Freud calls "the forcible imposition of mental infantilism." How it is that in our modern world religion seems to possess the power of forcible imposition, Freud never explains, unless he has in mind the Church's "forcibly" exploiting the frightened insignificance of the ordinary man. Even if we follow Freud's trend literally, we still will be unable to see clearly whether it is the Church that forcibly imposes upon the ordinary innocent man a primeval fear of the father, or whether this fear is merely utilized for a special idealization of the father image and consequent subjection of the ordinary man to the infantilism which stands ever ready to sweep over him from within. These and many other pertinent questions regarding faith in God and the tendency to conceive of God as having an anthropomorphic existence are not touched by Freud. Despite his incisiveness, it seems that Freud remained unclear as to what real religion is.

It is rather important to note that Freud did not come forward with any discussion of any of the Eastern religions. Again, it is rather difficult to understand why Freud limited himself to pointing out only the belief in a personal God and the ritualistic aspects of religion; the latter Freud considered a sign of the degeneration of true religion, which he seems to narrow down to some vague concept of justice and ethics and truth. The inner content of this justice and truth Freud does not describe—but he does seem to associate it with mono-

[37] *Ibid.*

theism, which came through Moses from the Egypt of Akhenaten, who most poignantly introduced monotheism to the world. In other words, whatever external meaning Freud chose to give the term "religion," he actually had in mind the Hebrew, Mosaic tradition and subsequent Christianity. Whatever Freud's conscious intent, it is the Judeo-Christian tradition that he seems to have in mind, for he talks really of no other. It is this religious thrust that came from the Jews through Moses and Christ that had for Freud a special fascination; he seemed not to be able to abandon the topic from almost the very beginning of his career as a psychoanalyst to almost the very end. Characteristically, when old and sick, already in London and ready to close his eyes on this world which had given him so much fame and so much pain, mental and physical, Freud was very eager to see the English translation of his *Moses* before he died. His wish was fulfilled.

What did Freud "do" with Moses? It will be recalled that Freud at first spoke of the *psychological* truth underlying the illusion called religious faith. This obviously was not sufficient for Freud, who, having once discovered the meaning of psychological reality, quite naturally had to come to the concomitant conclusion that that which might be psychologically real to a given person might possess no true reality whatsoever. If only the psychological truth which Freud saw in religion could be proven to rest on demonstrable historical truth, then Freud could have found himself in possession of what might be called tangible truth and thus confirmed historically his belief in religious disbelief and his profound though (as may be seen presently) somewhat unsteady faith in lack of faith.

For a period of over two decades, the idea germinated in Freud's meditations on the subject that just as man in his prehistory rose to the level of societal unity by way of parricide and through totemism, so did the religion of the Jews go through the same phase of parricide. Moses, Freud thought,

Freud and Religion

was not a Jew; he was an Egyptian priest who gave the Jews their monotheistic religion, and later on Moses was murdered by the Jews. Freud, in making the hypothesis that Moses was murdered, at once felt that (1) the very existence of Moses, an Egyptian priest who did not even speak Hebrew, lent *historical* basis to the religion of the Hebrews, and (2) the actual murder of Moses lent historical basis to Freud's theory of parricide and its role in the formation or glorification of God the Father.

Why should it be the father, and the father alone, that Freud saw so sublimely idealized? It has been difficult, if not impossible, to find even an approximation of a satisfactory answer to this question. The whole body of Freud's writing was patently androcentric, and the central man in Freud's system of thought remained always the father. There were among Freud's disciples some who tried to find a significant place for the mother of man in Freud's system of thought, but these attempts failed unless some radical turning away from the Freudian system took place. Such "splits" and "schisms" proved rather unsuccessful, because one cannot successfully fill a lacuna merely by rejecting a whole system and thus creating a new and more destructive lacuna. Be that as it may, it does seem that in *Moses* Freud attained the completion of a deeply seated and greatly cherished idea that demanded expression in some sort of rational order; it does appear that he rounded out, so to speak, into one system of thought the origin of neuroses in man as an individual and the origin of the belief in God in man as a race. The hypothesis of parricide seemed to be *the* missing link, and to Freud the clue to understanding man's yearning for a knowledge of God.

There is no doubt that Freud found this solution of his as to the psychological origin of religion a satisfactory one for himself, and there is also no doubt that Freud really offered no solution even by way of hypothesis. What he offers is a certain parallelism which seemed to satisfy his curiosity. Yet one doubts whether in this satisfaction Freud behaved like the natural scientist he considered himself to be. One is tempted to wonder whether Freud, in his odyssey about religion, did not actually live out one of his own deepest problems as a Jew and as a seeker of a faith which had preoccupied him from childhood on.

It will not do, of course, to label him, as Jones does, "a natural unbeliever... needing no explanation"; this certainly would not meet Freud's own standards for the understanding of a given person and of the ideas which had become such an integral part of him.

The time has not yet come for a thorough and definitive psychological evaluation of Freud as a personality and as an historico-sociological phenomenon. The passions that clustered around his name alone are still running high and, regardless of their best individual intentions and wills, the psychoanalytic groupings are still too prone to defend this or that aspect of Freudian tenets against attack from without. It is impossible to proceed with the necessary calm and to study Freud as he was rather than as he appears to be, or might have been, or ought to have been. Even the whole body of Freud's writings, and his correspondence with Fliess, and the volumes by Jones do not seem sufficient for a fully adequate assessment of the phenomenon known under the name Freud. The devoted group of his intimate followers, who spent so much energy and time and ingenuity in offering us what they finally have put at the disposal of the reading world, admittedly have kept back some letters, some data, some details which concerned the man and the people around him. We still lack the complete evidence of his unique capacity for learning and teaching, and also (just one of the peculiarities of Freud) his unique capacity for keeping himself throughout his life alone, seemingly without contact with or relationship

Freud and Religion

to the totality of scientific and philosophic thought in which he had grown up, a totality which he succeeded in keeping out of the visible foreground or background of his scientific and quasi-philosophical thinking.

It is difficult to forget, just as it is difficult fully to understand, a remark made to me by an intimate and ever loyal disciple of Freud, who said: "Freud had a remarkable capacity for forgetting some sources of his ideas." A reader unkindly disposed might interpret the above as a thrust at Freud's intellectual integrity. This would not be justified under any circumstances. Freud was a challengingly, provocatively, scrupulously honest intellect; but his apparent need to stand alone, his need to rid himself of any suspicion of intellectual dependence on others or spiritual dependence on a personal God, seems to have driven him frequently into a rigid, almost solipsistic intellectual attitude. This attitude must be understood in Freud, if we are to understand the many contradictions in his personality and thought, particularly as they touch problems of morals and religion, life and death.

One may say without any risk of exaggeration that Freud's preoccupation with the theme of death was real and lasted throughout his life. *Mutatis mutandis* one might accept Jones' remark to the effect that "Freud always had a double attitude or fantasy about death, which one may well interpret as dread of a terrible father alternating with desire for reunion with a loved mother." How far one's fantasies may carry one away from reality, one may judge from the fact that Freud's father was anything but terrible; and as to the reunion with a loved mother, Freud was always devoted to his mother, and lived in conscious dread lest she might survive him and suffer the pain of the loss of her son. (Freud was almost seventy-five years old when she died at the age of ninety-six.) Freud was also afraid, for the same stated reason, that his father might outlive him.

Freud suffered from death anxiety throughout his life. He

fainted once in Munich in 1912 (age 56), and as he was coming out of the faint he was heard exclaiming: "How sweet it must be to die." He was in the habit (even when young) of taking leave of friends by saying: "Goodbye, you may never see me again." Jones tells us that Freud said once that he thought of death every day of his life. Freud "more than once ascribed it [his attitude toward death] to the lasting influence of his death wishes in infancy."[38]

It is curious how Freud struggled between fear of and desire for death, desire for and fear of immortality—which all appeared quite often in a characteristically disguised and elaborated form. Early in his life, before he married, he once told his fiancée that he had destroyed all the letters he had received, and added with an ironic, triumphant anticipation that his future biographers would be hard put to find data about him after he had gone from this earth. Freud thus anticipated his lasting fame, to him a form of immortality which he himself created, and which he tried to obliterate by putting his future biographers in a very difficult, if not impossible, situation, presenting them with nothing instead of living documents of the past. One should not expect a consistency in such attitudes, for they are charged with many mutually contradictory emotions—a severe ambivalence, even multivalence, one might say. Thus, when Princess Marie Bonaparte, a devoted friend, loyal follower, and almost unquestioning disciple, came into possession of the letters which Freud wrote to Fliess at the close of the nineteenth century over a period of some fifteen years, Freud expressed regrets that he had not got hold of those letters first, because, he said with an irony bordering on bitterness, he would have destroyed them rather than let "so-called posterity" have them.

This "so-called posterity" is very telling. There is no doubt in anyone's mind, friend or foe of Freud, that Freud was an

[38] *Ibid.* 3, p. 279.

Freud and Religion

ambitious and intensely sensitive person. He hoped for world fame from the very outset of his career. He wanted greatness and recognition, and he hoped for a permanent place (immortality) in the history of human thought. At the same time he would prefer to die into nothingness without becoming the possession of a "so-called posterity." It is this antithetical attitude of Freud, this trend toward formulating polarities, this manner of becoming more dialectical than dialectics itself, that apparently led Freud to postulate the existence of a death-instinct which is supposed to coexist with the instinct of self-preservation. He even hinted that aggressiveness might be viewed as the death-instinct turned outward, instead of the death drives being the aggressive instincts turned inward. However, Freud himself was willing (even though he said it only indirectly) to consider the postulate of the death-instinct a theoretical viewpoint which orthodox psychoanalysts might or might not accept without injuring the theory and practice of psychoanalytic orthodoxy in any way.

The same, of course, must be said (Freud, I believe, would not object to this) about his views on religion. While it is true that a great number, if not the majority, of Freudian psychoanalysts look upon atheism as an earmark of scientific superiority, and upon religious worship as an atavism left over from primitive magic and animism, many of them recognize, even though not too pronouncedly, that being religious and practicing a religion does not exclude one from also practicing well the psychoanalytic profession.

It seems to become more and more clear that the problems of death, immortality, and religious faith (and each of them may have its own distinct psychology) are free problems, so to speak, and are for every individual to solve by and for himself, and that the Freudian views on these issues are not obligatory for psychoanalysts. The corpus of psychoanalytic knowledge does not require the obligatory inclusion of Freud's views on religion and ancillary matters. These are personal views of Freud, perhaps deeply personal, and bound up with his own intimate emotional life. And it is in the light of this emotional life, of which heretofore we have been vouchsafed only momentary glimpses and desultory lights, that it will become ultimately possible to understand the psychogenesis as well as the full emotional tone of Freud's views.

Whatever little we know about Freud thus far, this much seems clear: Freud stood in great admiration and awe before the image of Moses. If only Moses could be made fully human and *historical* and a foreigner, i.e., not a Jew, but an Egyptian who converted the Jews, then the full significance of Moses in the religion of the Jew would become more in harmony with Freud's personal, conscious, and unconscious attitude toward the Hebraic, Mosaic, and Christian tradition. That in some way, even though not explicitly so, Freud was preoccupied with the problem, is clear from the fact that he sees in Moses only one half, so to speak, of the dialectic pair which he always envisaged in every problem. Freud apparently was a great admirer of monotheism, particularly in its Mosaic version. He thought that the Jews would scarcely have survived without the Mosaic religion, which was, strictly speaking, a victory over the older tradition of the worship of Yahweh. But Moses was murdered in the wilderness. In some way the Jews fell away from "the pure conception" of Moses, and another man had to come to save the chosen people.

It is at this point that Freud begins to appear to us unclear. Why and how Moses was killed is never explained, but it is clear that Freud considers this murder one of the greatest falls in the history of the Jews. Things became empty, formalistic, lifeless; they degenerated into the formalities of ceremonies. It is at this point that Freud turns to St. Paul. It will be recalled that Freud always viewed St. Paul in a perspective of greatness and creative power. It was to St. Paul that he turned when he

Freud and Religion

tried to offer a clearer definition of his concept of libido, or Eros.

It is in St. Paul that Freud finds the Jew who created Christian theology. St. Paul accepted Jesus as the Messias, after Jesus, "whose ethical precepts surpassed even the heights attained by former prophets, had in turn been murdered."[39] It is curious that Freud, considering the references to original sin, says: "The unmentionable crime was replaced by the fault of the somewhat shadowy conception of original sin."[40] He seems to be so intent on stressing the murder of Moses and the murder of Jesus that he appears to overlook in the idea of original sin the sexual aspect of the fall of man. Freud does seem to overlook here the sexual component—one of the most conspicuous and distinctive elements of his own system. Says Freud further: "A Son of God, innocent himself, had sacrificed himself—and had thereby taken over the guilt of the world. It had to be a Son, since the sin had been the murder of the Father. . . . The Mosaic religion had been a Father religion; Christianity became a Son religion. The old God, the Father, took second place; Christ, the Son, stood in his place, just as in those dark times every son had longed to do. . . . From now on Jewish religion was, so to speak, a fossil."[41]

Even the casual reader of the above would not fail to notice that Freud saw a natural continuity, a spiritual unity, in the religious road from Moses through the prophets to Christ. Apparently he not only was impressed with this unity but saw in St. Paul the central spiritual power that lighted the road. Yet Freud was satisfied merely with a general interpretation—partly psychological and partly sociological. In all this he saw but an objective passing in review of great events under the sign of the murder of the Father and the rise of the Son, who

[39] *Ibid.* 3, p. 365.
[40] *Ibid.*
[41] *Ibid.*

too was then murdered. He saw, to be sure, that the new "Son religion" was also a religion of brotherhood, but it does seem singular that Freud did not go beyond the triumph of the Son. Brotherhood, mutual love, the love of one's enemy—all this Freud, the carrier of the banner of Eros which he accepted from St. Paul's Caritas, left aside. He even remarked somewhere with considerable emphasis that "love thy enemy as thyself" is untenable, since one ought to love only those who deserve one's love. Here again Freud leans on the naturalistic view of man's being closer to animal than to the image of God, whom Freud sees no reason to recognize, still less to accept.

We may note here parenthetically that most of the writings on the subject of religion by psychoanalysts other than Freud are merely variations on the same theme, but with less spiritual power, even though at times with considerable thrust. At times they sacrifice some of the things which Freud himself seems to have stood for. Thus, the most recent contribution from the pen of a psychoanalyst deals with St. Paul in an article entitled "Eros, Saul of Tarsus and Freud."[42] Forgetting apparently that Freud was openly inclined to accept St. Paul's Caritas, and overlooking the true meaning of Freud's Eros, the author of the article is emphatic about St. Paul's "disastrous" (*funeste*) influence on our Christian civilization because of his strict views on marriage, because of his asceticism, and because of his misogyny. The curious thing about it all is that the aspects of love in the teaching of Christianity are left out of consideration. What is presented is St. Paul's antihedonism and his ascetic turning away from narcissistic carnality, from the pleasure principle beyond which Freud himself tried to reach.

From the above example alone it would not be difficult to see that using the apparent parallelism of psychological

[42] Marie Bonaparte, "Eros, Saül de Tarse et Freud," *Revue française de psychanalyse* 21, no. 1 (Jan.–Feb., 1957) pp. 23–34.

mechanism, and confusing hedonism and love (actual confusion even if not actually stated), are poor methods for the adequate study of the inner aspects of life, particularly that of religious faith. These unreliable methods have proved insufficient and confusing. On the other hand, as an expression of Freud's own struggle within himself, the whole mode of Freud's thinking, and the manner of his presenting the problem of religion, is very revealing indeed—particularly in its manner of expressing itself in polarities.

Toward the latter part of his life Freud was wont to emphasize his Jewishness a little more definitely and more often than during the early years of his career. There was an overtone of pride in Freud's emphasis that St. Paul was a Jew and the founder of Christian theology. Yet, as has been noted, although this was not often or openly discussed, Freud "had" to "make" Moses an Egyptian, "had" to kill him—to set him aside, so to speak.

At the time *Moses and Monotheism* first appeared, there were scholarly, even though somewhat tolerant, voices who accused Freud of many things. T. W. Rosmarin considered Freud's effort impudent.[43] On the other hand, Abraham Shalom Yahuda published in Hebrew a review which was a refutation of Freud's views on Moses, and he concluded his review by saying: "It seems to me that in these words we hear the voice of one of the most fanatical Christians in his hatred of Israel and not the voice of a Freud who hated and despised such fanaticism with all his heart and strength."[44] The words of Reb Abraham Shalom Yahuda sound a bit strong; yet there seems to be a kernel of truth in what that Hebrew scholar says. He apparently sensed the fundamental, albeit unconscious, ambivalence which Freud showed in relation to the Hebraic tradition. That ambivalence, like everything that is

[43] Jones, *op. cit.* 3, p. 369.
[44] *Ibid.* 3, p. 370.

deeply repressed, manifests itself so obliquely and so much under the cover of rationality that one would be hard put to demonstrate it with accuracy, without making a totally new study of all Freud's writings from this particular point of view.

Yahuda, who visited Freud in 1938, told him about the work of the Hebrew and Arabic scholar, Ernst Sellin, who at one time was inclined to agree with Freud's hypothesis and who thought that some of the passages in Hosea (Osee) might suggest that Moses was actually murdered. Yahuda told Freud that Sellin later on recanted, and Freud riposted with a shrug of his shoulders: "It might be true all the same."[45] If we recall Freud's own original hesitancy about publishing his *Moses,* his confession that he was not certain of his facts, that originally he referred to his *Moses* as a historical novel—the impression will be confirmed that it was more emotion than scientific endeavor that determined Freud's hesitations and doubts and moments of anxiety ever since he was confronted with Michelangelo's Moses, which fascinated and seemingly worried him. Freud used to sit for hours at the right end of the railing of the altar of San Pietro in Vincoli in Rome, facing the right wall against which was the Moses. All this occurred almost twenty years before the arrival of Hitler. It seems, therefore, that Freud's preoccupation antedated the revival of interest in the fate of the Jews which Hitler's atrocities reawakened.

With regard to Moses, as with regard to many other things close to his heart, Freud seems to have been in a state of searching and painful conflict in which the positivist scholar (conscious) and the potential believer (unconscious) fought an open battle. Be it noticed that Freud with all his antireligious positivism *was* inclined to be superstitious in many respects. Jones, in speaking of this aspect of Freud's personality, does

[45] *Ibid.* 3, p. 373.

not hesitate to say "acceptance and rejection are both operative" in many of us with regard to many superstitions, and Freud was no exception in this respect.[46] Witness the tendency to believe in some sort of thought transference, his attaching some esoteric meaning to certain figures like 17, or 61, or 62, which latter denoted to him the age at which he was to die. Once while discussing various phenomena commonly called "psychic," Jones made the remark: "If one could believe in mental processes floating in the air, one could go on to a belief in angels." Freud closed the discussion at this point (about three in the morning!) with the remark: "Quite so, even *der liebe Gott.*"[47] Jones goes on to say that the words of Freud were said in a jocular, a slightly quizzical tone. "But," adds Jones, "there was something searching also in the glance, and I went away not entirely happy lest there be some more serious undertone as well."[48] Says Jones a little further:

In his correspondence there are many current allusions to the mysterious numbers [he learned from Fliess]. If he tells Ferenczi that an attack of migraine came on 23 plus 2 days after his birthday, or reproaches Jung that he has had no letter from him even 28-3 days from the last, we are bound to conclude that such pointless remarks, half-jocular as they doubtless were, indicated some lingering belief in the significance of such numbers.[49]

Freud was fascinated for a time by the so-called "media." He was not inclined to be skeptical about telepathy. He did state that even among educated people, who as children at least believed in the return of the spirits, one finds not infrequently a tendency to believe in that which one rationally

[46] *Ibid.* 3, p. 379.
[47] *Ibid.* 3. p. 381.
[48] *Ibid.*
[49] *Ibid.* 3, p. 383.

disbelieves. Freud relates then one of his own experiences; he met a sister of a former patient who had died some time before. This sister bore a resemblance to her dead brother, and a thought, quite spontaneously, passed through Freud's head: "So after all, it is true that the dead may return."[50] Even though Freud related that this thought was followed at once by a sense of shame, the fact remains undeniable that there was a strong emotional "streak" in Freud which bordered now on superstition, then on belief in the physical immortality of man here on earth.

It becomes also clear that Freud fought deliberately against certain spiritual trends within himself. These trends tried to assert themselves by way of the well-known mechanism of distortion and secondary elaboration, described by Freud as characteristic of the unconscious and dreams. The trend took the form of anxious little superstitions, of involuntary and unreasonable beliefs in what the common jargon calls spiritism.

The foregoing sketchy outline of some of Freud's "automatisms" in the direction of superstition, or telepathy, or spiritism, or parapsychology (as the more modern usage calls certain aspects of human naïveté which are woven out of a too simple materialism or even a more simple materialized spiritualism)—this outline ought not to be considered as a reproach of any kind. There is nothing in these propensities of Freud that diminishes his greatness. Their presence only emphasizes the tremendous will power Freud had to exert all his life in order to remain balanced on the tightrope of scientific materialism strung over the whole field of the psychological functioning of man.

In addition to having to accomplish this Herculean task of remaining in constant scientific balance, Freud endeavored to accomplish yet another thing. He seems to have been

[50] *Ibid.*

Freud and Religion

inspired with the need to get religion out of his way—perhaps it disturbed or embarrassed him a little. But in order to "abolish" religion, Freud did not first set himself to grasp the full meaning of religion through the ages. Instead, he somewhat cut religion to a size chosen by himself. As pointed out earlier, he reduced religion to the concept of the man in the street. Such a reduction, if applied to science, would make science come off as an art of making mechanical toys or cutting out paper dolls, or as a diabolic vision of gigantic derricks and bulldozers. The man in the street would hardly have a real comprehension or even a feeling of what science truly is. The man in the street is pragmatic, utilitarian, direct, and equal unto his daily prosaic needs; his religion, too, inevitably shows the weaknesses of his platitudinous psychology of literalness. To make him the measure of religion means to create an artifact which one chooses to call religion for the sake of the argument.

And Freud did have an argument to offer. Time and again, when speaking of religion, Freud points out that he measures it by its ceremonials (he does not specify which), and by the fact that it offers an illusory immortality to the credulous man in the street who, like a child, believes in it all. Freud seems to be almost bitter about what he calls the ceremonials of religion. By means of very vivid and almost inspiring descriptions of the murder of the father, the murder of Moses, the murder of Christ, Freud leaves for himself a humanity not redeemed but laden with external guilt of murder, whose wages are irrevocable, absolute death—nothingness.

Yet, every now and then Freud would rise to sublime heights of inspiration. Thus, he seems inspired when he speaks of St. Paul, and he seems inspired when he describes the ties which keep a group together. He pointed out that the Christian community is tied into a unit not only by the devotion of each of its members to the Father or Father Image, the leader, but also by the identification of each of its members with Christ. The members are thus admonished to remain faithful not only by loving Christ and not only because of the love Christ bestows upon them, but by loving one another even as Christ does. The uniqueness of this series of ties based on love, in which the "moral masochism" which Freud saw in the Hebraic community just before the advent of Christ appears absent, does not seem to have escaped Freud, but he appears to have passed over it without further ado.

It does seem singular that the aspect of love-Caritas-Agape, which was often the leitmotiv of Freud's ideal man and ideal community, was glossed over by Freud without any comment. This aspect was beyond Freud's model of the pedestrian religion of the man in the street. More than that, I believe that religion in which the theme of death, while ever present, is anything but a mark of finality seems to have left a vacuum in Freud's meditations. He seemed to need the theme of death before him in all its starkness. Jones has a terse and excellent few lines regarding this theme:

> He [Freud] had been increasingly looking forward to the promised date of his own death in February, 1918, with mingled feelings of dread and longing. Furthermore, we should not forget that the theme of death, the dread of it and the wish for it, had always been a continual preoccupation of Freud's mind as far back as we know anything about it. We can even trace the beginning of it all to the sinful destruction of his little brother in his earliest infancy.[51]

Thus, the theme of death again is closely related to this psychological murder of the little brother by the infant Freud in the small town of Freiberg around 1857. Jones is inclined

[51] *Ibid.* 3, p. 42. Cf. also *ibid.* 2, p. 196, regarding the prediction of Freud's death.

Freud and Religion

to stress Freud's sense of isolation deriving from being Jewish in a small town predominantly Catholic. This appears somewhat doubtful because, after all, where a racial minority is really small, the prejudices against it are not apt to be very strong. Freiberg was a town of five thousand inhabitants, of which about one hundred were Protestants and as many were Jews; the remainder were Roman Catholics. Freud had his devout Catholic nurse who seems to have served as a bridge between the synagogue and the five churches of Freiberg, among which the 200-foot-high steeple of the Church of St. Mary stood out.

The little Freud was attached to his nurse and spoke her Slavic language. "More important," writes Jones, "she was a Catholic and used to take the young boy to attend the church services. She implanted in him the ideas of Heaven and Hell, and probably also those of salvation and resurrection. After returning from church the boy used to preach a sermon at home and expound God's doings."[52] Jones would wish us to believe that the chimes of the Catholic churches rang out not brotherly love (to the ears of the little Freud) but hostility to the little circle of nonbelievers. "Perhaps there was an echo of these chimes in that night long after when his [Freud's] sleep was disturbed by church bells so that, to put an end to the annoyance, he dreamed that the Pope was dead."[53] It is difficult, of course, to say what the deeper motivations were of that dream in which the pope was dead, but one at once suspects that we deal here with a more deep-seated hostility than at first appears. This is how Freud reported the dream:

In another dream I similarly succeeded in warding off a threatened interruption of my sleep which came this time from a sensory stimulus. In this case it was only by chance, however,

[52] *Ibid.* 1, p. 6.
[53] *Ibid.* 1, p. 12.

that I was able to discover the link between the dream and its accidental stimulus and thus to understand the dream. One morning at the height of summer, while I was staying at a mountain resort in the Tyrol, I woke up knowing I had had a dream that *the Pope was dead.* I failed to interpret this dream—a non-visual one—and only remembered as part of its basis that I had read in a newspaper a short time before that His Holiness was suffering from a slight indisposition. In the course of the morning, however, my wife asked me if I had heard the frightful noise made by the pealing of bells that morning. I had been quite unaware of them, but I now understood my dream. It had been a reaction on the part of my need for sleep to the noise with which the pious Tyrolese had been trying to wake me. I had taken my revenge on them by drawing the inference which formed the content of the dream, and I had then continued my sleep without paying any more attention to the noise.[54]

The dream just cited appears in the chapter entitled "Material and Sources of Dreams," under the subheading "Somatic Sources." The interpretation as given by Freud seems to point out a special aspect of the psychic economy of dreams—namely, that the function of dreams is the preservation of sleep and that this particular dream may have got its stimulus from somatic sources, in this case the church bells. While there is no reason to doubt Freud's candor and correctness of interpretation, some questions do arise in this connection which Freud's interpretation as given does not seem fully to answer.

First, it was Freud's wife who asked him whether he had heard "the frightful noise" of the church bells. Freud himself was not aware that the bells were ringing. Nor does he tell us that he recalled hearing the bells after his wife asked

[54] Sigmund Freud, *The Interpretation of Dreams (First Part),* in *Complete Psychological Works,* tr. James Strachey (London, 1953) 4, p. 232.

Freud and Religion

him the question. The assumption at hand is that Freud was right, but the phenomenon of overdetermination in psychic functioning that Freud himself discovered permits us to go one or two steps further. Why the pope? This could be answered simply and in accordance with Freud's own principles of the interpretation of dreams. He had read in the newspapers a short time before about the pope's illness. Thus the subject theme of the dream (the pope) could be considered a remnant of some impression of the previous day (*Tagrest*) which had woven itself into the dream. The last question: why should the death of the pope make the pealing of the bells become innocuous? There might as well have been a dream, "the pope recovered." Hence, it is nothing important, let them ring and one may go on sleeping. Freud gives us a clue in his "I had taken my revenge"—an obvious and rather direct acknowledgment of hostility.

One might arrive at the same conclusion if one thinks of Freud's dream a little more simply. "The pope is dead" is a simple wish-fulfillment dream. Freud had read about the pope's illness. This touched upon his usually sensitive spot of hostility—the Roman Catholic Church. This hostility then expressed itself in the characteristic manner, i.e., directly. Children, Freud pointed out, usually have dreams in which the unconscious wish is fulfilled in the dream without any disguise. Freud's experience in dealing with dreams was unsurpassed, and therefore he might as well dream a "direct" dream. It does not require any effort to assume that the simple dream, "The pope died," was a direct expression of a wish— an expression which, by the way, was not a plastic image as characteristic of most dreams, especially those of children, but a thought without images, a sort of apperception that became conscious in Freud's sleep.

Freud reported this dream about 1913 and again, more fully, in 1914, and again in 1916. It would not be surprising if some day we discovered that Freud had this dream some time during the last illness of St. Pius X and the election to the papal throne of Benedict XV. The fact that Freud in reporting the dream refers to the pope as His Holiness is rather revealing. This more or less ecclesiastical and diplomatically correct reference to the pope was not entirely in harmony with Freud's usually rather reserved and somewhat cold, forbidding tone and manner when he referred to religion and Church matters. Perhaps this "His Holiness" may be looked upon even as an overcompensatory deference on the part of the critical Freud, who particularly at that moment was beset with an unconscious death wish against the Holy Father.

Where did it come from, this carping hostility against the Church and against religion in general? It is obviously a caricature which Freud created in order to demolish it with greater ease by fitting it into the mold of the murder of the primeval Father, the murder of God, and the murder of the Son of God, a murder which was transformed by the anguished and credulous murderers into an illusory, nonexistent resurrection from the dead and immortality.

As has been hinted at several times, it is doubtful whether a complete and incontrovertible answer can be given at this stage of our knowledge of Freud's personal life. But the little we have been vouchsafed to learn does permit us to formulate a plausible psychological reconstruction.

Heavy was the heart of the little Freud when his wish that his little brother die was fulfilled. For the rest of his life he felt guilty, for the rest of his life he felt he deserved to die, and so he wished death to come and dreaded its possible approach throughout his life. How afraid he was of the Day of Judgment one sees in the fact that it is the theme of the Day of Judgment that Freud missed entirely when he recalled the great impression Signorelli's frescoes in the Duomo of Orvieto had made upon him.

To rid himself of his guilt in relation to the much-yearned-for death of his little brother, little Freud and later the adult, grown-up, and old Freud (in the "unconscious" of his psychic apparatus) wished perhaps that the day of the rising of the dead would come and his brother would return. But would not that resurrection reawaken again that murderous hostility which started him onto the path of dread of death, of the Judgment Day? Perhaps, too, the sudden disappearance of his nurse was in itself a shattering betrayal of his hopes and a constant reminder (to Freud) that there is no resurrection, that death is death, a nothingness, a betrayal by fate of the very greatness and hope of man on this earth.

Perhaps it is this sense of the betrayal of hopes and promises that made Freud so bitter about religion, as if it were (to use his, Freud's, own terms) a forcible imposition on the infantile credulity of man. Did not Freud as a child believe in his nurse, only to be disappointed and to find his faith shattered into the dust of eternal disappearance?

As far as Freud is concerned, psychological as well as historical reality point to the early fascination which religion had for him and to the bitter disappointment a simple Slovak woman caused him by not fulfilling her promise of protection and resurrection. Perhaps it was that simple Slovak peasant woman who later became Freud's "ordinary man," whose religion he treated with contemptuous bitterness and haughty disregard.

Jones was right when he hinted that Freud would not accept his nurse's theology. But he was not quite right when he saw in Freud's attitude toward her "theology" anything more than an autobiographical excrescence. His nurse made Freud see religion in an astigmatic manner. This vision fortunately can be set aside, because it is not something one must accept if one accepts psychoanalysis. Freud's psychopathology may thus be utilized without bowing to Freud's militant atheism.

If this be true, what of the practice of psychoanalytic therapy? The answer is the same. The atheistic surfacing of Freudian psychoanalysis has neither insulated nor otherwise protected psychoanalysis from the ever-present impact of those human aspects of psychotherapy which reveal the human personality as something much more than a complex labyrinth of psychological mechanisms, and point to the transcending relationship between man and the unknown.

Ever since man started his so-called "conquest of nature," he has tried to fancy himself the conqueror of the universe. In order to assure himself of the mastery of a conqueror, he grabbed the trophy (nature, universe). He had to feel that the Maker of the trophy was annihilated, or his own fantasied sovereignty over the universe would be endangered. It is this trend that is reflected in Freud's unwillingness to accept religious faith in its true meaning. It is the same trend which wishes to conceive and take seriously "morality without sin" (Hesnard) and "religion without revelation" (Julian Huxley) —that is to say, a man-made universe and only man-made, with man-made laws for life and living. It is no surprise, therefore, to find that in the field of human psychology a man, no matter how great—a man like Freud—had constantly before him the vision of a man who is always unhappy, helpless, anxious, bitter, looking into nothingness with fright, and turning away from "so-called posterity" in anticipatory, almost snobbish, disgust. Such a man feels pressed by his own civilization, tormented by his own culture, isolated by his own society, always threatened with defeat by the willfulness and aggressiveness of others or by his own "death instinct." And yet, one cannot help but feel that this aspect of Freud is but a testimony to human frailty, and that means Freud's frailty too. Somewhere, in some way, Freud seems to have

Freud and Religion

sensed the transcending truth about man when he said that to be normal meant to him *arbeiten und lieben*.

It seems to me that one of the greatest failures of the last century, in the center of which Freud stands out so boldly, is the failure to recognize that man's true greatness lies in the humble recognition of his task and mission, to follow the mysteries of the world of man and the world of things without superstitious occultism and without megalomanic scientism.

GEORGE ALLEN & UNWIN LTD
London: 40 Museum Street, WC1

*Auckland: P.O. Box 36013, Northcote Central, N.4
Barbados: P.O. Box 222, Bridgetown
Beirut: Deeb Building, Jeanne d'Arc Street
Bombay: 15 Graham Road, Ballard Estate, Bombay 1
Buenos Aires: Escritorio 454-459, Florida 165
Calcutta: 17 Chittaranjan Avenue, Calcutta 13
Cape Town: 68 Shortmarket Street
Hong Kong: 105 Wing On Mansion, 26 Hankow Road, Kowloon
Ibadan: P.O. Box 62
Karachi: Karachi Chambers, McLeod Road
Madras: Mohan Mansions, 38c Mount Road, Madras 6
Mexico: Villalongin 32-10, Piso, Mexico 5, D.F.
Nairobi: P.O. Box 4536
New Delhi: 13-14 Asaf Ali Road, New Delhi 1
Ontario: 81 Curlew Drive, Don Mills
Philippines: P.O. Box 4322, Manila
Rio de Janeiro: Caixa Postal, 2537-Zc-00
Singapore: 36c Prinsep Street, Singapore 7
Sydney, N.S.W.: Bradbury House, 55 York Street
Tokyo: P.O. Box 26, Kamata*